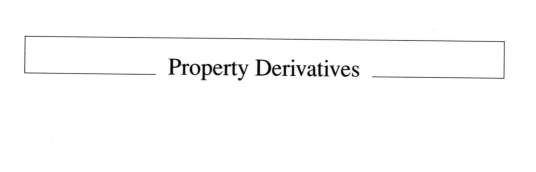

Property Derivatives

Property Derivatives

Pricing, Hedging and Applications

Juerg M. Syz

John Wiley & Sons, Ltd

Copyright © 2008   John Wiley & Sons Ltd, The Atrium, Southern Gate, Chichester,
West Sussex PO19 8SQ, England

Telephone   (+44) 1243 779777

Email (for orders and customer service enquiries): cs-books@wiley.co.uk
Visit our Home Page on www.wiley.com

Other Wiley Editorial Offices

John Wiley & Sons Inc., 111 River Street, Hoboken, NJ 07030, USA

Jossey-Bass, 989 Market Street, San Francisco, CA 94103-1741, USA

Wiley-VCH Verlag GmbH, Boschstr. 12, D-69469 Weinheim, Germany

John Wiley & Sons Australia Ltd, 42 McDougall Street, Milton, Queensland 4064, Australia

John Wiley & Sons (Asia) Pte Ltd, 2 Clementi Loop #02-01, Jin Xing Distripark, Singapore 129809

John Wiley & Sons Canada Ltd, 6045 Freemont Blvd, Mississauga, ONT, L5R 4J3, Canada

Wiley also publishes its books in a variety of electronic formats. Some content that appears in print may not be
available in electronic books.

Library of Congress Cataloging-in-Publication Data

Syz, Juerg M.
   Property derivatives : pricing, hedging and applications / Juerg M. Syz.
      p. cm. — (The Wiley finance series)
   Includes bibliographical references and index.
   ISBN 978-0-470-99802-1 (cloth : alk. paper)   1. Real estate investment.   2. Real property—prices.
3. Hedging (Finance)   I. Title.
   HD1382.5.S99 2008
   332.63′24—dc22

                                                              2008015121

British Library Cataloguing in Publication Data

A catalogue record for this book is available from the British Library

ISBN 978-0-470-99802-1 (H/B)

Typeset in 10/12pt Times by Aptara, New Delhi, India
Printed and bound in Great Britain by CPI Antony Rowe, Chippenham, Wiltshire

To My Family

Contents

Preface   **xi**

PART I   INTRODUCTION TO PROPERTY DERIVATIVES   1

1   A Finance View on the Real Estate Market   **3**
  1.1   Real Estate is Different from Other Asset Classes   4
  1.2   Limited Access to Real Estate Investments   5
  1.3   New Instruments needed   5

2   Basic Derivative Instruments   **7**
  2.1   Forwards, Futures and Swaps   8
  2.2   Options   12

3   Rationales for Property Derivatives   **23**
  3.1   Advantages and Disadvantages of Property Derivatives   23
  3.2   Finding a Suitable Real Estate Investment   25
  3.3   Usage of Property Derivatives   26

4   Hurdles for Property Derivatives   **29**
  4.1   Creating a Benchmark   30
  4.2   Education and Acceptance   31
  4.3   Heterogeneity and Lack of Replicability   31
  4.4   Regulation and Taxation   32
  4.5   Building Liquidity   33

5   Experience in Property Derivatives   **35**
  5.1   United Kingdom   36
  5.2   United States   43
  5.3   Other Countries and Future Expectations   47
  5.4   Feedback Effects   49

6   Underlying Indices   **53**
  6.1   Characteristics of Underlying Indices   54
  6.2   Appraisal-Based Indices   57
  6.3   Transaction-Based Indices   68

PART II   PRICING, HEDGING AND RISK MANAGEMENT   87

7   Index Dynamics   **89**
   7.1   Economic Dependencies and Cycles   89
   7.2   Bubbles, Peaks and Downturns   90
   7.3   Degree of Randomness   92
   7.4   Dynamics of Appraisal-based Indices   93
   7.5   Dynamics of Transaction-based Indices   96
   7.6   Empirical Index Analysis   97
   7.7   Distribution of Index Returns   99

8   The Property Spread   **101**
   8.1   Property Spread Observations   101
   8.2   The Role of Market Expectations   106
   8.3   Estimating the Property Spread   107

9   Pricing Property Derivatives in Established Markets   **109**
   9.1   Forward Property Prices   109
   9.2   Pricing Options on Property Indices   112

10   Measuring and Managing Risk   **117**
   10.1   Market Development and Liquidity   117
   10.2   Early and Mature Stages   118
   10.3   Property Value-at-Risk   121

11   Decomposing a Property Index   **127**
   11.1   General Explanatory Factors   127
   11.2   Tradable Explanatory Factors   129
   11.3   Example: The Halifax HPI   129

12   Pricing and Hedging in Incomplete Markets   **131**
   12.1   Hedging Analysis   131
   12.2   Pricing without a Perfect Hedge   136
   12.3   Example: Hedging a Trading Portfolio   138
   12.4   Risk Transfer   140

PART III   APPLICATIONS   143

13   Range of Applications   **145**
   13.1   Professional Investers and Businesses   146
   13.2   The Private Housing Market   146

14   Investing in Real Estate   **149**
   14.1   Properties of Property   150
   14.2   Property Derivatives and Indirect Investment Vehicles   156
   14.3   Investing in Real Estate with Property Derivatives   162

15 Hedging Real Estate Exposure   **165**
  15.1   Short Hedge   166
  15.2   Long Hedge   169
  15.3   Hedge Efficiency and Basis Risk   170

16 Management of Real Estate Portfolios   **173**
  16.1   Tactical Asset Allocation   174
  16.2   Generating Alpha   174
  16.3   Sector and Country Swaps   176

17 Corporate Applications   **183**
  17.1   Selling Buildings Synthetically   183
  17.2   Acquisition Finance   186

18 Indexed Building Savings   **187**
  18.1   Linking the Savings Plan to a House Price Index   187
  18.2   Engineering a Suitable Saving Plan   190

19 Home Equity Insurance   **193**
  19.1   Index-Linked Mortgages   193
  19.2   Collateral Thinking   198
  19.3   Is an Index-Hedge Appropriate?   200

Appendix   **203**

Bibliography   **209**

Index   **215**

Preface

Properties are not only a place to live and work but are also one of the oldest and biggest asset classes. While architecture dramatically changed the shapes of buildings over the years, the financial aspects of real estate were not less revolutionized.

After the land of monarchs, lords and feudal dynasties was broken into parcels and sold on a free market, the arrival of mortgages radically innovated real estate. During the industrial revolution, banks opened themselves to mortgage loans for common people, which changed homeownership completely. Mortgages allowed individuals to own their homes, which in turn changed the way people live.

Homeownership has moved from being established by force to being something you can buy, sell, trade and rent. However, the freedom to own something comes with a good portion of risk. Now as then, real estate is the single biggest asset of many households, and mortgages are their main liability. The recent subprime crisis and its associated foreclosures in the United States painfully reveal the risk of external financing. In addition to the extensive use of mortgages, which are a relatively crude tool that does not address asset-liability management, the next step is to establish new instruments that enable homeowners and investors to actually manage real estate risk.

Today, financial markets have the potential to revolutionize real estate again. Property derivatives offer ease and flexibility in the management of property risk and return. However, most markets are at an embryonic stage and there is still a long way to go.

Participating in the establishment of this new market filled me with quite some excitement. At Zuercher Kantonalbank (ZKB), I had the chance to work on the first residential derivatives in Switzerland, launched in February 2006, as well as on the first commercial swap on the Swiss IPD index, which was traded in September 2007. Moreover, we structured a mortgage that includes a property derivate to protect home equity.

My work at ZKB as well as the numerous conferences, seminars and meetings on property derivatives helped a great deal in getting the very valuable contacts from both academia and practice. In this respect I would like to thank Dr. Kanak Patel from the Department of Land Economy at the University of Cambridge, Prof. Susan Smith from the Department of Geography at Durham University, Peter Sceats from Tradition Financial Services, Stefan Karg from UniCredit, the Zuercher Kantonalbank, the Swiss Finance Institute and Marcus Evans for giving me the opportunity to present and discuss specific issues of the topic. The exchange of ideas led to many beneficial insights and aspects from sometimes very different angles.

Most of all, however, I would like to give great thanks to my dissertation advisor Prof. Paolo Vanini for his support and guidance. Because of his suggestions and challenges, the quality of this work has been brought to a level that I could never have reached myself.

Furthermore, the numerous inspiring discussions in and outside the bank have led to a strong improvement of the work. I would like to thank Aydin Akguen, Zeno Bauer, Thomas Domenig, Silvan Ebnöther, Philipp Halbherr, Moritz Hetzer, Ursina Kubli, Adrian Luescher, Claudio Mueller, Paola Prioni, Marco Salvi, Patrik Schellenbauer, Peter Scot, Nikola Snaidero and Roger Wiesendanger from ZKB, as well as Alain Bigar, Rudi Bindella, Christian Burkhardt, Andries Diener, and Marco Mantovani for their many valuable inputs. Last but not least I would like to thank my employer ZKB for allowing me time to complete this book as part of a PhD Thesis for the Swiss Banking Institute of the University of Zurich.

Part I

Introduction to Property Derivatives

1

A Finance View on the Real Estate Market

Financial risks of bricks and mortar.

Real estate is not only a vital part of the economy, involving tens of thousands of businesses and jobs worldwide, but also the primary financial asset of many companies and citizens. In the United States, US$ 21.6 trillion of wealth is tied up in residential property, representing about one-third of the total value of major asset classes. This is far more than the US$ 15 trillion value of publicly traded US equities (Property derivatives, 2006). Moreover, commercial real estate in the US accounts for about US$ 6.7 trillion. Economists observe similar relations worldwide. The European commercial real estate market size is estimated to be about € 3 trillion. In fact, no other asset class reaches the value of real estate.

Real estate is not only a big asset class, but also a risky one. It is in fact a ubiquitous industry that faces risk on many fronts. For example, the health of the housing industry is subject to changes in mortgage rates, building and energy costs, and a range of pressures from the economy overall. Homeowners, renters and corporations as well as investors are all subject to property risk.

Price and performance risks of properties are higher than those of many asset classes that are well established in financial markets. Given the size and risk of real estate, there should be a sufficiently large demand for instruments to transfer the associated risks and returns easily. According to Karl Case, the economic significance of such instruments, in the form of property derivatives, could even be much greater than that of all other derivative markets (Case *et al.*, 1993).

Asset and risk managers apply modern finance to more and more asset classes. Paradoxically, real estate has only experienced this finance revolution marginally yet. Despite its size and importance, investors often classify real estate as an alternative asset class, along with hedge funds, private equity or commodities. This comes as a surprise, given the ubiquity of the property market. However, many individuals do not fully realize the financial risks in "bricks and mortar." Accordingly, instruments to manage property risk are still rare.

Over only the last ten years there has been growing evidence of more innovative approaches in real estate markets. Debt securitization, asset-backed securitization and income-backed securitization have become popular in North America, Western Europe and Asia. Property securitization allows real estate to be converted into small-lot investments, just as stocks or trust units for equities, which are then sold to investors. Rental income and other profit from the real estate portfolio are distributed to these investors.

But property is still the last major asset class without a liquid derivatives market. Other industries, such as the agricultural or the financial sectors, have had access to a wide range of financial risk management tools for a long time. Such tools have not been available at all to the housing industry until recently. Real estate index futures and options have been introduced since the early 1990s in an attempt to increase the liquidity of real estate investments, although the property derivatives market is still in its nascent stage.

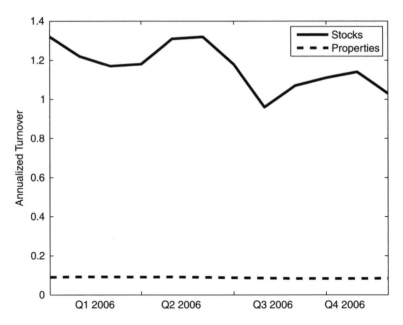

Figure 1.1   Two different worlds of liquidity: monthly annualized turnover rates of single family properties versus turnover of stocks in the US. Turnover of properties is about one-tenth of turnover of stocks

1.1   REAL ESTATE IS DIFFERENT FROM OTHER ASSET CLASSES

Real estate has some characteristics that make it difficult to value and trade real estate performance and to track its price development. First of all, properties are very heterogeneous and typically not fungible; i.e. every single real estate object is idiosyncratic and unique by definition, since no location is equivalent to another. Given the uniqueness, valuing properties and tracking their prices is usually done on an individual basis. Transaction values are rare, since real estate is typically held for longer periods of time and turnover is much lower than, for example, for stocks. Figure 1.1 compares the annual turnover for stocks and properties in 2006.[1]

Given these characteristics, standardization is needed to make the real estate market as a whole more tangible and trackable. The popular hedonic method allows for such standardization. It assumes that market prices of traded properties contain information about the valuation of the attributes of the object under consideration. The method decomposes a property into single attributes that are valuable to buyers, e.g. size in square meters, location, age of the building, proximity to a large city and so on. All attributes that are valuable to potential buyers should be considered. In turn, when prices of attributes are known, a new object can be valued using the factor prices. A property is thus treated per se, but as a bundle of standard attributes. Regression analysis is used to find the prices for the attributes. Hedonic models became standard for transaction-based, quality-adjusted property indices and are mainly used

---

[1] Data obtained from www.realtor.org/Research.nsf/Pages/EHSdata, Federal Reserve Statistics and the New York Stock Exchange.

for residential properties (see Chapter 6 on property indices). On the other hand, when no or only a few transactions are observable, appraisals are substitutes for transaction prices. Appraisal-based indices became standard for commercial properties.

1.2   LIMITED ACCESS TO REAL ESTATE INVESTMENTS

Once investors are able to measure risk and return of real estate, it can be treated in a similar context as other asset classes. However, despite its attractive risk-return characteristics and great diversification benefits, real estate was and still is considered a boring and old-fashioned investment category in many markets. One reason for this attitude might be the fact that investable instruments are available only in very limited quantity.

So far, real estate has been a huge market in which the only way to gain exposure was to buy physical assets, either directly or indirectly through a fund, a Real Estate Investment Trust (REIT) or a real estate company. Investing directly is time-consuming and out of reach for most small investors. Direct investments are risky and difficult to manage, and require a lot of due diligence, and expensive taxes and transaction costs. Once an investor has established a portfolio of properties, it is further difficult to shift exposures from one sector of the market to another or to generally reduce exposure.

Indirect investments, on the other hand, are typically traded much more conveniently than direct investments. Besides the eased trading and handling, their main advantage compared to direct investments is the diversification of specific risk to multiple properties. However, costs of transaction and maintenance still occur, since the indirect investment vehicle needs to buy, sell and administer its properties.

In most countries, indirect investment vehicles are not available in sufficient quantity to satisfy demand, so they often trade at a premium over the net asset value. Moreover, since investors value and discount cash flows, real estate funds and companies often behave like a fixed income or equity investment. Changes in property prices, which have typically a low correlation to equities and bonds and would thus provide diversification benefits, are rarely fully reflected.

Also, it is usually not possible to take a short position in a property investment vehicle. Thus, they cannot be used as a hedge against a price decline for an existing real estate portfolio. Finally, the risk of asset mismanagement is inherent in any actively managed fund or company.

1.3   NEW INSTRUMENTS NEEDED

New instruments that enable investors, at least in part, to overcome these shortcomings would provide substantial benefits to all property stakeholders. Property derivatives are financial instruments that are valued in relation to an underlying asset or price index. Derivative instruments can be used to hedge risk in portfolios and business operations. With these new property instruments, investors for the first time have an efficient opportunity for protection in down markets. In addition, they create new means of risk transfer to a broad range of investors. When used as investment instruments, they provide exposure to the price movements of an underlying market. Participation in the real estate market becomes possible without having to buy and sell properties. Recently, property derivatives started gaining traction in Europe, making it easier for institutional investors such as pension funds as well as private investors such as homeowners to assume or hedge positions in the property market.

New financial tools could bring benefits to the property market that previous innovations have brought to other markets. Property derivatives could close the gap of lacking investable instruments in the real estate market, enlarge the universe of financial tools that address market needs, reallocate risk and returns to where they suit best and broaden acceptance for real estate as an asset class. Derivatives, when used properly, have the potential to foster stability in the housing industry.

2

Basic Derivative Instruments

Derivatives came slowly, but massively.

Derivative instruments range from very simple to highly complex. The aim of this chapter is to introduce the derivative types that are relevant in the context of property derivatives.

Derivatives are powerful instruments to hedge, transfer and manage risk, to tailor payoffs in accordance with investors' risk-return profiles and to optimize investment portfolios. Moreover, a derivative can make any good or index tradable. According to the Bank of International Settlement (BIS), worldwide notional amounts of over-the-counter contracts totalled roughly US$ 410 trillion in 2006, while exchange-traded contracts summed to about US$ 70 trillion;[1] i.e. the notional value of derivatives was about 10 times the 2006 global GDP. The engagement of more and more banks in property derivatives is a sign of the willingness to expand the profitable world of derivatives.

The derivatives users base is extremely large. The agricultural sector was the first to apply derivatives, in the form of forward contracts. Farmers and millers agreed on price and quantity of wheat to be delivered at some point in time in the future. This hedged the risk of rising wheat prices for the miller. Farmers, on the other hand, hedged themselves against falling prices, e.g. in case of an excess supply of wheat. Many other examples of early forward and option contracts exist, e.g. on cotton in the UK, on tulips in Holland and on rice in Japan. Probably the first organized trading platform for derivatives was the New York Cotton Exchange, established in 1870.

In the 1970s, derivatives experienced a revolution, for several reasons. Myron Scholes and Fischer Black developed the so-called Black–Scholes formula in 1973 (Black and Scholes, 1973). The formula laid a base for option pricing, based on one basic assumption: the absence of arbitrage. Formalizing this argument that a profit cannot be made without taking risk and without investing money led to the well-known formula. At the same time, information technology evolved quickly, such that complex calculations could be done within fractions of seconds. Further, organized exchanges, on which derivatives could be traded transparently and liquidly, were founded, such as the Chicago Board Options Exchange (CBOE) in 1973.

A derivative is a financial instrument whose value is derived from the price of one or more underlying assets; hence the term derivative. The underlying asset may not necessarily be tradable itself. Examples of underlying assets or instruments are equities, interest rates, commodities, currencies, credits, all kinds of indices, inflation, weather temperatures or freight capacity. Anything that has an unpredictable effect on any business activity, i.e. anything that is risky, can be considered as an underlying of a derivative. The trading of derivatives takes place either on public exchanges or over-the-counter (OTC), i.e. as a direct agreement between two or multiple counterparties. Derivatives can be divided into two general categories:

- *Linear claims.* The payoff depends linearly on the underlying asset's value. Basic linear claims include forwards and futures as well as swaps.

---

[1] Data obtained from the Bank for International Settlement (BIS).

- *Nonlinear claims*. The payoff is a nonlinear function of the underlying asset's value. Basic nonlinear claims include options and any combination of options.

2.1   FORWARDS, FUTURES AND SWAPS

Forward and future contracts are binding bilateral agreements to buy or sell a specific asset in the future. While forwards are typically traded over-the-counter (OTC), futures are standardized contracts that are traded on a public exchange. Standardization makes contracts fungible; hence they can be traded more easily. On the other hand, more individual specifications of OTC contracts are able to address particular needs of the counterparties.

The buyer and seller of a forward or future contract agree on a price today for an asset to be physically delivered or settled in cash at some date in the future. Each contract specifies the terms of payment as well as the quality, the quantity and the time and location of delivery of the underlying asset. A change in value of the underlying asset induces a change in the contract value. Institutions and individuals that face a specific financial risk based on the movement of an underlying asset can buy or sell forwards or futures. This offsets the respective financial risk. Such transactions are known as hedging. Institutions and individuals can also buy and sell forwards and futures hoping to profit from price changes in the underlying asset. These transactions are considered speculation. Swaps are agreements to periodically exchange payments that are derived from an underlying asset between two counterparties. They are equivalent to a series of forward contracts.

2.1.1   Forwards

A forward is a contract between two parties agreeing that at a specified future date one counterparty will deliver a pre-agreed quantity of some underlying asset or its cash equivalent in the case of nontradable underlying assets. The other counterparty will pay a pre-agreed price, the so-called strike price, at the same date. If the strike price is set such that zero upfront payment is required from either of the counterparties to enter the contract, it is also called the forward price. The two counterparties are legally bound by the contract's conditions, i.e. the time of delivery, the quantity of the underlying and the forward price.

The buyer of a forward takes a so-called *long* exposure, while the seller is said to go *short*. These definitions are commonly used in academia and practice. A long position in an asset is a position that benefits from price increases in that asset. An investor who buys a share has a long position, but an equivalent long position can also be established with derivatives. A short position benefits from price decreases in the asset. A short position is often established through a short-sale. To sell an asset short, one borrows the asset and sells it. When one unwinds the short-sale, one has to buy the security back in the market to return it to the lender. One then benefits from the short-sale if the asset's price has decreased. Figure 2.1 shows the payoffs at maturity for both the long and the short forward position.

While the delivery time and the delivery quantity of the underlying asset can be fixed without any problem, the question is how the parties can agree on the future price of the underlying asset when the latter can change randomly due to market price fluctuations. The argument that defines the forward price is that there must be no trading strategy allowing for arbitrage, i.e. a risk-free profit. The fair forward price of a forward contract can be found as follows.

Suppose an investor sells a one-year forward contract, meaning that he takes the obligation to deliver in one year a certain quantity n of the underlying asset whose current market price is

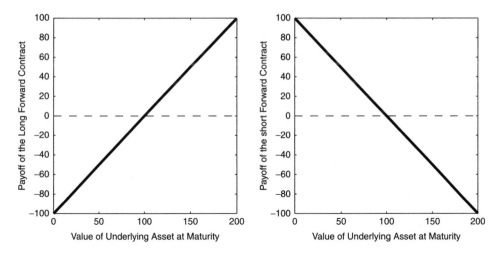

Figure 2.1   Payoff of a forward contract with a strike price of 100

S. In order to avoid any exposure to market risk, he borrows from a bank the amount $n \times S$ and buys the necessary quantity of the underlying asset today t with that money. In other words, he sells a *covered* forward. At maturity T, he delivers the asset to the buyer of the forward contract who pays the forward price F times the quantity n to the investor. From this amount he has to repay the bank his loan, which grew to $e^{r(T-t)} \times S$, where r is the one-year continuously compounded risk-free interest rate and $T - t$ is the time to maturity. Thus, the investor's cash flow in T is

$$F - e^{r(T-t)}S \tag{2.1}$$

Since he or she started with no money and took no price risk (the forward contract has offset the price fluctuations of the underlying asset), the investor ends up with no money. Otherwise, by selling or buying forward contracts, he or she would be able to make unlimited profits without taking any risk. This would be a *risk-free arbitrage*. Therefore, the fair price F solves

$$F - e^{r(T-t)}S = 0 \tag{2.2}$$

i.e.

$$F = e^{r(T-t)}S \tag{2.3}$$

F is the only forward price so none of the counterparties will be able to make a risk-free profit by selling or buying the contracts and lending or borrowing money.

The above relation only holds for nondividend paying financial underlying assets such as, for example, nondividend paying equities. For dividend paying equities or physical underlying assets, factors such as yield, temporal utility or storage costs must be taken into account. The formula for the forward price is then adjusted to

$$F = e^{c-y(T-t)}S \tag{2.4}$$

where c is the *cost-of-carry* that includes the interest rate r as well as storage and mainte-nance costs and y is the yield that is earned if the underlying asset is owned during the time until maturity. The yield can be, for example, dividends of an underlying stock or, for oil as the underlying asset, the possibility to heat during an unexpectedly cold winter when oil would temporarily be very expensive. For commodities, the yield is thus commonly called the *convenience yield*.

2.1.2 Futures

Futures are standardized forward contracts that are traded on exchanges. All futures positions are *marked-to-market* at the end of every working day. To illustrate this procedure suppose that a three months' futures contract on crude oil is bought for US$ 60 per barrel. The next day the futures closing price for the same delivery date is US$ 61 per barrel. This means that the contract has gained one dollar. In this case, the seller of the futures contract immediately pays US$ 1 into the buyer's account. Suppose that one day after, the futures closing price dropped to US$ 59. Then the buyer has to pay two dollars to the seller's account. This process continues to the maturity date.

While forward contracts bear the risk of default of the counterparty, the payoffs of futures are typically guaranteed by a clearing house. The clearing house acts as the intermediary and counterparty for all parties that trade on the respective public exchange. Trading is done anonymously. To reduce default risk, the clearing house requires daily settlement of margins that cover the current liability of a counterparty; i.e. a future contract's gains and losses are accumulated over time. In contrast, the compensation payment of a forward contract is only done at expiry and involves a higher degree of counterparty risk.

Because of the specific mechanism adopted by futures exchanges, contracts are settled in cash and only in some special cases the seller has to physically deliver the underlying asset. For property derivatives, as for most index derivatives, physical settlement is not possible because administration and execution would be much too complex, costly and time consuming.

2.1.3 Perpetual futures

Shiller and Thomas propose perpetual futures with no maturity as suitable property derivatives (Shiller, 1993; Thomas, 1996). The construction of such an instrument requires an underlying index that includes the perpetual net cash income of properties. The contract then periodically pays these cash flows to the investor. This is similar to a perpetual bond with fixed or floating interest payments. A property owner could pass on the collected rents to another investor through such a contract.

However, the price of such a contract must be the present value of all expected payments in the future. That makes the price of the contract sensitive to the discount rate, which in turn is, at least partly, driven by prevailing interest rates. As a result, perpetual contracts will be very sensitive to interest rates and might thus behave in a similar way to a traditional fixed income investment. This potentially reduces the diversification benefits that properties typically have. The advantage of a perpetual future is that trading volumes in property derivatives with different maturities could be pooled into one contract and liquidity would consequently be improved.

2.1.4 Swaps

Swaps are instruments that allow periodic payments to be swapped between two counterparties. Typically, one party receives a floating rate from and pays a fixed rate to the other swap party for a certain period of time. Swaps can be arranged in various ways. For example, there are swaps between different currencies, in which case the parties swap a domestic and a foreign

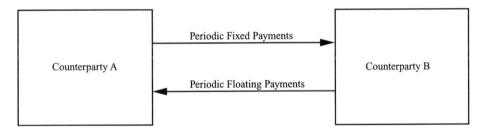

Figure 2.2   Swap agreement between two counterparties

rate. Figure 2.2 illustrates the agreement between the *swap payer* who pays the floating leg and the *swap receiver* who receives it and pays a fixed rate in return. Swaps are typically not traded on public exchanges but on the OTC market. Most common are interest rate and currency swaps.

A swap is now considered in the context of property performance. Suppose an insurance company wants to hedge part of its real estate exposure by using a swap contract on the UK Investment Property Databank (IPD) All Property Index, which measures the performance of commercial properties in the United Kingdom. The basic swap agreement consists of exchanging the yearly return of the IPD index against the three-month London Interbank Offered Rate (LIBOR) plus a fixed spread. Both the interest rates and the property index performance are paid on the same fixed notional principal. The interest leg (LIBOR based) is typically paid quarterly while the property return is paid only annually; i.e. the frequency of payments does not need to be the same. Since January 2008, many banks and brokers started quoting in fixed percentage return format. Figure 2.3 illustrates the payment streams of a typical swap contract on the IPD index.

2.1.5   Counterparty risk

Counterparty risk is created in the above structure because of the mismatch in the timing of payments: the LIBOR leg is paid quarterly whereas the IPD return leg is paid annually in arrears. The intermediary is exposed to the seller's default risk for the period until the total return of the IPD index is paid. This risk will increase if the property market performs strongly and the seller may be due to pay a large amount to the intermediary. The buyer is exposed to the counterparty risk of the intermediary to a similar extent. To reduce counterparty risk under

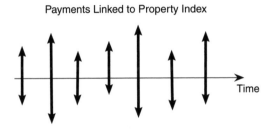

Figure 2.3   Payoff streams for a property swap contract

either swap, more frequent payments of the total return leg as well as netting of payments could be considered.

2.2 OPTIONS

Options are some of the most successful financial products to be introduced in the last decades. They are contracts through which a seller gives a buyer the right to buy or sell an underlying asset at a predetermined price within a set time period. There are two basic types of options, call options (the right to buy) and put options (the right to sell). An option thus allows investors to fix the price, for a specific period of time, at which an investor can buy or sell an underlying asset, against the payment of a premium which is only a percentage of what would be paid to own the underlying asset outright. This allows investors to leverage an investment, i.e. to increase both its risk and return.

Unlike other investments where the risks may be unlimited, the risk of buying options is limited to losing the premium, i.e. the price a buyer pays for an option. The premium is paid upfront at purchase and is not refundable, even if the option is not exercised. Because the right to buy or sell the underlying security at a specific price expires on a given date, the option will expire worthless if the conditions for profitable exercise or sale of the contract are not met by the expiration date.

As for all derivatives, the value of an option is derived from the value of an underlying asset. Most frequently, the underlying investment on which an option is based is a stock of a publicly listed company. Other underlying investments on which options can be based include stock indexes, government securities, foreign currencies, or commodities like agricultural or industrial products.

Options are traded on securities marketplaces among institutional investors, individual investors and professional traders. An option contract is defined by the following elements: type (put or call), underlying asset, unit of trade (number of shares, respectively notional amount), strike price and maturity date.

The use of options gives market participants the leverage of futures with a more limited risk, but at a higher price. Options provide the opportunity to limit losses while maintaining the possibility of profiting from favorable changes in the underlying asset. To the holder, options are the most flexible of all derivatives because they give a multiple choice at various moments during the lifetime of the option contract. However, the option seller always has to fulfill the option holder's requests. In contrast to the option buyer, the option seller may face unlimited risk. That is the reason why the option buyer has to pay a premium to the option seller.

2.2.1 Basic option types and strategies

Both basic option types, calls and puts, can either be bought or sold. This defines four basic option strategies.

A call option represents the right, but not the obligation, of the holder to buy a specified underlying asset at a predetermined price, the strike price, at a preset period of time, i.e. until maturity. The seller of a call option is obligated to sell the underlying asset if the call option holder exercises his or her right to buy on or before maturity. For example, a *General Electric May 60 Call* entitles the buyer to purchase 100 shares, the contract size, of General Electric common stock at US$ 60 per share at any time prior to the option's expiration date in May.

A put option, on the other hand, represents the right, but not the obligation, of the holder to sell a specified underlying asset at the strike price until maturity. The seller of a put option is obligated to buy the underlying asset if the put option holder exercises his or her right to sell when or before the option matures. For example, a *General Electric May 60 Put* entitles the buyer to sell 100 shares of General Electric common stock at US$ 60 per share at any time prior to the option's expiration date in May.

The seller of an option receives a premium from the buyer and assumes at the same time the obligation to deliver (for call options) or take (for put options) the underlying asset against the payment of the strike price. The seller's profit is therefore limited to the premium amount. The buyer can lose only the paid premium, since he or she buys a right and assumes no obligation. The profit of a call option is unlimited, as the underlying asset can gain in value without limits. The maximum profit of a put option is the strike price less the paid premium, in case the value of the underlying drops to zero. Figure 2.4 shows the payoff diagrams of the four basic option strategies.

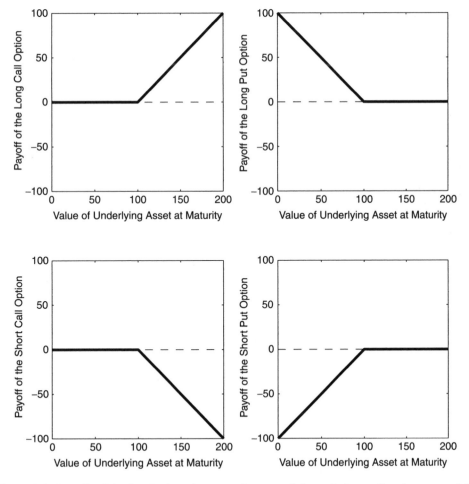

Figure 2.4 Payoffs of the four basic option strategies: upper left graph, long call option; upper right graph, long put option; lower left graphs, short call option; lower right graph, short put option

The basic option types, i.e. call and put options, are commonly referred to as plain vanilla options. Besides call and put options, there are many more types of options that differ in their payoff structures, path-dependence, payoff trigger and termination conditions. Pricing some of these options is a complex mathematical problem.

Options holders do not actually have to buy or sell the underlying asset that is associated with their options. They can and often do simply resell their options. If they do choose to purchase or sell the underlying asset represented by their options, this is called exercising the option.

The two main styles of exercise possibilities are:

- *American-style.* The option holder can exercise the option at any time from purchase until the maturity date. Most stock options traded on the marketplaces are American-style.
- *European-style.* European-style options can only be exercised at maturity. Index options are typically European-style.

2.2.2 Pricing options

Option valuation is different from traditional, discounted cash-flow valuation methods. The value of an option is inferred from the value of a portfolio of traded assets, which has the same payoff as the option, rather than from discounted cash flows. The composition of the replicating portfolio is adjusted dynamically and mimics the option fluctuations over time. If the value of the option and the portfolio are not equal, an arbitrage opportunity would exist. The law of one price enforces that two assets that have the same future payoffs must have the same current value.

Option pricing uses the no-arbitrage argument to ensure dynamically that the value of the option equals the value of the replicating portfolio as the price of the underlying asset evolves. The option and the replicating portfolio are combined in an offsetting manner into a hedge position. For any change in the price of the underlying asset, the change in value of the option will equal the change in value of the replicating portfolio. As a consequence, the value of the hedged position is independent of fluctuations in the underlying asset. The hedge position has no other source of uncertainty and so it earns a risk-free rate of return.

Under the assumption that an option can be replicated and that the underlying asset follows a so-called geometrical Brownian motion, i.e. asset returns are independent and identically distributed (i.i.d), the Black–Scholes formula provides option prices for a European-style call option. The formula reads

$$C = S_t e^{-y(T-t)} \Phi(d_1) - K e^{-r(T-t)} \Phi(d_2) \qquad (2.5)$$

where

$$d_1 = \frac{\text{Ln}(S_t/K) + (r - y + \sigma^2/2)(T - t)}{\sigma\sqrt{T - t}}$$

and

$$d_2 = d_1 - \sigma\sqrt{T - t}$$

where K is the exercise price and Φ represents the cumulative normal probability distribution. The risk-free interest rate r as well as the underlying price S can be directly observed. The volatility σ and the yield on the underlying asset y must be estimated. The strike price K and the time to maturity $T - t$ are specified in the option contract.

The first term on the right-hand side of Equation (2.5) represents the position in the underlying asset and the second term represents the cash position in the replicating portfolio. With every move in S, the portfolio must be reallocated; i.e. the replication strategy is an ongoing, dynamic process. A European put option, on the other hand, is priced as

$$P = Ke^{-r(T-t)}\Phi(-d_2) - S_t e^{-y(T-t)}\Phi(-d_1) \tag{2.6}$$

The value of options is derived from the value of their underlying assets. Obviously, the value of an option will rise or decline based on the related asset's performance. However, there are some more elements that enter the Black–Scholes formula. The following parameters must be considered when pricing options:

- The price of the underlying asset S
- The strike price K
- The risk-free interest rate r
- The volatility of the underlying asset σ
- The time to maturity $T - t$
- The cash and noncash yield/cost on the underlying asset y

Each of these elements has an impact on the option's price. In contrast, no information is needed on probability estimates of possible future prices of the underlying asset (they are captured in the current price of the asset itself and in its volatility), the expected rate of return for the underlying asset (the ability to build a replicating portfolio that completely offsets market risk implies a risk-free discount rate), the expected return of the option (the option has the same value as the replicating portfolio) or the market participant's risk aversion (independent from taste of risk, as subjective valuation would create an arbitrage opportunity). Options can be priced using only very little input and are very objective. The reason is that the valuation is based on a no-arbitrage principle, which holds as long as the option's payoff can be replicated.

The price of the underlying asset

The price of the underlying asset determines the payoff at maturity. Therefore, it directly influences the price of the option before maturity. A call option holder, for example, can expect a higher payoff if the price of the underlying asset rises. The current price of the underlying asset can typically be directly observed in the market.

The strike price

The strike price of an option is the price at which the underlying asset is bought or sold if the option is exercised. Strike prices are generally set at narrow intervals around the market price of the underlying asset. The strike price is defined in the option contract.

The relationship between the strike price and the actual price of the underlying asset determines, in the language of options, whether the option is in-the-money, at-the-money or out-of-the-money.

An *in-the-money* call option has a strike price that is below the actual price of the underlying asset. For example, a call option at a US$ 95 strike price for a stock that is currently trading at US$ 100 is in-the-money by US$ 5. These US$ 5 are called the intrinsic value of the call option. On the other hand, an in-the-money put option has a strike price that is above the actual stock price. For example, a put option at a US$ 110 strike price for a stock that is currently trading at US$ 100 is in-the-money by US$ 10.

An option is called *at-the-money* if the strike price is near or equal to the actual price of the underlying asset.

Finally, an *out-of-the-money* call option has a strike price that is above the actual price of the underlying asset. An out-of-the-money put option has a strike price that is below the actual price of the underlying asset.

The risk-free interest rate

The risk-free interest rate also influences an option's price. Part of the replicating portfolio that mimics the option consists of a risk-free asset and thus earns its rate. Proxies for the risk-free interest rate can be directly observed in the market. For example, a Treasury bill is considered to be as good as risk-free.

The volatility of the underlying asset

Volatility does not affect prices of noncontingent claims such as forwards and futures. That is because they have symmetric payoffs; i.e. increased price fluctuations can result in both higher gains and losses. For contingent claims such as options, however, volatility impacts the price considerably. That is because payoffs are asymmetric; i.e. increased price fluctuations can result in higher gains to the holder, but not in larger losses (since the maximum loss is the paid premium). Thus, options generally gain in value when volatility increases.

Figure 2.5 displays two distributions of underlying asset values after one year as well as the payoff function of a call option. The higher the volatility, the wider is the distribution of

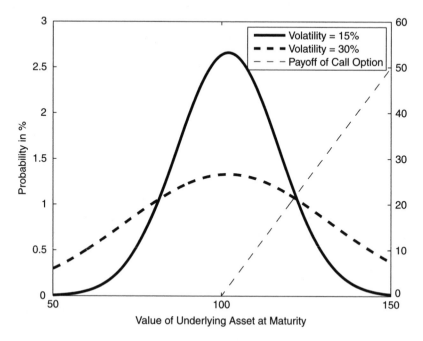

Figure 2.5 Distribution of the underlying asset value at maturity (one year), for volatilities of 15 and 30 %. The interest rate is assumed to be 2 % and the dividend yield is zero. The underlying asset value stands at 100 at the beginning of the year. The payoff of a call option is scaled on the right-hand side

outcomes. The kinked payoff function of options creates a one-sided effect to volatility. On the one hand, higher volatility would lead to a higher probability of a very bad outcome, but since losses are limited, the option holder does not care by how much the option is out-of-the money at maturity (below 100 in the graphed example). On the other hand, higher volatility leads to a higher chance of a very positive outcome. Since gains are not limited to the option holder, he or she directly benefits from increased volatility. Volatility is a critically important determinant of option values.

However, historic volatility and future volatility are not the same. Volatility can change over time. The expected future volatility cannot be directly observed, so volatility must be estimated when an option is priced.

However, volatility can easily be estimated as long as the result of the option pricing model can be observed, i.e. the prices of options. Volatility levels that are extracted from observed option prices are called *implied volatilities*. These implied volatilities can in turn be used to calculate prices of new option contracts, using the model again the other way round.

The time to maturity

The time to maturity is determined in the option contract. Generally, the longer the time to maturity, the more valuable is the option. The reason for this relation is straightforward for the American-style option: the holder of the option can always exercise the option prior to maturity. In addition, there is the possibility to wait and exercise the option at a later point in time. The longer the time to maturity, the greater is the value of the possibility to wait.

For European-style options, the relation of time to maturity and option price needs further explanation. A start is made by showing that an early exercise does not make much sense. Assume that an investor holds a call option with a strike at US$ 100 and a two-year maturity on a nondividend paying stock. The price of the underlying stock is currently at US$ 90. Obviously, an early exercise makes little sense, since the out-of-the money option would be worth zero immediately. Suppose the stock rises to US$ 110 over the next year. If the investor were to exercise the option now, he or she would need to put down US$ 100 (the strike price) and get the stock worth US$ 110. The difference between the actual stock price and the strike price of US$ 10 would have been gained, called the intrinsic value.

Alternatively, the investor could wait another year (i.e. to maturity of the option), and observe where the stock price has gone. If the stock price has gone down to, say, US$ 80, he or she would be happy to have waited since a loss would have been avoided. If, on the other hand, the stock rose further to, say, US$ 130, the investor could still exercise the option and put down the strike price of US$ 100. If he or she had exercised earlier, a stock worth US$ 130 would be held. However, the later the strike price needs to paid, the more interest can be earned on that money. Therefore, also in this scenario, it was wiser to wait as long as possible, i.e. until maturity. It follows that a longer maturity is more valuable, i.e. results in a higher option price, even if the option cannot be exercised before maturity.

As just seen, the remaining time to maturity is valuable. Consequently, the option price must be worth more than the intrinsic value (i.e. the US$ 10 that are collected in the above example if exercised immediately). That additional value is related to time to maturity and volatility. Higher volatility makes it more valuable to wait and see, i.e. to have the chance of avoiding

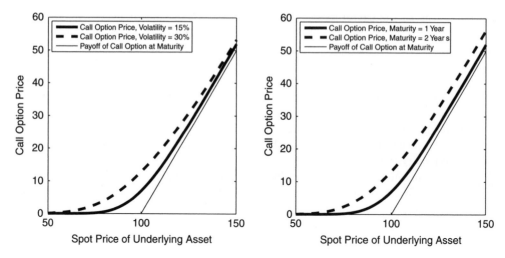

Figure 2.6 Price of a European call option and the impact of volatility and time to maturity on the option price. In the base case, maturity is one year, volatility is 15 %, the dividend yield is zero and the interest rate is 2 %

a large loss by not exercising early. This difference between the option value and its intrinsic value is thus often called the time or volatility value.

$$\boxed{\text{Option price} = \text{intrinsic value} + \text{time value}}$$

The left graph in Figure 2.6 shows how an increase in volatility increases the value of an option. The graph on the right shows the result of increased time to maturity on the option's price. The time value is increased similarly in both cases.

The cash and noncash yield/cost on the underlying asset (net yield)

Just as for forward and futures contracts, the holder of an option is not entitled to earn any yield on the underlying asset before the option is exercised and the underlying asset is owned directly. The yield on a directly owned asset is called the convenience yield. On the other hand, the option holder does not need to bear the cost that is related to the storage or maintenance of the underlying asset, called cost-of-carry. A large yield such as a big dividend payment can make it worthwhile to exercise an option early. Suppose a stock pays a dividend of 5 % tomorrow and an investor holds a deep in-the-money call option (i.e. the option is highly likely to be exercised) that matures next week. If the investor could exercise the option today, he or she would need to put down the strike price today but would capture the dividend. If he or she were to wait until maturity, there would only be a need to pay the strike price in a week but the dividend payment would be missed. Clearly, the possibility of an early exercise can be valuable if the underlying asset provides a yield. In that case, an American-style option is worth more than a European-style option.

The net yield can be directly observed in the market (announced dividend payments) or estimated from related markets.

2.2.3   Sensitivities of option prices

Since options depend on a number of input factors, they must change in value when an input factor changes in value. The strike price as well as the maturity date are deterministic; i.e. once they are set, they do not change any more. The other input factors, price of the underlying asset, volatility, interest rate and net yield, can change over time. For example, the impact of a change in volatility on the option price, all else being equal, is the *sensitivity* of the option price to volatility.

Most important and obvious, the option price is sensitive to a movement in the underlying asset. The change in the option value divided by the change in the underlying asset is called the *delta*. The delta of a call option is between zero and one while the delta of a put option is between minus one and zero. The delta is an important parameter with regard to the replicating portfolio. Since it measures the price change of an option due to a price change in the underlying asset, the delta actually is the exact number of underlying assets that must be held in the replicating portfolio. Somebody who intends to hedge an option should therefore hold a delta amount of underlying assets. This procedure is called *delta hedging*.

However, since options are nonlinear derivatives, the delta itself will change with every move of the underlying asset; i.e. the hedger must adjust the hedge amount dynamically, in order to correctly mimic the option to be replicated. Since in reality it is not possible to continuously adjust the hedge, the hedger is exposed to the risk of the delta changing quickly. The hedger with the delta position is always one step behind the true actual delta. The risk of unanticipated changes in the delta is called the *gamma* risk. In other words, the gamma is the sensitivity of the delta with respect to the underlying asset. If a trader wants to hedge gamma risk in addition to delta risk, he or she needs a security with a nonlinear payoff depending on the same underlying asset in addition to the underlying asset itself. By just using the underlying asset (which is an instrument with a linear payoff) the trader could never hedge gamma risk (which arises only in nonlinear payoffs). Formally, the delta Δ of a European-style call option is defined as

$$\Delta_{\text{Call}} = e^{(y-r)(T-t)}\Phi(d_1) \tag{2.7}$$

while the gamma Γ of a European-style call option reads

$$\Gamma_{\text{Call}} = \frac{\phi(d_1)e^{(y-r)(T-t)}}{S\sigma\sqrt{T-t}} \tag{2.8}$$

Figure 2.7 shows the delta of a European call option with respect to the price of the underlying asset, while Figure 2.8 equivalently displays the option's gamma.

Similarly, option price sensitivities with respect to volatility (called *vega*), to interest rates (called *rho*) and to net yield can be calculated and used as a hedge measure for a change in the respective parameter. These sensitivities, which were developed for options on liquidly traded assets (e.g. equity), will generally be appropriate for property options as well.

In the context of property derivatives, it makes sense to focus on delta and gamma, which are the most dominant sensitivities that must be considered when managing related risks. Chapter 12 describes how delta and gamma come into play when a trading book consisting of property derivatives is to be managed.

Volatility on property returns is quite stable and the impact of interest rates on option prices is typically small. Thus, the sensitivities vega and rho are not of major importance when hedging a property derivative. For details of sensitivities of option prices, see, for example, Hull (2000).

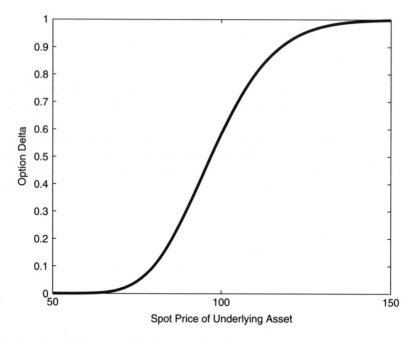

Figure 2.7 Delta of a European call option along the price of the underlying asset. Maturity is one year, volatility is 15 %, dividend yield is zero and the interest rate is 2 %

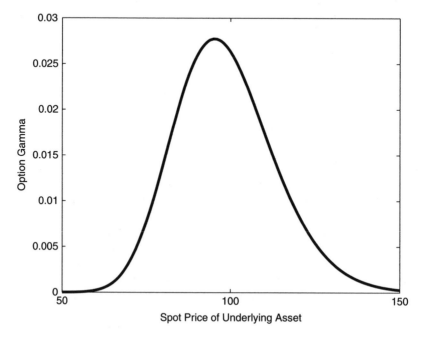

Figure 2.8 Gamma of a European call option along the price of the underlying asset. Gamma is highest at-the-money. Maturity is one year, volatility is 15 %, dividend yield is zero and the interest rate is 2 %

2.2.4 Benefits and risks of options in short

It is interesting to consider why an investor would want to get involved with complicated options when they could just buy or sell the underlying asset. There are a number of reasons.

An investor can profit on changes in an asset's price without ever having to actually put up the money to buy the asset. The premium to buy an option is a fraction of the cost of buying the underlying asset outright. When an investor buys options, the investor hopes to earn more per dollar invested than by buying the underlying asset; i.e. options have a *leverage*. Further, except in the case of selling uncovered calls or puts, risk is limited to the premium paid for the option, no matter how much the actual asset price moves adversely in relation to the strike price. Given these benefits, why would everyone not just want to invest with options?

Options are very time-sensitive investments. An options contract lasts for a short period, typically a few months. The buyer of an option can lose the entire premium, even with a correct prediction about the direction and magnitude of a particular price change if the price change does not occur before the option matures. Hence, investors who are more comfortable with a longer-term investment generating ongoing income, i.e. a buy-and-hold investment strategy, will rarely invest in options. Also, options are more difficult to understand than, for example, stocks. Investors who are not comfortable with derivatives might be hesitant to use them.

In a world of perfectly complete and efficient markets, derivatives would be redundant. They could be replicated by a combination of the underlying asset and other securities. Nobody would need a call option if its exact payoff could be achieved just by trading the underlying security. In reality, however, derivatives serve purposes that cannot be implemented by other instruments. Many underlying instruments are not directly tradable themselves, e.g. interest rates or inflation. In many aspects, derivatives have made markets more complete and efficient. The larger the frictions in the base market, the greater is the potential benefit derivatives can create. These benefits include, among others, a reduction in transaction costs, an acceleration in transaction speed and an improvement in information availability. Real estate seems to be a perfect candidate for a derivatives market. Chapter 9 describes in detail how to price options on property indices in a Black–Scholes framework.

3

Rationales for Property Derivatives

Saving time, money and more.

A market is liquid if large volumes can be traded anytime, without affecting market prices. The liquidity of the property market is low compared to its market size. Turnover in the real estate market is much lower than for most security markets. Moreover, in market downturns, turnover and liquidity "dries out." The illiquidity of the property market arises mainly due to its heterogeneity, and certainly not due to a lack of market participants.

In an illiquid base market such as the property market, derivatives can ease the transfer of risk and thus be of great benefit to market participants. Unlike some of the more exotic classes of derivatives that have been launched in recent years, property derivatives have a very simple appeal and a potentially huge base of end-users. They allow managing property risk quickly and cheaply, removing long transaction lead times and saving on transaction costs.

Derivatives only make sense if the underlying asset exhibits sufficient market risk that many participants are willing to transfer, hedge against and speculate on. The three fundamental requirements for an asset class to be a suitable underlying asset for derivatives seem to be fulfilled by the property market. First, the size of the market is sufficiently large, such that demand to buy and sell exposure should exist sufficiently to make a derivatives market desirable. However, the size of the spot market alone is not sufficient to qualify the market as a meaningful underlying for derivatives. Second, risk in terms of volatile returns is present, meaning that it makes sense to invest or hedge. Third, a credible index that is accepted as a common benchmark must exist in order to have a reference for payoffs. It will be seen later on that such indices exist in some countries but are not fully established in others (see Chapter 6 on property indices).

However, a large part of the property market consists of owner-occupied residential housing. Most homeowners do not consider real estate to be an investment, but only consumption. An emotional component as well as the personal and financial situation in their lives drive the buying and selling decision. Institutional investors, who generally act more rationally on real estate investments, are the primary target for most property derivatives. Involving the limiting factors of low turnover, illiquidity and owner-occupiers, the property market is still large enough for a derivatives market to face sufficient demand and supply.

3.1 ADVANTAGES AND DISADVANTAGES OF PROPERTY DERIVATIVES

The cost of buying and selling physical property (so-called round-trip costs) are generally estimated to be between 5 and 8 % of the value of the property investment. The use of derivatives allows investors to avoid a large part of these costs. This appears to have been the trigger for property derivatives in the UK and mainland Europe.

However, the rationale for property derivatives is not just about saving transaction costs. Besides avoiding costs, the most obvious benefit is that they make real estate investable in a flexible way. Property derivatives can be traded quickly and easily, contrary to physical property transactions.

In addition to saving time and money, there are more advantages to property derivatives. For example, by investing in an index, the investor gets not only exposure to a few single objects but to a diversified property investment. Such a synthetic investment in the broad market avoids the idiosyncratic risks of single objects. Moreover, tax authorities of many jurisdictions treat property derivatives favorably compared to direct investments. Table 3.1 lists the most obvious advantages of property derivatives over physical property investments.

A result of a liquid, established derivatives market is the improvement of market information. By observing transaction prices, it is possible to assume implications on the base market. For example, derivatives can reveal the volatility that is expected by market participants. Improved market information in turn results in better transparency and finally contributes to more efficiency in the real estate market.

Table 3.1   Advantages and disadvantages of property derivatives
compared to direct and indirect real estate investments

Advantages of property derivatives

Allow liquid and short-term investment (instant exposure)
Significantly reduce transaction costs in buying and selling
Increase diversification within property portfolios
Tactical flexibility
Make regional and sectoral diversification easy
"Direct" exposure to property (property prices, not real estate stock)
Ability to transform risk
Divisibility of investment amounts
Improvement of market information and liquidity
Low administrative costs
Tax efficient (some countries)
Legal aspects (restrictions for foreign direct investments)
Exposure to real estate without direct ownership of properties
Opportunities for hedging that until now have not been possible
True portfolio diversification
Opportunity to benefit from both rising and falling property markets
Allowing leverage and thus reducing capital intensity
Market access for retail investors with small volumes
Possibility of capital guarantee and other optional payoffs

Disadvantages of property derivatives

Temporal disadvantages
   Large bid–ask Spreads
   Low volume/liquidity
   No permanent secondary market
   Appropriateness of underlying index
   Credibility of underlying index
   Hedge accounting practice

Permanent disadvantages
   No management discretion
   No ability to generate alpha
   No ability to scale property management business

Table 3.2   Potential buyers and sellers of property derivatives

Buyers	Sellers
Retail investors	Corporates with nonstrategic properties
Institutional investors	Mortgage lenders
Building savers	Homeowners
Real estate portfolio managers	Real estate portfolio managers
Hedge funds	Hedge funds
	Developers
	Home suppliers

There are also some disadvantages for property derivatives. It is important to distinguish between temporary disadvantages due to the actual illiquidity and permanent disadvantages. The disadvantages of property derivatives are also listed in Table 3.1. Note that management discretion can be both an advantage or a disadvantage. As long as management is able to create value, i.e. beat the overall property market by skillful 'cherry picking,' it is an advantage that management can actively influence the composition and use of the real estate portfolio. On the other hand, the risk of potential mismanagement is a disadvantage, since the investor would have been better off by investing in the diversified overall market.

The numerous advantages suggest that buyers as well as sellers can benefit from the use of derivatives. This observation is a necessary condition for the establishment of any efficient derivatives market. Table 3.2 lists potential buyers and sellers of property exposure through derivatives. The Property Derivatives Interest Group (PDIG) conducted a survey that suggests that there is considerable demand for property derivatives. In the UK, companies controlling nearly GB£ 45 billion of commercial property had been cleared to trade in this new market by mid 2005 (Use of property derivatives, 2005). Also, there seems to be enough of a divergence in views regarding the performance of a property investment. A survey conducted by the UK Investment Property Forum (IPF) in August 2006 showed that forecasts for overall UK property total returns 2008 ranged from 0.0 to 9.8 %.[1] The divergence of opinion was centered on the degree to which returns will be positive for the period. Figure 3.1 shows the 35 forecasts of the survey, which on average are 5.31 %.

Given a variety of views, the opportunity to implement market timing strategies, cross border and asset class diversification, combined with low transaction costs, will eventually drive trading volumes.

3.2   FINDING A SUITABLE REAL ESTATE INVESTMENT

Some investors welcome possibilities to invest in property without having to make direct investments. Further, there is a growing demand for new instruments that allow for greater liquidity than the existing indirect investment vehicles. It can be argued that increasing volatility, which is observed in many property markets, brings property risk to investors' minds and makes instruments to hedge the risk more desirable (Plewka and Pfnür, 2006).

Many private and institutional investors faced difficulties in finding suitable, diversified real estate investments, since supply was much lower than demand. The gap would be even wider

---

[1] Data obtained from Investment Property Forum (IPF).

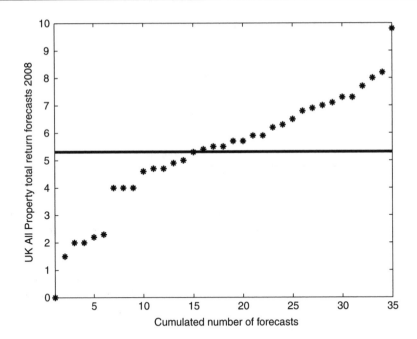

Figure 3.1   A diverse range of forecasts is needed to establish a market for derivatives

if all investors strictly targeted a Markowitz-efficient allocation (see Chapter 14 for an optimal portfolio allocation including real estate). Consequently, many real estate investment vehicles traded at a premium over their net asset value (NAV). The risk factor of premiums and discounts increase volatility and can result in sharp downturns, once excess demand vanishes.

Although indirect investment vehicles have become more popular recently, derivatives offer an alternative that allows more sophisticated uses such as hedging real estate portfolios or swapping sector or country exposure. Most indirect investment vehicles need to comply with a number of regulations. Typically, they are required to distribute most of their income as dividends and thus resemble a fixed income investment rather than an investment that tracks property prices. Consequently, indirect investment vehicles lose a part of the diversification benefits that investors expect from real estate.

Market participants are generally only motivated to trade new instruments if no acceptable substitutes already exist (Fitzgerald, 1993). If a property derivative could be easily mimicked using existing real estate vehicles in combination with, for example, interest rate derivatives, there would be little interest in developing and using a market for property derivatives. However, it seems that such substitutes do not exist for property derivatives. This provides a strong rationale for these new instruments.

3.3   USAGE OF PROPERTY DERIVATIVES

An over-the-counter (OTC) derivative, e.g. a swap between a bank and an investor, can be arranged in a few minutes with no significant transaction costs. Contracts can be written against the total return, income-only or capital value-only components of the underlying index.

Derivatives generally improve transparency. The development of a property derivatives market is not just good for itself but for the industry as a whole, because many people still think of property as an illiquid asset class with very poor transparency. So far, transparency is prevented since fund managers hesitate to disclose information publicly and make it available to competitors.

Derivatives enable investors to move exposures around much more easily. A derivative allows quick implementation of investment decisions and therefore makes tactical allocation possible. It allows investors to enter short real estate positions and to get a hedge at a reasonable price.

The derivatives market of many other asset classes has matured to at least the same size as the underlying market within a few years. Derivatives could unlock the potential of the commercial property market by removing physical delivery and thereby enabling faster, cheaper and more effective execution of allocation strategies, short-term hedges, risk transfer and geographical diversification. Heterogeneity of the base market make physical delivery impossible for property derivatives, so only cash settlement is practicable and desirable.

The use of property derivatives should not be limited to the investment market. Corporate occupiers could use derivatives to manage their property risk through rental swaps in much the same way that a company's treasury manages financial risk with interest rate swaps. Hedge funds could also become major players in the market. In fact, their early participation may help establish a liquid market more quickly.

In sum, property derivatives unite many of the advantages of direct and indirect real estate investments. Since they follow closely a specified property price or performance index, an investor benefits from the asset class diversification effect without actually buying property directly. At the same time, administration and transaction costs, which indirectly result in every traditional investment vehicle, are saved. However, indirect investment vehicles and property derivatives should not primarily be seen as substitutes but as complements, just as equity derivatives and stocks.

4
Hurdles for Property Derivatives

Nobody said it was easy.

Both professional real estate investors and private homeowners can benefit greatly from a property derivatives market. Today, investors can buy shares of real estate companies, real estate funds, Real Estate Investment Trusts (REITs) or other indirect investment vehicles. In terms of liquidity and divisibility, they are comparable to shares in equity. However, prices of these investments rarely follow property prices but are rather correlated with interest rates and equity markets. Thus, they do not provide the valuable diversification effect an investor expects from the asset class real estate. Homeowners on the other hand face difficulties to hedge the risk of a sharp price drop of residential house prices. Often, the only admissible strategy is to sell the property. Why is real estate, given its size and economic importance, an asset class without a liquid derivatives market that would make it easier to hedge and invest in real estate?

Today, the United Kingdom is by far most advanced in trading property derivatives. In the late 1990s, a group of fund managers formed the Property Derivatives Users' Association, now part of the Investment Property Forum (IPF). This lobbyist group helped persuade the UK's Financial Services Authority (FSA) that there could be sufficient liquidity in a property derivatives market. New regulations in November 2002 meant that insurance companies could treat property derivatives as admissible assets. Before, they were subject to different tax rules from other derivatives, resulting in concern that any losses might not be tax deductible. Besides tax accounting restrictions, stamp duty has been lifted, provided that no rights in the land exists.

These changes in regulation and taxation boosted activity in the UK property derivative market. However, these were unfortunately by far not the only hurdles for the property derivatives market.

A survey of institutions, investment managers, property companies and investment banks undertaken by Hermes in May 2006 was targeted to find out the most significant hurdles to trading property derivatives. The results were as follows:

- Require trustee/investment committee approval (38 %)
- Insufficient market liquidity (27 %)
- Insufficient systems and controls (5 %)
- Insufficient understanding (5 %)
- Other (5 %)
- None (20 %)

Getting trustee/investment committee approval to engage in property derivatives is not likely to impede the development of the market in the long run as the cost and speed advantages of derivatives over direct investments are clear. Further, as the market develops, the level of liquidity will also increase and so this second reason for nonparticipation will disappear. The mentioned hurdles actually apply for any new market, and will typically disappear over time.

Table 4.1 Hurdles for property derivatives in four categories: benchmarking, education, replicability and regulation and taxation

---

Hurdles for property derivatives

Creating a benchmark
  Heterogeneity of properties and aggregation
  Lack of underlying indices that enjoy a broad acceptance
  Low calculation frequency of indices

Education and acceptance
  Little awareness of property risk
  Understanding of prices and volatility for these new contracts
  One-sided market expectations
  Resistance of conservative market participants

Heterogeneity and Lack of Replicability
  Tracking error when used as hedging instrument
  Limited arbitrage possibilities
  Lack of replicability by underlying assets

Regulation and taxation
  Unfavorable tax treatment
  Unfavorable accounting and legal treatment

Also of interest is the fact that 20 % of those surveyed indicated that there were no major hurdles to investing.

In February 2007, the Japanese Ministry of Land, Infrastructure and Transport (MLIT) established a study group to assess the potential development of property derivatives in Japan. The resulting report finds that three main actions should be taken. First, indices should be enhanced to reflect realistically the Japanese real estate market. Second, a legal and regulatory framework to monitor and control property derivative transactions effectively should be put in place. Third, market education, including studies on property derivative pricing, indices and trading systems, should be performed.

In a survey conducted at a Seminar of Investment Property Databank (IPD) on Japanese property derivatives in 2007, only 5 % of the participants claimed that they knew "a lot" about derivatives. Around 45 % said they knew "a little," 40 % said "not much," while 9 % admitted they knew nothing at all. The seminar was attended by 300 Japanese real estate investors, portfolio managers, developers and government officials. Moreover, 64 % said they came from institutions that would be able to use property derivatives in future, with 52 % of those expecting their company to do so in the near future.

There are some obvious and some less obvious hurdles that made and still make the quick establishment of a liquid property derivative market difficult. Some of them depend on the respective jurisdiction, while others are inherent in the property market. Table 4.1 lists the most important hurdles. In addition, to start the property derivatives market, a sufficient number of counterparties must be found to build liquidity.

4.1 CREATING A BENCHMARK

A main characteristic of the property market is illiquidity, arising from heterogeneity and the lack of transparency. Property prices are thus rarely observed and cannot be looked up daily on a screen. The construction and establishment of an appropriate index is a first necessary step to establish a derivatives market.

The UK was able to embrace derivatives well before the rest of the world, mainly due to the availability of relevant property indices. The London-based private firm Investment Property Databank (IPD) originally focused on building its UK index. Most other countries failed in the past to define good indices.

IPD now collects information on property market performance across a variety of countries and its indices are considered to be the leading benchmarks. By the end of 2007, IPD UK collected portfolio records capturing 12234 properties with a market value of GB£ 183769 billion. It benchmarks property unit trusts and publicly traded instruments, but also takes direct investment portfolio data sent by pension funds, and benchmarks performance against data sent by peers. It publishes individual country indices for 15 European and 6 non-European countries as well as a pan-European and a global index. Many practitioners hope to see an IPD-led global benchmarking index emerge. This is likely to happen as more and more banks enter the property derivatives market and start trading contracts on the IPD indices. So far, however, the UK is fairly unique in terms of the IPD index, which benchmarks the asset class of property as a whole as well as different property sectors (see Chapter 6 on IPD indices).

4.2 EDUCATION AND ACCEPTANCE

The availability of a reliable underlying index is a necessary condition, but not sufficient for a derivatives market. A further challenge is to educate investors and potential market participants. Brokers in particular were embarking on education programs to encourage traditional property investors to look at trading derivatives. Besides the big players, smaller participants should get educated in the same way.

The idea of derivatives as instruments to gain exposure to property has not yet been fully accepted by real estate industry leaders. Growth in the property derivatives market must be led by an increased understanding and acceptance of reliable indices and instruments on them, as well as a better understanding of their potential benefits. Managers of property portfolios need to see that risk can be dealt with quickly and relatively cheaply, saving transaction time and costs. If a real estate portfolio manager wants to reduce property exposure temporarily, he or she must be aware that derivatives allow this to be done without selling a portfolio that the manager may not be able to get back.

4.3 HETEROGENEITY AND LACK OF REPLICABILITY

The lack of replicability inhibits banks from launching a derivative product and simply replicating it by buying the properties contained in the underlying index. The more heterogeneous the underlying market is, the more difficult it will be to establish a replicating portfolio. In order to have a portfolio with prices closely related to those of the derivatives, a large number of properties must be bought in a very short time. Physical replication is thus inefficient, time-lagged and costly. In the absence of perfect replicating strategies, a hedging error exists. In order to reduce or eliminate this error, the bank needs to find a counterparty that is willing to take the opposite side of the deal. In other words, banks simply act as intermediaries, matching supply and demand. If the bank keeps a risk position, it will try to reduce the hedging error by engaging in various hedging strategies (see Chapter 12 on hedging).

Lack of replicability does not necessarily inhibit the establishment of a derivatives market. As observed in, for example, the weather and inflation derivatives market, volume can still grow even if there is no way to replicate the underlying instrument. Thus, it is sufficient to have an objective, trustworthy measurement of the underlying value. As long as potential users of derivatives accept the measurement, a derivatives market can be very well established.

4.4 REGULATION AND TAXATION

As for any new market, taxation and regulation are potential hurdles in the buildup period. How property derivatives are treated when a manager uses them as a hedge is one important regulation issue that may impact the evolvement of the market. The use of property indices to hedge a specific portfolio assumes that the portfolio composition matches the index composition. Given the heterogeneous nature of property, this is impossible to achieve and will therefore not lead to a perfect hedge. However, if the hedge is good enough, i.e. correlation between the portfolio and the index is high, sellers would not be prevented from entering the market. Whether and how actuaries can apply hedge accounting for property derivatives, i.e. offset their risk and return against the ones of the hedged property portfolio, is currently under discussion. To apply hedge accounting, regulators require hedging effectiveness to be demonstrated using statistical or other numerical tests.

If hedge accounting is not applicable, portfolio managers have little incentive to hedge their position. In that case, property derivatives may even increase actuarial profit fluctuations, although economically the fluctuations would partially cancel each other out. While local jurisdictions vary from country to country, international regulatory authorities are setting guidelines for the use of property derivatives. For example, the US Financial Accounting Standards Board (FASB) is currently reviewing its requirements for the application of a property derivative as a hedge for real estate.

In the UK, the removal of regulatory and tax impediments revealed the tax efficiency of property derivatives over direct investments. In 2002, the Financial Services Authority (FSA) decided to allow life insurance companies to include real estate swaps and forward contracts as admissible assets in the computation of their solvency ratios. Further, the inland revenue legislation from September 2004 established a regime for taxation of property derivatives, thereby removing tax as a barrier to trading property derivatives. Key points were that no stamp duty is levied, be it land tax or reserve tax, on the issue or transfer of property derivatives. This gave rise to an immediate benefit over purchasing property, as stamp duty of up to 4 % of the property value is saved.

UK regulators ruled that property derivatives are taxed under derivatives contracts legislation, which broadly taxes all profits and losses as income. There are some exceptions for property derivatives. The taxation of income and capital gains will depend on what type of entity enters the derivatives transaction. The law defines two categories of institutions:

- Derivatives as a primary business. In such a case, the gains and losses are treated, and taxed, as income.
- Derivatives not as the primary business of the respective company. In this case the capital element will be subject to capital gains and the income element will be charged by a corporation tax.

Capital losses arising on contracts can be carried back against capital gains on similar derivatives arising in the previous two accounting periods. In general, capital gains may also be offset against other existing capital losses. Property Index Certificates (PICs), some of the earliest property derivatives in the UK, are treated as loans for tax purposes. Often, the PIC is split for accounting purposes into a loan and an embedded derivative. The latter is taxed separately under the derivative contracts legislation. The new collective investment scheme "Sourcebook COLL" allows authorized retail and nonretail funds to hold property derivatives.[1]

Two key legislative changes have cleared the way for a commercial property derivatives market in the UK. To summarize, companies can include property derivatives in their solvency calculations and capital losses can be offset against tax.

4.5 BUILDING LIQUIDITY

A successful derivatives market needs liquidity. Yet many potential participants are wary of entering the property derivatives market as liquidity is currently lacking. If and when the vicious circle is broken, property derivatives could be used by the major property investors, occupiers, hedge funds and, eventually, retail investors. Liquidity could attract players outside the traditional real estate community.

In the early days, trading in property derivatives had been impeded by a lack of diversity in the investor base, given that all investors were going in the same direction at the same time. Uniformity of opinion makes trading difficult to impossible. As long as market participants mostly agree on forecasted property prices, it will be hard to find counterparties for both sides of a deal. Investors must have a sufficiently large dispersion in beliefs, expectations, goals and horizons to catalyze trading. With the entry of a wider range of participants holding different views, trading prospects are brightening. Some of them might speculate as contrarians. In particular, hedge funds that seek returns from distorted prices could play an important role in building liquidity.

In April 2004, IPF reports that the range of property return expectations in the UK has widened considerably compared to earlier years. Their consensus forecast was based on contributions of 31 forecasters, of which 12 were property advisors and research consultants, 12 were fund managers and 7 were equity analysts specializing in the property sector. The average expectation for each group was similar, but the range of individual forecasts was very diverse. Table 4.2 shows the forecast statistics for rental value growth, capital value growth and total return according to *The Survey of Independent Forecasts* (2004). The 7.7 % range on the 2004 total return encouraged the development of the UK property derivatives market that started to take off in that year. Derivatives allow investors to take advantage of differences in views. Diversity in views is needed to build liquidity.

On the side of residential owner-occupied housing, Hinkelmann and Swidler (2006) are sceptic as to whether the market can take off. Mentally, homeowners tend to treat their home just as a consumption good rather than as an investment that involves price risk. Moreover, they would always be subject to a huge tracking error risk when hedging their homes with derivatives based on house price indices. This limits the effectiveness of hedging, and individuals may not use derivatives to manage house price risk. Ultimately, a lack of hedgers in the marketplace may lead to failure of residential housing derivatives such as the Chicago Mercantile Exchange (CME) housing futures contracts. It remains to be seen whether the involved challenges and hurdles can be successfully addressed.

---

[1] See www.fsa.gov.uk.

Table 4.2   Forecast statistics of 31 contributors in April 2004 (in %).

	Rental value growth			Capital value growth			Total return		
	2004	2005	2006	2004	2005	2006	2004	2005	2006
Maximum	1.6	3.4	4.5	8.0	5.1	5.0	14.1	11.4	12.0
Minimum	−2.0	−0.3	1.0	−0.7	−1.1	−1.0	6.4	6.0	6.0
Range	3.6	3.7	3.5	8.7	6.2	6.0	7.7	5.4	6.0
Standard Deviation	0.8	0.8	0.8	1.8	1.5	1.5	1.7	1.6	1.5
Median	0.5	1.2	2.3	3.3	1.0	2.0	10.0	8.0	8.8
Average	0.3	1.4	2.4	3.3	1.4	1.8	10.2	8.3	8.7

History shows that the buildup period of a new market is very fragile. Property derivatives were launched in the early 1990s and actually failed. The debut on the London Futures and Options Exchange (FOX) crashed in a combination of bad timing and scandal over false trades designed to create the impression of higher activity (see Chapter 5 on experience in property derivatives).

Today, liquidity in the property derivatives market has a good chance of being increased. In 1981, the first interest rate swap was done. Although people were sceptic at the time, it is now a trillion dollar market. The property market could experience a similar sort of growth in derivative instruments.

5

Experience in Property Derivatives

The early bird catches the worm.

By December 2007, property derivatives deals have been made public in Australia, France, Germany, Hong Kong, Italy, Japan, Switzerland, the UK and the US. Deals were referenced to both commercial and residential properties. Derivatives that reflect commercial real estate are typically tied to appraisal-based indices while derivatives that reflect owner-occupied residential housing usually use transaction-based indices as the underlying instrument (see Chapter 6 on property indices).

Most contracts are still executed as matched bargain trades between a buyer and a seller, with pricing determined through negotiations between them. As the market becomes more liquid, standardized contracts will become available directly from intermediaries. They will price the contracts and assume the risk of finding a suitable counterparty.

Several derivative structures have been developed and traded. So far, the bulk of trades has been structured as over-the-counter (OTC) swap contracts. In addition, a few derivatives are listed and traded on public exchanges. Most market participants are aiming to create derivatives that replicate the familiar characteristics of direct property investment, i.e. quarterly rental income and annual capital growth. As the market expands, the variety of structures increases. Derivative markets have a particular order of development and it is not unusual for options to develop after futures and swaps, because the option writers require these instruments to be liquid in order to hedge their positions.

The Property Total Return Swap (PTRS) is the most popular format and, in principle, swaps a fixed or floating interest payment for an amount calculated with reference to total returns on the property index, which consists of both rental income and capital gains (see Chapter 2 on swap transactions). The swap structure is quite simple and the variations usually only involve the choice of the index (country, sector and rental, and/or capital growth index), the tenor and the payment conventions.

A PTRS is a simple exchange of cash flows between two counterparties based on a notional amount. On one side, the buyer, taking a long position on commercial property, pays a fixed percentage interest rate or LIBOR plus a spread. In return, he or she receives a cashflow based on the annual total return of the property index. The seller, taking the equivalent short position, pays and receives cashflows that are exactly opposite.

The interest rate used by the market is typically the three-month LIBOR. The spread that is added reflects expectations of the future performance of the index, and what buyers and sellers are prepared to accept to take the position (see Chapter 8 on the property spread). In January 2008, many banks switched from the LIBOR-based to a fixed interest rate convention.

In the event that the annual total return is negative, i.e. if the capital value drops sufficiently to wipe out income returns, the total return buyer pays that negative return to the seller, in addition to the quarterly interest payments. The property index commonly used is an annual index, which is based on the actual performance of a large number of institutional portfolios and comprises an income or rental and a capital growth element.

In addition to swaps, contracts-for-difference (CFDs) are used as trading instruments. For deals on residential indices, such as the Halifax House Price Index, CFDs are already common. A CFD represents an index that is artificially set at 100 when the deal is done. Investors and hedgers then state the price at which they are willing to buy or sell the index at maturity. If two counterparties agree on a three-year deal at 112 and the index rises to 116, then the buyer receives $116 - 112 = 4$ times the contract size from the seller. The transactions are cash free until maturity, when profits and losses are settled. Many market participants find CFDs more intuitive than swaps.

Alternatively to an unfunded swap or CFD, it is also possible to make a funded investment. Rather than paying LIBOR plus a spread quarterly and receiving property returns, the investor pays the notional amount of cash upfront and receives property returns net of the spread. For example, on a two-year swap an investor could choose, rather than paying LIBOR plus 1 % on the swap, to pay 100 % of the notional amount and receive the property return minus 1 % each year and 100 % redemption after two years.

The basis for property derivatives documentation is the International Swaps and Derivatives Association (ISDA) documentation. Just as for other derivatives, ISDA has prepared standardized documents for property swaps, in order to facilitate trading. The Property Index Derivatives Definitions were published in May 2007. Standardization aims to reduce transaction costs, legal risk and transaction time, to increase transparency and confidence in the market, and to improve efficiency and liquidity. In addition to the definitions, ISDA provides confirmation templates for forwards and swaps in the US (Form X) and in Europe (Form Y), as well as an annex that describes the indices on which the trades are based. By September 2007, the Association has included the Standard&Poor's/Case–Shiller Index, the Office of Federal Housing Enterprise Oversight (OFHEO) Index, the National Council of Real Estate Investment Fiduciaries (NCREIF) Index, the worldwide Investment Property Databank (IPD) Indices, the UK Halifax House Price Index, the FTSE UK Commercial Property Index and Radar Logic's Residential Property Index (RPX). The definitions booklet covers issues such as disruption events on these indices. More indices, as well as confirmation templates for options and basket trades, are likely to follow.[1]

5.1 UNITED KINGDOM

After years of a hesitant existence, the UK property derivatives market is developing confidence and stability that has generated a momentum of excitement. Property derivatives had a small cohort of advocates since the mid 1990s, but for most of that period only Barclays Capital was involved. The market remained illiquid and one-sided. Apart from rare activity, the market did not start to grow until 2005. Transactions happened occasionally but volumes were very low.

The first publicly traded property derivatives were the futures that were traded on the London Futures and Options Exchange (FOX), introduced on 9 May, 1991. Pension funds used property derivatives when they first came out. The exchange offered four contracts based on indices for commercial property capital value, commercial rent, residential property and mortgage rates. The underlying indices of the FOX contracts were the IPD capital growth index, the IPD rental growth index, the Nationwide Anglia House Price (NAHP) index and the FOX Mortgage Interest Rate (MIR) index. While the IPD indices are based on appraisals and reflect

---

[1] See www.isda.org.

commercial properties, the NAHP is a transaction-based hedonic index on residential properties (see Chapter 6 on property indices).

Unfortunately, trading was suspended just a few months after the launch. It became public that trading volumes were artificially boosted using so-called wash trades, i.e. offsetting deals that in the end produce neither a gain nor a loss. However, real trading volume was much lower than expected. The discovery of this mischief hastened the contracts' demise. In sum, the market was open only from May to October of 1991.

Throughout the 1990s, several other initiatives were launched to get derivatives started. Iain Reid, a property consultant, realized that property funds could benefit hugely from the ability not just to build synthetic exposures to different segments of the market but also to hedge existing long positions by creating off-setting short positions. Reid moved to Barclays and found that its bankers were similarly enthusiastic about his plans to develop a product that could hedge property exposures. The UK real estate market had just been through a crash, and Barclays had property exposure as a result of bad loans made to property developers. To them, the idea that they could hedge that exposure was a revelation and they were very keen to launch something.

Together with Aberdeen Property Investors, Barclays Capital structured a tradable bond that pays out IPD index returns. They called these bonds Property Index Certificates (PICs). PICs link their coupon payments to the IPD All Property Income Return Index and the capital redemption value to the IPD All Property Capital Growth Index. Investors who wanted to gain exposure to the property market paid upfront to buy the bond and received income based on property valuations in the form of quarterly coupon and redemption payments. By issuing PICs, Barclays basically exchanged its long property exposure for a fixed income. The PICs were seen as bond instruments that pay a return based on an IPD index rather than pure derivatives. The instruments enable investors to bet on the market, but not against it. Since its release, the certificate has mainly created interest from high-net-worth, private bank and institutional investors.

In addition, Barclays launched exchange-traded Property Index Forwards (PIFs). These forward contracts on the IPD Capital Growth or Total Return Index included some standardized elements, to make the products tradable. However, in contrast to exchange-traded future contracts, not the market itself but the bank took the role of the market maker. Since the bank never really succeeded in developing a liquid secondary market, the concept was still based on matching buyers and sellers. Barclays continuously quoted prices for the contracts (Roche, 1995).

In 2004, the authorities loosened the legal and tax bindweed on the growth of a wider derivatives market. One of the earliest derivatives swap was arranged between Deutsche Bank and Eurohypo in 2005, and brought together a buyer and a seller of UK property risk. The seller exchanged a total property return (based on the IPD Index) for a LIBOR-based return paid by the buyer based on a notional principle. Prudential, the UK life assurer, and British Land also agreed on a commercial property swap at about the same time.

The formal launch of the Property Derivatives Interest Group (PDIG) on 16 September 2005 has set the crucial signal for the property market in the UK, which may serve as a role model for property derivatives trading elsewhere. However, the UK is somewhat fortunate because the available indices that are run by IPD are mature and widely accepted as accurate. That is not (yet) the case in most other countries.

In 2006, the market could build on the growth of the previous year and attracted further investment banks. Several banks started to quote option prices on IPD's main index. Further, it was hoped that the arrival of sectoral transactions would deliver a further boost to the market.

However, after a few trades on sector and even subsector indices in 2006, there were no more such deals in the first half of 2007. In essence, it remained a simple swap and forward market on the All Property Index with a few option trades, before trading volume soared in the wake of the US subprime mortgage crisis. The uncertainty introduced by the crisis attracted a number of new participants in the property derivatives market.

5.1.1   More market participants and banks joining the market

The British commercial property market is estimated to be about GB£ 600 billion. Pension funds, property companies and other professional investors own about half of this amount according to the Investment Property Forum (IPF) the parent company of PDIG.

On the buy-side, a diverse range of institutions, investment banks and individuals exists. Either they are unable to get quick access to the property market or want to rebalance an existing property portfolio. On the sell-side, there are large property funds that worry about a market downturn and want to reallocate a property investment to bonds or stocks. In other words, sales involve larger volume trades and buys smaller ones.

In 2006, the buy-side was easier to see and to find than the sell-side. Investors were keen to take exposure to the underlying property index, while few investors with physical property exposure were willing to sell. In 2007, the situation has changed. Many investors such as large insurance companies are now concerned about their property investment and willing to hedge, while it is no longer clear who wants to take on the exposure.

For professional real estate investors, derivatives on the IPD All Property Index are a relatively crude tool since these investors often want to express a view on more finely differentiated subsectors, such as retail warehouses or offices in central London. Sector swaps started to bring the market closer to the needs of fund managers. Disaggregation could further play an important role in the property swap market, since the All Property side could feed off growth in the sector trades.

ABN Amro, Goldman Sachs, Merrill Lynch and the Royal Bank of Scotland were among the most active from 2005 to 2007. Starting in 2006, Goldman Sachs offered property swaps and promised full liquidity; i.e. the bank was ready to warehouse a substantial amount of market risk. ABN Amro and Merrill Lynch also started to warehouse risk to an undisclosed limit. Some trades had a milestone character for the UK property derivatives market:

- ABN Amro and Merrill Lynch claim to be the first banks that traded a sector-specific property derivative in November 2005, a 15-month swap based equally on the All Property Index on one hand and the Retail Sector Index on the other hand. The notional was GB£ 30 million for each transaction leg. The deal was brokered by a joint venture between the London property adviser CB Richard Ellis (CBRE) and interdealer broker GFI, set up to handle property derivatives transactions.
- It was followed by the first subsector deal in August 2006, a GB£ 10 million total return swap linked to the IPD Shopping Centre Index, again between ABN Amro and Merrill Lynch. It was also brokered by the CBRE–GFI joint venture at an undisclosed price. Merrill Lynch brought structured notes on this index to the market the same year.
- In August 2006, Goldman Sachs launched the first London Stock Exchange-listed certificate linked to the IPD All Property Index. The denomination of such a certificate is as small as GB£ 10 and it has a maturity of five years. The investor receives a one-for-one exposure to the performance of the index return, subject to the fixed annual index adjustment of 2.8 %. Goldman Sachs marketed the product to both institutional and private investors.

Table 5.1   The 22 investment banks that are licensed to IPD by February 2008

Abbey National	HSBC
ABN Amro	HSH Nordbank
Bank of America	HypoVereinsbank
Barclays Capital	JP Morgan
BNP Paribas	Lehman Brothers
Calyon	Merrill Lynch
Commerzbank	Morgan Stanley
Credit Suisse	National Bank of Canada
Deutsche Bank	Royal Bank of Scotland
EuroHypo	Toronto Dominion
Goldman Sachs	UBS

Several brokers have joined forces with property agents to work as intermediaries, which is an example of how the physical property world and the financial world are converging. The alliance between the commercial property firm Cushman and Wakefield Finance and the interdealer broker BGC Partners is called Cushman and Wakefield BGC (CW BGC), and draws on a client base that owns more than half of the GB£ 330 billion in the UK institutional property market. Similarly, as already mentioned, the real estate firm CB Richard Ellis (CBRE) joined forces with the interdealer broker GFI Group. Also, the property service provider DTZ, as well as Tullet Prebon, Cantor Fitzgerald, ICAP, Vyapar Capital Market Partners and OTC broker Traditional Financial Services (TFS) started brokering property derivatives. In March 2007, TFS has agreed a cooperation with the UK property group Strutt and Parker on the UK property derivative business. TFS has also formed a partnership with Property Investment Market, a platform that allows property investments to be exchanged. Combining the strengths in property with those in derivatives could help to educate potential users of property derivatives, including both banking and property clients.

By February 2008, there were 22 investment banks that are licensed to market derivatives on the IPD indices, but only a few of these are also prepared to warehouse risk. This means that there is so far only a small interdealer market. Some investment banks make available firm prices to their clients on a weekly or even daily basis, which will enable the investor to either value their position or to close it out early. The licensed banks are listed in Table 5.1.[2]

The convergence of a number of factors is creating the conditions for a significant and lasting market to take hold. The recent increase in demand for UK property investment is supported by a shift in UK institutional portfolio allocation towards property and by increased demand from a number of overseas sources. The increased turnover in the investment market and growth in the invested property stock improves confidence in both valuations and liquidity, which in turn support confidence in the reliability and liquidity of derivatives. Also, the recent high performance of commercial property and today's uncertainty about future returns has stimulated interest from new investor types, including hedge funds, private equity and private investors. There is a larger variety of views and positions on the direction of the property market, which is creating both sellers and buyers of risk. The rapid growth of debt finance for commercial real estate has brought a variety of participants, particularly the banks, into the property market. Derivatives are an obvious extension of the suite of tools used to access and manage risk in both the debt and equity spheres.

---

[2] See www.ipdindex.co.uk.

5.1.2 Volumes and activity

All of the banks that are licensed to trade IPD-based property derivatives are required to report their market participation quarterly on a deal-by-deal basis to IPD. Since January 2004, IPD has published aggregated trading volumes on the IPD indices, where it counts both sides of a deal. The cumulative notional value of executed trades on the IPD UK Index reached GB£ 12.215 billion by the end of the fourth quarter of 2007. The total accumulated number of deals was 923, making an average deal size of about GB£ 13 million. There were 553 new trades reported in 2007, with a total volume of GB£ 7219 billion. The first quarter of 2007 was particularly strong with GB£ 2.927 billion of activity. Although the majority of the trades was referenced to the UK All Property Index, few swaps have also been taken out on the property sector indices, i.e. offices, retail, shopping centers and industrial. End-users are used to deal with slots between GB£ 10 and GB£ 100 million. The shape of the market has altered since 2004. The early deals were for relatively long periods, few in number and large in size. In 2007, there is a larger number of trades, but on average much smaller sizes and often short maturities. Table 5.2 shows the size of the property derivatives market traded on IPD Indices since January 2004.[3]

The UK property swap market offers a good liquidity, i.e. daily tradable bids and offer prices, out to five years. In August 2005, the only thing traders considered were three-year total return swaps on the All Property Index. In 2007, maturities range from six months to 15 years, but most trades are still between one to three years maturity. Short-term trades on the next available maturity resemble more an auction on the consensus for the returns of the running year rather than a long-term investment or hedge. UK IPD swaps often take the form of strips that use the monthly IPD index estimate as the initial fixing level and the actual annual index levels for the fixings thereafter.

In contrast to sector trades, contracts on the All Property Index experience good demand. Liquidity seems to have retreated from the sector indices back to the All Property Index. The sector indices would provide a more precise hedge for actual portfolios, but as long as there are only a few sector trades, investors still prefer the more liquid All Property swaps. As the market develops further, it is hoped that more and more contracts on regional or sectoral indices take place.

Moreover, the variety of property derivatives will increase with the further introduction of more contingent claims, i.e. call and put options. UK property derivatives have been traded mostly over-the-counter, but there are indications that a considerable exchange-traded market could emerge.

Banks and brokers are optimistic about market growth. In early 2007, Deutsche Bank estimated the total notional value of outstanding deals to be between GB£ 75 billion and GB£ 100 billion by 2010. For the same horizon, Goldman Sachs is seeing a volume of GB£ 150 billion. Back in 2005, TFS Brokers forecasted a cumulative notional value of GB£ 2 billion for 2006, GB£ 6 billion for 2007, GB£ 30 billion for 2008 and GB£ 240 billion for 2009. Further potential is certainly massive. Certain oil derivatives are said to be 16 times the underlying market.

5.1.3 It is not all just about IPD

IPD indices cover the commercial real estate market. On the side of residential property derivatives, contracts on the Halifax House Price Indices (HPIs) have been around since 1999

---

[3] See www.ipdindex.co.uk.

Table 5.2 Trading volumes of property derivatives on IPD indices. The trade information is provided to IPD by the banks licensed to trade derivatives on IPD indices

	Q1–Q4 2004	Q1 2005	Q2 2005	Q3 2005	Q4 2005
Total outstanding notional value (mGB£)	260	485	806	927	1,100
Notional value of trades executed each quarter (mGB£)	260	225	321	121	183
Total outstanding number of trades	10	14	42	56	80
Number of trades executed each quarter	10	4	28	14	24
Average outstanding deal size (mGB£)	26	35	19	17	14
Average deal size executed each quarter (mGB£)	26	56	11	9	8

	Q1 2006	Q2 2006	Q3 2006	Q4 2006	Q1 2007	Q2 2007	Q3 2007	Q4 2007
Total outstanding notional value (mGB£)	1963	2466	4124	6686	6769	7266	7916	9032
Notional value of trades executed each quarter (mGB£)	853	513	1658	864	2927	970	1660	1662
Total outstanding number of trades	139	189	279	415	428	473	543	703
Number of trades executed each quarter	59	54	90	87	153	90	96	214
Average outstanding deal size (mGB£)	14	13	15	16	16	15	15	13
Average deal size executed each quarter (mGB£)	14	10	18	10	19	11	17	8

(see Chapter 6 on property indices). City Index Financial Markets and IG Index, two London-based spread betting firms, offer bets on UK average house prices on the nearest two quarters. The bets are based on the Halifax House Price Survey. Goldman Sachs introduced call and put warrants and certificates on the Halifax All Houses, All Buyers and Standardized Average House price indices in 2004. The contracts of this first series expired in June 2006.

Unlike the commercial property derivatives market, the residential property derivatives market started not as a brokered market in which counterparties would transact matched deals but was intermediated by a risk-taking institution. By 2007, over GB£ 2 billion of derivative trades based on the Halifax HPI have been executed.

Santander Global Banking & Markets claims to be the number one provider of residential property derivatives in the UK, with over GB£ 1.5 billion traded by 2007.[4] The bank deals over-the-counter contracts as well as structured products such as capital guaranteed residential property bonds and warehouses the corresponding risk according to Andrew Fenlon, Head of Property Derivatives at Santander Global Banking & Markets. In conjunction with property agent Knight Frank, it developed a residential property plan, linked to the HPI and targeted at retail clients. Although the main interest and volume of property derivatives is in the commercial sector, i.e. on the IPD indices, several interdealer brokers also intermediate contracts on the HPI. Users of HPI derivatives mainly include mortgage banks and hedge funds.

Quotes on the HPI include maturities up to 30 years, i.e. a range much wider than for IPD derivatives. Trades on the HPI often take the form of CFDs with maturities quoted in steps of 12 months. The market uses the monthly, nonseasonally adjusted version of the Halifax HPI.

Santander has also provided the seed capital for the FTSEpx fund launched by MSS Capital, an asset manager in the UK, in June 2006. This fund was launched along with the FTSE UK Commercial Property Index Series. The index series is designed to reflect the investment performance of retail, office and industrial property in the UK. The performance data for the index is derived directly from the dedicated FTSEpx open-ended fund. The fund is a Guernsey Property Unit Trust, listed on the Channel Islands Stock Exchange, and was invested in an underlying portfolio with exposure to more than GB£ 10.5 billion across all subsectors by March 2007 according to the FTSE press release, 1 March 2007. FTSE claims its index is an important advance for the market because it offers daily published figures, which should increase liquidity and make the index suitable for short-term trades (see Chapter 6 on property indices).

The FTSEpx offers a readily available hedging solution for derivatives writers. Since the FTSE index is based on investable funds, replication of the index performance is easier than with the IPD Index. However, there has been very little trading volume in the FTSEpx derivatives so far.

First, the Royal Bank of Scotland (RBS) started to link its derivative products to the FTSE UK Commercial Property Index. RBS sold several five-year capital-guaranteed products tied to the FTSE index to high-net-worth individuals, and plans to develop products that will appeal to the retail market in the near future. FTSE and RBS claim that the index is much better suited for retail clients than the IPD index family. According to RBS, the lack of a liquid underlying asset remains a key issue with IPD indices. On the other hand, IPD claims that the FTSE index is not sufficiently accurate and robust, as it is drawn from a single fund. One fund is not going to behave exactly like the rest of the market, particularly when subsectors are considered. The annual IPD index references a portfolio of property that is valued at GB£ 192 billion, about 18 times larger than the FTSEpx reference portfolio.

---

[4] Abbey Financial Markets, a subsidiary of Abbey National, was the leading institution in the UK residential property derivatives market. Abbey National was acquired by the Santander Group in 2004.

However, Santander is also working on a range of structured investments based on the FTSE index for both retail and institutional investors. According to MSS Capital, other investment banks have also applied for an FTSE license, to use the index to create property derivatives including swaps and options. Mostly, banks intend to structure products based on the FTSE Commercial Property Index for retail investors. The FTSE brand for distribution of structured products is well known to these investors. There are many vehicles designed for the commercial real estate market, but besides the IPD derivatives market, there is so far no possibility of taking a short position in property. Further, property fund managers are benchmarked against the IPD Index and so will want to engage in derivatives relative to the IPD Index.

5.2 UNITED STATES

One of the largest potential markets for property derivatives is the United States. In 2007, the Chicago Mercantile Exchange and Global Real Analytics estimate the US property derivatives market to grow to US$ 106 billion in three to five years.

In the past two decades, the US housing market has experienced strong growth. In the early 1980s, the median home value in the US was about US$ 60 000. By the end of 2004, it had grown to US$ 190 000. From 1999 to 2004, house prices on the coast sides more than doubled.

This increase in housing prices was paralleled by declining mortgage rates. In the early 1980s, mortgage rates approached 18 %. Then they gradually decreased to 6 % by 2000. Given today's high prices and the recent increase in mortgage rates, there is much speculation about what lies ahead. However, even if housing bubbles exist and do not burst, minor shifts in value and sales can result in substantial losses for entire sectors of the economy. Such an overheated market attracts both investors that seek a hedge and speculators. The possibility to transfer the market's risk is thus becoming more important. Actually, the decline in house prices in 2007 that triggered the so-called subprime crisis has brought more attention to the property derivatives market and its hedging possibilities.

In the US, there are early examples of house price securities. Financial assets based on real estate include stocks and bonds that began trading on the New York Real Estate Securities Exchange (NYRESE) in 1929. Unfortunately, with the collapse of real estate security prices, and capital markets in general, the SEC decertified the NYRESE as a national market in 1941.

After a long break, property derivatives came into discussion again. The first property swap, linked to the National Council of Real Estate Investment Fiduciaries (NCREIF) Property Index (NPI), was completed in January 1993 (see Chapter 6 on property indices). Morgan Stanley intermediated the two counterparties. The seller was a large US pension fund that wanted to reallocate assets from property to equity, but did not want to buy or sell any property. The buyer, a medium-sized life insurance company, agreed to pay US$ LIBOR in exchange for income payments generated by properties.

In April 2005, NCREIF has awarded a mandate to Credit Suisse First Boston (CSFB) (renamed Credit Suisse Investment Bank on 1 January 2006) to develop derivative products based on the index. The derivatives were aimed at managers of institutional real estate portfolios, which Credit Suisse sees as a significant untapped opportunity for sophisticated risk-management products.

CSFB began marketing those products during the summer of 2005 and subsequently completed the first transactions. In January 2006, a real estate fund entered into a swap agreement to receive the total return on the NCREIF Office Index while paying the total return swap on the NCREIF Apartment Index. The US$ 10 million transaction was structured as a two-year trade according to Centennial Realty Advisors/National Real Estate Investor/Parke Chapman.

A Credit Suisse-related entity was counterparty to all trades. The Swiss bank was exclusively licensed for two years to distribute derivatives on the NPI. However, it waived those rights in October 2006 to build up market liquidity after executing only a handful of trades. According to *The Financial Times*, 3 May 2007, there have been only two trades, worth US$ 50 million. The exclusive agreement with NCREIF to provide derivative solutions based on the property index would have expired April 30, 2007.

In early 2007, further banks were granted licences to trade the NCREIF property index and are planning to launch a US platform to trade property derivatives (Four more banks, 2007). By December 2007, seven banks were licensed to trade derivatives on the NCREIF commercial property index. Besides Credit Suisse, Bank of America, Deutsche Bank, Goldman Sachs, Lehman Brothers, Merrill Lynch and Morgan Stanley are involved. The traded volume reached US$ 300 million by late 2007. More banks are expected to sign up for a licence contract within a few months (Banks move, 2007; Property derivatives, 2007). Given the potential, hedge funds and insurance companies are also starting to show interest in developing the US market for property derivatives.

Credit Suisse initially offered three basic trades to investors: Price Return Swaps on the capital value return component of the NPI, Property Type Swaps on the total return by property type subindices (for all reported property types except hotels, as hotels comprise only less than 3 % of the overall index) and Total Rate of Return Swaps for the NPI total return:

- In a *Price Return Swap*, the capital value return component, published quarterly by NCREIF, is exchanged against a fixed spread. The fixed spread is used to balance demand on both the long and short sides of the trade (see Chapter 8 on the property spread).
- A *Property Type Swap on the total return by property type subindices* is a total rate of return swap transaction in which an investor takes a long position in one property type and a short position in a different property type, based on the respective property type subindices. Depending on the property type swap that is entered into, the investor will either pay or receive a fixed spread to enter into this swap. The fixed spread will be determined by supply and demand in the market, and therefore could be positive, negative or zero.
- In a *Total Rate of Return Swap for the NPI total return* the quarterly total return published by NCREIF is exchanged against a three-month LIBOR plus or minus a spread. The spread is used to balance demand on both the long and short sides of the trade.

All trades are notional based. This means that they are unfunded and the only cash needed upfront to enter the trades are margin requirements necessary to manage counterparty risk evaluated on a counterparty-by-counterparty basis. The trades settle quarterly and have a maturity of two to three years. In April 2007, the property company CBRE claimed that the first trade on a US subindex had been closed.

5.2.1 US housing

Beyond commercial property, the second current initiative for property derivatives in the US considers owner-occupied residential housing. This market, estimated to be more than US$ 21 trillion, is much larger than its commercial counterpart. However, large institutions have shown little appetite to trade derivatives on residential property indices, consisting of privately owned houses. Institutional investors focus on commercial property, and do not trade residential property in volumes needed to encourage growth in a derivatives market.

Several derivative products based on a housing index have been proposed to hedge housing exposure in academic literature. To improve the possibilities to pool and share housing
investment risks, Case, Shiller and Weiss (1993) propose a market in futures contracts tied
to regional house price indices. Englund, Hwang and Quigley (2002) suggest that there are
large potential gains from policies or instruments that would permit households to hedge their
lump investments in housing. Case *et al.* attribute the failure of the London FOX contracts in
1991 to the public's lack of appreciation and understanding of such markets. Whether such
appreciation for housing markets now exists remains an open question.

The US market is still looking for a common benchmark. Multiple public exchanges or
platforms try to promote housing derivatives for builders, developers, lenders and professional
investors with large positions in real estate based on different index families. Although the
platforms have many differences, they all operate in a similar way to an ordinary stock market.

The Chicago Mercantile Exchange (CME) offers futures and options contracts designed to
follow home prices in 10 US cities, as well as an aggregated national index. CME opened
trading in contracts based on the S&P/Case–Shiller Home Price indices on 22 May 2006.
CME housing futures and options are cash-settled to a weighted composite index of national
real estate prices, as well as to specific markets in the following US cities: Boston, Chicago,
Denver, Las Vegas, Los Angeles, Miami, New York, San Diego, San Francisco and Washington
DC. Trading in the housing contracts has been relatively thin in the first year, with an average
daily volume of about 50 contracts. The notional value of all outstanding futures contracts was
slightly above US$ 77 million in August 2006. In total, the traded notional was approximately
US$ 340 million in 2006. In early 2007, volume was still low and only about 25 contracts a
day were traded on average. According to the CME, there is a "huge educational need" for this
new derivatives market.

Critics say that the design of the contracts has held the market back, as they only go out
to one year while most investors want to hedge for longer periods of time. This issue was
addressed in September 2007, when the CME extended its contracts on the S&P/Case–Shiller
index out to 60 months.

The Chicago Board of Options Exchange (CBOE)'s Future Exchange (CFE) offers futures
contracts that track prices nationally and regionally (North-east, South, Midwest and West)
and eventually in 10 metropolitan areas as well.[5] CFE contracts are linked to the median price
of existing home sales as tracked by the National Association of Realtors (NAR).

Further, HedgeStreet allows anyone with a US$ 100 deposit and an internet connection
to trade financial instruments called "housing price hedgelets" based on single-family house
prices in six different cities (Chicago, Los Angeles, Miami, New York, San Diego and San
Francisco). Just as the CFE contracts, the HedgeStreet hedgelets are based on indices of
NAR. CBOE and HedgeStreet announced on 22 February 2006 that they collaborated on retail
distribution of their contracts via joint marketing initiatives and that they would share certain
technologies and hosting facilities to achieve cost and distribution synergies. The agreement
also involved an equity investment by CBOE in HedgeStreet.

Moreover, the London-based International Real Estate Exchange (INREEX) intends to offer
contracts tied to average home prices published by the Office of Federal Housing Enterprise
Oversight (OFHEO), the agency that regulates the mortgage organizations Fannie Mae and

---

[5] See www.cboe.com/CFE.

Freddie Mac. The exchange's trading technology allows investors to trade the national or a state index online.[6]

The low trading volume in the contracts based on the S&P/Case–Shiller index caused Radar Logic, an analytic and data company providing a range of daily indices and analytic tools, to launch a further index family for residential property. The Residential Property Indices (RPX) represent the median transaction prices per square foot paid in one of 25 Metropolitan Statistical Areas (MSAs) on any given day. In addition, there is a national composite index, representing over US$ 10 trillion in residential properties. The RPX market targets investors that are exposed to mortgage credit or to the housing market cycles in general.

Derivatives trading in the RPX started on 17 September 2007 on an over-the-counter (OTC) basis with maturities expected to be from one to five years. Initially, licensed banks to offer products in the RPX market included Morgan Stanley, Lehman Brothers, Merrill Lynch, Deutsche Bank, Goldman Sachs and Bear Stearns. Trades are quoted in terms of price appreciation in percent for a given maturity date and executed as quarterly price return swaps exchanging a fixed payment against the quarterly index appreciation. For example, if one counterparty buys the index with a maturity of one year at 4 %, he or she pays 1 % every quarter in exchange for the actual quarterly index returns.

The interdealer broker ICAP announced the creation of a joint venture with Radar Logic to develop the RPX market in August 2007. In September 2007, ICAP intermediated the first derivative transaction, a total return swap, based on the RPX. The counterparties were two of the licensed banks. Further, Radar Logic has plans to roll out similar indices that allow trading in commercial real estate.

5.2.2   CME Expanding to Commercial Real Estate

After the launch of futures and options on regional home prices, CME announced a partnership with the commercial real estate index provider Global Real Analytics (GRA) on 6 September 2006. They listed future and option contracts based on the S&P/GRA Commercial Real Estate Indices (CREX) on 29 October 2007.

The S&P/GRA CREX indices capture underlying real estate dynamics by tracking transaction-based price changes in diverse property sectors and geographic regions. GRA has a 20-year history of capturing data and sees the new indices as a natural extension, suited for the use of publicly traded futures contracts.

Ten quarterly cash-settled contracts are available: a national composite index, five regional indices (Desert Mountain West, Mid-Atlantic South, Northeast, Midwest and Pacific West) and four national property type indices (retail, office, apartment and warehouse properties).

CME expects the users of the new property contracts to be different from those trading in housing derivatives. If someone hedges against house-price declines in an area, he or she develops or buys a house there. The commercial contracts, on the other hand, are designed for larger investors who hold commercial properties in their portfolios, such as pension funds and REITs.

To hedge real estate or home price declines, individuals can purchase put options based on a particular index. If prices fall, investors will naturally see the value of their real estate holdings decline, but they offset the losses with gains in the put options. The CME hopes that there will be enough speculators in the market to take the other side of the transactions.

---

[6] See www.inreex.com.

5.2.3   The ISE property derivatives market

The International Securities Exchange (ISE) launched a derivatives market based on the Rexx commercial real estate property indices in November 2006. The market will operate using the Longitude framework, a matching engine based on a Dutch auction process.

At the launch, a subset of the Rexx indices was chosen based on anticipated demand. For each index offered, a series of auctions was held prior to publishing the Rexx index, which allows market participants to trade digital and vanilla options as well as forward contracts on the index value.

The auction format differs from a traditional, continuously quoted market in several ways. Instead of requiring a discrete match between a buyer and a seller, the auction aggregates liquidity across all strikes and derivatives. The prices in the auction are determined by the relative demand represented by all the orders received up to that point. As the auction operates as a Dutch auction, all trades are cleared at the final auction market price, even if that market price is better than a trade's limit price. According to ISE, auction participants include pension funds, commercial property managers, investment banks, hedge funds, portfolio managers, REITs and CMBS. Besides serving as an underlying part for the ISE platform, the Rexx index is also said to be used in the OTC market.

5.3   OTHER COUNTRIES AND FUTURE EXPECTATIONS

The development of the property derivatives market has so far centered on the UK and the US. However, both interest and transaction volumes are growing throughout Europe and Asia. Market participants expect first trades in Denmark, Ireland, the Netherlands, Spain and Sweden after first trades in Australia, France, Germany, Hong Kong, Japan and Switzerland. As the quality of indices improve, more and more countries will see first trades. Also, the Pan-European IPD index creates strong interest from retail investors and from US pension funds. The trend is unlikely to spread to some countries where the data basis, needed to construct a reliable index, is insufficient.

Quickly increasing volumes are also expected due to the interest of insurance companies to hedge their liability risk, which depends heavily on real estate price changes. Liquidity will probably only change if more banks are willing to warehouse risks, i.e. take a risky position. More mature markets will lead to more standardized derivatives traded on exchanges. However, the OTC market is likely to be the dominant derivative format in the near future.

5.3.1   Australia

The property group Grosvenor and ABN Amro traded the first property derivative in Australia, based on the Property Council/IPD Australian Property Index, in May 2007. The trade took the form of a two-year total return swap.

5.3.2   France

The first French property swap was traded by Merrill Lynch and AXA Real Estate Investment Managers in December 2006. The undisclosed notional amount was linked to the IPD Total Return French Offices Annual Index. By mid 2007, the French market has developed a permanent two-way pricing, i.e. bid and offer prices are constantly quoted. By the end of the fourth quarter of 2007, GB£ 787 million have been transacted in 63 trades. Most trades have been done on the office component of the French IPD index.

Moreover, market participants report enquiries on derivatives relating to the National Institute for Statistics and Economic Studies (INSEE) residential house price index.

5.3.3 Germany

The first option on an IPD index outside the UK was traded in January 2007, referenced to the German IPD/DIX Index. Goldman Sachs acted as intermediary for this trade, which was one of the first property derivative transactions in Germany. Subsequently, BNP Paribas offered a capital protected note on a basket consisting of IPD UK All Properties, IPD France Offices and IPD Germany All Properties. IPD publishes official transaction data starting with the second quarter of 2007.

The market picked up quickly, with 44 trades on a total notional value of GB£ 283 million from the second to the fourth quarter of 2007. In May 2007, Deutsche Bank Research expects the German market to reach € 25 billion by 2010. HypoVereinsbank states that a volume of € 150 billion is possible in the long run for Germany and € 300 billion for the European Union. The numbers represent about 1 % of the respective physical property market.

5.3.4 Hong Kong

Starting in November 2006, Colliers International and interdealer broker GFI formed a joint venture, GFI Colliers, that offers brokerage services for derivative contracts on the Hong Kong University–Hong Kong Residential Price Index (HKU–HRPI). The index, complied by the University of Hong Kong, is based on transaction figures from the Land Registry. Hong Kong has long attracted attention in the global property world due to the volatility of its real estate prices. The HKU–HRPI was offered at 650 basis points over HIBOR or a total of roughly 10.5 %. ABN Amro and Sun Hung Kai Financial announced in February 2007 that they had traded a property swap based on Hong Kong's residential market. The inaugural transaction in Asia, at less than HK$ 100 million (US$ 13 million), was traded as a one-year price return swap. As buyer of the derivative, ABN Amro gained exposure to the city's housing market by receiving the annual change in the index. By September 2007, five global banks have received licenses to trade Hong Kong residential property derivatives.

5.3.5 Italy

The first Italian property derivative transaction, based on the IPD Italian Property Index, was carried out between Grosvenor and BNP Paribas in October 2007. ICAP acted as a broker for the trade that took the form of a two-year swap.

5.3.6 Japan

Further, Grosvenor and Royal Bank of Scotland have traded the first Japanese property derivative in July 2007. The monthly IPD Japan Property Index was used as the basis for the two-year total return swap. It was the first derivatives trade on commercial property in Asia, following the launch of a residential property derivatives market in Hong Kong. IPD uses data provided by Japanese real estate investment trusts (J-REITs) to calculate the index.

5.3.7 Singapore

GFI and Colliers claim they are working with the National University of Singapore to create residential indices for Singapore's housing market. The main issue is that there are few countries that have an adequate amount of transparency to develop credible and robust indices on which to trade.

5.3.8 Switzerland

The first property derivatives in Switzerland were launched by the Zuercher Kantonalbank (ZKB) in February 2006. The bank issued two structured products that were offered to institutional as well as retail investors as a new solution to invest into the asset class of real estate. One of the products was capital-protected while the other was structured as a discount certificate. The products could be subscribed in small denominations and the bank guaranteed a daily secondary market. The two products were based on the "Zuercher Wohneigentumsindex (ZWEX)," which tracks owner-occupied house prices in the Zurich greater area. The index is calculated and published quarterly and is based on transaction prices. The bank says that demand exceeded expectations, especially for the product with capital protection.

In September 2007, the first swap on commercial property was transacted. ZKB and ABN Amro traded the IPD Switzerland All Property TR Index against Swiss LIBOR plus an undisclosed spread.

5.4 FEEDBACK EFFECTS

Property derivatives will improve transparency in the real estate market. According to Tsetsekos and Varangis (2000), an active derivatives market plays an important role in facilitating an efficient determination of prices in the underlying spot market by improving transparency on current and future prices. A successful property derivatives market may have several feedback effects on its underlying properties and indices.

Derivatives and their prices generate information about supply and demand of market participants. After the establishment of a derivatives market and due to more and better information, efficiency in the spot market can very well improve. Derivatives make nontransparent prices visible. In particular, the observed derivative prices reveal the market's expectations. The result could be that market participants anticipate price expectations faster, and nonrandom price moves such as cyclical behavior could partly be washed out. It is important not to confuse true cycles with autocorrelation in an index that may simply arise due to the index construction method. It can be assumed that prices of physical properties adapt faster to new information if there is a derivatives market.

5.4.1 Impact on Volatility

There is mixed evidence on the impact of a derivatives market on its underlying asset market. Some studies have found a reduction in volatility after the introduction of derivatives while others conclude that volatility was not affected or even increased (see, for example, Bollen, 1998; Conrad, 1989; Harris, 1989).

The general reasoning for an increase in volatility states that derivatives attract speculators who may destabilize the base market and create bubbles, and that the closing out of hedging positions shortly before expiration creates additional price variation. On the other hand, a decrease of volatility could result as derivatives make a market more complete, reduce transaction costs and enhance information flows. Also, the transfer of speculative activity from the base market to the derivative market may dampen volatility.

Ross (1976) suggests that derivatives improve the efficiency of incomplete markets by expanding the opportunity set faced by investors. This in turn should reduce the volatility of the underlying asset.

Kumar *et al.* (1998) show that option listings have beneficial effects and improve the market quality and liquidity of the underlying stocks. They analyzed the impact of derivatives on their underlying assets for 174 stocks that had an option listed on either the American Stock Exchange (Amex), the Chicago Board Options Exchange (CBOE), the New York Stock Exchange (NYSE), the Pacific Stock Exchange (PSE) or the Philadelphia Stock Exchange (PHLX) from 1983 to 1989. In particular, they observed a decrease in the bid-offer spreads and increases in quoted depth, trading volume, trading frequency and transaction size after the introduction of derivatives. In summary, the listing of options resulted in reduced transaction costs for the underlying stocks. Further, they found that information asymmetries decreased and pricing efficiency increased.

Hwang and Satchell (2000) address the question of whether derivative markets destabilize asset markets. Based on the FTSE100 stock index, they found that introducing options reduces fundamental volatility and that the new options market has stabilized the underlying asset market. McKenzie *et al.* (2001) examined the impact of individual share futures on the volatility of the underlying shares. They found a reduction in both systematic risk and unconditional volatility.

Finally, Platen and Schweizer (1998) describe feedback effects that arise due to the hedging procedure of derivatives. They explain a stochastic behavior of volatility by incorporating the technical demand induced by hedging strategies. Exotic derivatives such as barrier options, where a hedger eventually quickly needs to unwind large positions in the underlying asset, can well increase volatility in the short term. However, as physical properties, unlike stocks, do not serve as a liquid hedge for derivatives, such an adverse effect on the volatility of the property market cannot be expected.

5.4.2   Impact on Risk Premium

Derivatives reflect the market's sentiment and expectation quickly in their prices. Improved understanding and transparency could foster the acceptance of real estate as an asset class. Further, derivative markets should provide accurate signals for an optimal allocation of capital and risk (Geltner *et al.*, 1995).

Higher attractiveness and better risk management possibilities due to property derivatives could drive property prices generally upward. In other words, the risk premium and accordingly the cost of capital shrinks, since risk can better be measured and managed. However, this will only occur when there is enough liquidity and risk management opportunities. The investment bank Merrill Lynch estimates that this scenario can begin to happen if derivative volumes traded reach at least the transaction value of direct property. The bank estimates the critical size in the UK to be GB £50 billion turnover per year for the commercial sector. With the rapid growth of the UK property derivatives market, such a feedback effect could soon be seen to start.

5.4.3 Impact on Appraisal Practice

The introduction of the commercial property derivatives market in the UK has raised some issues related to the valuation process of appraisers (according to the Royal Institution of Chartered Surveyors (RICS)). A sufficiently liquid market of commercial property derivatives would offer useful information about how the market expects property values to evolve. Appraisers could take this information into account when performing a valuation. However, appraisers may pay little attention to derivatives prices in the early stages of the market development.

When performing a valuation, appraisers prefer using comparable evidence. However, this approach has a number of shortcomings. First of all, it will always be retrospective by definition. Further, the illiquid nature of the physical commercial property market means that transactions are only rarely observed. Moreover, comparable deals may include covenants, incentives and lease clauses that are undisclosed but clearly price relevant and thus distort the comparability.

A forward price curve implied from derivatives could facilitate valuations and increase valuation accuracy by providing market forecasts for rents, yields and capital values on a daily basis. Such forecasts could be incorporated into the valuation process and would provide a timelier indicator than retrospective transaction data. Some appraisers already use derivative prices on the IPD All Property Index and its subsector indices as a starting point for the valuation process. Note that the valuations in turn are used to calculate the IPD indices. In effect, if appraisers follow more closely the forward curve of property prices, the index could follow the prices of the derivatives on them.

However, a property price forward curve will not make appraisals obsolete. The heterogeneous nature of the property market leads the appraiser to place a higher weighting on bottom-up analysis rather than a top-down analysis starting from an index that does not reflect local market conditions. In order to do so, the appraiser must still use comparable transactions for reference or discounted cash flow (DCF) techniques. The problem of heterogeneity and of the associated basis risk arising when valuing a single property based on an index will be less important if index coverage expands to incorporate property at a regional, city and even local level.

5.4.4 Impact on Transaction Volumes

Another feedback effect concerns activity. Baum (1991) says that the introduction of a derivatives market potentially reduces trading volume in the spot market, since the transfer of risk and return through derivatives make physical transaction at least partly obsolete. However, evidence is mixed. Other studies show that the existence of derivatives have actually improved activity in the related spot market (see Dresig, 2000).

However, there is some concern that a successful derivatives market will lead to fewer transactions in the underlying property market, reducing the base market's liquidity and increasing its volatility. This may have a significant impact on the underlying indices used to measure property returns, particularly the capital growth indices, which rely on valuations based on transactional evidence. Derivative advocates argue that there will always be demand for physical property from investors who believe they can beat the market through picking individual properties and actively managing them.

6
Underlying Indices

Apples and oranges.

Key to the success of a property derivatives market is the existence of a transparent and reliable index that can be used as an underlying value. Creating such an index for properties is by no means an easy task. No two buildings are identical; i.e. properties are heterogeneous constituents of an index. Consequently, recording and averaging only prices or valuations lead to a poor-quality index. All characteristics of a property that determine its value also need to be considered, so that prices can be adjusted for heterogeneity and finally be aggregated.

Most existing indices were initially constructed as descriptive measures, typically targeted as a benchmark instrument. Thus, it is not clear that these indices are suitable as underlying instruments for derivatives, i.e. as operative measures. To achieve a high accuracy and to earn wide trustworthiness, the following basic criteria should be fulfilled:

- *Representativeness.* The index must truly reflect risk and performance of the respective real estate market and idiosyncratic risk should be reduced to an acceptable level by including a large enough number of objects. Just as for the stock market, where an index with a limited number of titles represents the overall market well, a large enough sample represents the property market as a whole.
- *Transparency.* The calculation method of the index has to be publicly available.
- *Track record.* A long track record helps people to understand the index and to judge its representativeness and behavior in past economic circumstances.
- *Objectivity and minimization of potential fraud.* The input data must be free of subjective preferences and valuation practices. A large number of independent data providers further reduces the risk of manipulation, as the data of each provider gets a smaller weight in the overall index.
- *Actuality and high frequency.* High-frequency indices are typically preferred. However, high frequency requires a lot of data. By the time data are used in the index calculation, it must still be actual and representative. A new index point is usually calculated after a time period that observes a sufficiently large sample of new transactions or valuations. Frequency is directly dependent on the number of observations: the more observations, the higher the possible frequency. On the other hand, if the period is too long, the problem of temporal aggregation can introduce a significant bias; i.e. an observation that occurred at the beginning of a period is only used for calculations when the period has ended, resulting in a time-lag for that observation.

The real estate market as a whole is an aggregate of many submarkets such as owner-occupied housing, offices or land. Usually the performance of a submarket and not the overall market is the focus of an investor. It is important to take indices as underlying instruments that have a large community of potential users. Primary users are generally institutional investors, but private investors should also be able to understand and benefit from property derivatives. While investors see real estate as an asset class that must generate a return as high as possible, homeowners see their house as a consumption good with some price risk. The submarkets for the two are completely different. The choice of an index as a suitable underlying instrument for derivatives depends mainly on the criteria of the region, property type and data base (rents, transaction prices or appraisal values). Types with a potential volume that is sufficiently large for a reasonable derivatives market include offices, residential properties, retail space and industrial space. It is doubtful whether more special property types such as hotels or even land would find a big enough market.

Owner-occupied housing is treated very differently around the globe. While homeowners borrow relatively moderately and stay for decades in their home in central Europe, households in the UK and in the US are much more sensitive to property price movements. Often, they are ready to realize gains by selling their home or they increase the mortgage once prices have appreciated. Only the latter mind-set may lead to a broadly supported desire for protection against falling house prices. The market for owner-occupied housing is huge, and the sufficiently large number of transactions make indices more reliable.

From a geographical view, national, regional or local coverage could be considered according to the needs of potential investors. Homeowners who look for protection prefer a local focus to minimize their tracking error. Investors seeking broad diversification instead prefer a nationwide index. Institutional investors with large positions in office buildings probably prefer the office index of a particular city to hedge their exposure.

In general, a significant correlation still exists between submarkets and the overall property market, since they substitute each other to a certain degree. Thus, a broader index instead of a regional one can be used as proxy-hedge. Brown and Matysiak (1995) show that for a reduction of 95 % of idiosyncratic risk, 171 objects are needed, under the assumption of a low correlation of 0.1 between the objects in the portfolio.

6.1 CHARACTERISTICS OF UNDERLYING INDICES

6.1.1 Representative sample size

The number of prices or valuations per index point is crucial for the index representativeness. The smaller the sample size, the larger the bias due to idiosyncratic risk of the included objects. Figure 6.1 shows the dependence of idiosyncratic risk in an index as a function of the number of objects. The variance of the index is a function of the variance of the objects σ^2, the number of objects contained in the index N and the correlation between the objects ρ. For simplicity, it is assumed that variance for all objects as well as correlation between any two objects are the same and constant. Hence,

$$\sigma^2_{index} = \frac{\sigma^2}{N}[1 + (N - 1)\rho] \tag{6.1}$$

For N to infinity,

$$\sigma^2_{index} \rightarrow \sigma^2 \rho \tag{6.2}$$

Therefore $\sigma^2 \rho$ is the risk that cannot be diversified away.

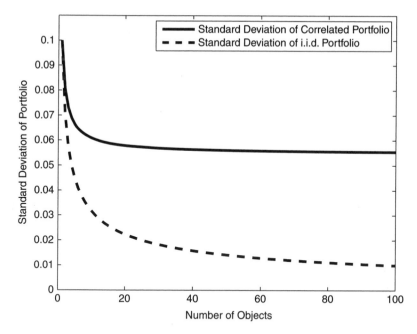

Figure 6.1 Idiosyncratic risk in an index. A standard deviation of 0.1 is assumed for the objects and a correlation of 0.3 respectively zero between the objects

6.1.2 Residential and commercial indices: transactions versus appraisals

Transaction-based indices are widely seen as the best to reflect movements of true market prices. The hedonic method is able to solve the problem of heterogeneity very well, by adjusting for quality. The shortcoming of transaction-based indices is the necessity to observe enough individual transactions. For office buildings in a mid-size city, there are just not enough transactions to have the representative sample that is needed to calculate a transaction-based index on a reasonably frequent basis. In such a case appraisal-based indices apply.

Property indices are classified along two main dimensions: type of property and geographical expansion. Geltner and Miller (2001) define the categories:

- Residential owner-occupied housing
- Residential apartment renters
- Retail
- Office
- Industrial
- Hotel and convention

Except owner-occupied residential housing, the categories cover commercial purposes. Data sets are very different for owner-occupied housing and commercial real estate. For owner-occupied housing, no rent is observed and thus a discounted cash flow (DCF) method cannot be applied. On the other hand, prices of many transactions and the corresponding property characteristics can be recorded. For the commercial categories, fewer transactions are typically observed. However, DCF methods and other valuation methods can be applied due to the generated income stream. In summary, owner-occupied housing indices are usually based on transactions, while commercial property indices are based on appraisals.

In addition, there are indices that are based on indirect real estate vehicles such as REITs, funds and real estate companies. The advantage of using these indices as underlying instruments for derivatives is their public observability in the market. The disadvantage, however, is the typically relative low correlation to direct property investments. Hence, they do not accurately represent real estate prices and are rarely suitable as a substitute for direct property indices. Also, real estate companies are subject to management risk.[1] A derivative on an index of property companies is simply a derivative on a stock basket. On the Chicago Mercantile Exchange (CME) and the Chicago Board Options Exchange (CBOE), options on REIT indices (e.g. the Dow Jones Equity REIT Index) have already been traded for quite a while. The question is which market is reflected by the index performance. Indices consisting of property companies are typically much more volatile than indices of direct property investments and are influenced by the general equity market.

6.1.3 Geographical focus

Besides the type of use of properties, the geographical focus is of interest to index and derivatives users. A geographical focus is typically represented by urban and rural or by local and national indices. In general, the narrower the geographical focus is defined and measured, the better an index is able to track individual properties. The tracking error is a major concern when a property owner wants to hedge an estate.

However, the level of geographical focus has a natural limitation. To be representative, unbiased and stable, and to minimize the impact of outliers and limit potential manipulation, a reasonable index must include a significant number of transactions or valuations regularly. Thus, the regional focus cannot be too narrow from a practical point of view. There is a trade-off between idiosyncratic risk of the index and geographical focus.

6.1.4 Single objects

Single objects that are owned by one individual are typically not suitable as underlying assets for derivatives. Too many moral hazard problems arise. For example, a homeowner who bought a put on his house has an incentive to sell it too cheaply to a related person. Also, if the occupier does not bear the risk of a bad sales price any more, he or she has less incentive to keep the house in good shape.

6.1.5 Vacancy levels

Vacancy risk is a major concern for property managers. Thus, the possibility to hedge against rising vacancy would be attractive to them. However, before a derivatives market on vacancy can arise, reliable and representative vacancy indices need to be established. Also, hedging vacancy with an index can result in substantial basis risk, especially for property portfolios with few objects.

---

[1] For an analysis of the relation between real estate companies and real estate market prices, see, for example, Barkham and Geltner (1995), Gordon *et al.* (1998), and Moss and Schneider (1996).

6.1.6 Total return and price indices

While price indices reflect the pure price development of the underlying property universe, total return indices also include rent income and its changes. In addition, income indices that solely track the development of rents exist. Appraisal-based indices can include both appraisals on the properties and rental income. Such appraisal-based total return indices are typically used for commercial property indices.

6.1.7 Index weighting

Stock indices are usually price, capitalization or equally weighted. Since properties are typically not split into shares, price and capitalization weightings are equivalent. An equally weighting scheme would give small objects the same importance as very large objects. This does not represent the market properly. As for stock indices, weighting according to capitalization of the components seems most reasonable for property indices.

For appraisal-based indices, a problem arises if objects are bought or sold. As long as the former respectively subsequent owner also submits a valuation data to the index data pool, there is no inconsistency. A large number of objects should be able to make the impact of a single object, which drops out of the index or is newly included, small enough so that no significant bias occurs.

6.2 APPRAISAL-BASED INDICES

Since properties are often held for longer periods of time, there is relatively little data of real market transactions. This is especially the case for commercial properties. To track possible changes in value during such a holding period, appraisal valuation is used as a substitute for market valuation. The appraisal value should reflect the most probable price that could be achieved if the property was sold in the market (Wofford,1978). The appraisal valuation is usually done by using discounting methods and/or by looking at market prices of comparable objects. Especially in the Anglo-Saxon countries, appraisal-based indices are widely applied and accepted as performance benchmarks. Here three index families of appraisal-based indices are discussed: the IPD indices, the FTSE property indices and the NCREIF indices.

In Europe, the British group Investment Property Databank (IPD) is the most popular provider of appraisal-based indices. The group has cooperations in many European as well as in some Asian countries with regard to sourcing data. In the US, the NCREIF NPI Index is the dominant appraisal-based index that measures commercial real estate performance. The basic principle behind the indices is the pooling of performance data of institutional real estate investors. The data are based on the periodic appraisals of chartered surveyors. In the UK, appraisers approved by IPD must be members of the Royal Institution of Chartered Surveyors (RICS). Definitions and guidelines for the valuation methods are collected in the so-called "Red Book."

Appraisal data are typically used to calculate a number of indices, e.g. a Total Return All Property Index. Indices are differentiated along components such as value growth, income return or total return and along properties included, i.e. along property type and geographical focus. While value growth indices measure the change in value of a pool of properties, income return reflects the net cash return generated by rents. The total return is a combination of the two.

6.2.1   Problems in constructing an appraisal-based index

Several construction issues arise with appraisal-based indices. Discrepancies between appraisal valuation and market (transaction) prices do not only come from bad appraisals but also from systematic biases (Gau and Wang, 1990; Geltner, 1989). A main source of biases in the aggregation of different data into one index number is that they are temporally lagged; i.e. the index reflects the real market prices only with a delay (Guttery and Sirmans, 1998). Further, since not all aggregated valuations are done at the same time, a smoothing effect results. Valuations are done typically only once a year, but at different dates for different objects. Valuations that influence the index could thus be lagged by up to a year. Another smoothing effect arises through the use of a backward-looking valuation process; i.e. past returns or past transactions are used to calculate the valuation. The smoothing leads to an underestimation of index volatility. Critics say valuation indices often fail to reflect a market turning point in time (Fisher *et al.*, 1994).

A further problem in aggregation is autocorrelation, which is related to smoothing. Brown and Matysiak (1995) find an autocorrelation of single objects close to zero. However, temporal aggregation can result in significantly autocorrelated values for an index. More precisely, the index shows a cyclical behavior. The asynchronous inclusion of information results in a kind of moving average.

6.2.2   Appraisal practices

An appraisal is an estimate of a property's current market value. There are different appraisal methods and techniques that apply. Appraisers take into account recent sales of comparable properties, replacement cost and other appraisals of similar types of assets, if such information is available. Appraisals should be distinguished between internal and external ones. An internal appraisal is one prepared for the investment manager or institutional investor by in-house professional real estate staff. External appraisals are performed by independent parties, typically official appraiser institutes.

In the UK, the International Valuation Standards Committee (IVSC) defines appraisal methods and practices. In the US, the Appraisal Institute (AI) takes a similar role, according to the US National Index Valuation Guidelines.

The open market value (OVM) is the best price that could be achieved from a property sale, without any obligations and against cash payment, on the valuation day under the following requirements:

- The owner is willing to sell.
- There is a reasonable time frame for the sale.
- There are unchanged market conditions and circumstances during the sales process.
- Special interests of potential buyers are ignored.
- The acting of the counterparties is rationale and unforced.

The OVM is typically evaluated using an income or investment method. This DCF method reflects the actual rental income of a property, net of administration cost, by discounting them to a present value.

The data that contributing property managers submit periodically are market values for each property that qualifies for the index. The values that the data contributors submit are the values that they believe are the properties' fair actual market values. A change in value from one period to another can have several reasons:

- The property was externally appraised by a new appraiser.
- Changes in market conditions such as occupancy, rental, capitalization and interest rates during the period were observed.
- A property value may be adjusted only for capital expenditures made during the period. This is a pure accounting adjustment which reflects the amount of the capital expenditure.

The main risk of a valuation-based process is that information entering the index is not correct or not reliable. Most significantly, valuers may tend to be backward-looking in making their valuation, referencing to recent valuation values. This has the mentioned effect of smoothing property return volatility. Drawbacks of the valuation process and the appraisal-based indices arise because valuers may be:

- under pressure from investors and so overestimate the property's value;
- overly influenced by certain factors, e.g. local markets;
- not reacting to changing markets appropriately;
- relying on comparables that are outdated;
- reluctant to mark-up (mark-down) property when markets move.

To ensure a high degree of process quality, the UK and US have a well-supervised surveying practice. The methodology is standardized, and there are professional guidelines for the use and citing of comparable transaction data.

Several studies have been performed to measure the errors between valuations and subsequent sale prices. For example, a study by property consultants Drivers Jonas and IPD analysed 8500 transactions between 1982 and 1995. The number of valuations lying within a $\pm 10\%$ band around the sale price was 30% and within a $\pm 20\%$ band it was 67%. In years with a strongly rising market, the accuracy drops to only 56% within $\pm 20\%$ in 1998 and 52% in 1989.

Further, a study by RICS jointly with IPD showed that accuracy of valuations in the UK, France, Netherlands and Germany improved recently in a steadily rising market environment. The bias towards undervaluation was again confirmed in this study with these countries experiencing 80, 70, 70 respectively 38% of properties sold at a higher price than the most recent valuation. Additionally, the study shows for all four countries that the larger the property, the higher the valuation accuracy. Generally, valuation accuracy tends to be directly related to the capital growth rates.

In summary, the studies suggest improving accuracy with a bias towards conservative undervaluation.

6.2.3 Investment Property Databank

The European market for property derivatives is primarily based on a set of benchmark market indices, published by the Investment Property Databank (IPD).[2] By the end of 2006, IPD published individual country indices for 15 European countries, as well as a Pan-European index. The quality of the European IPD indices varies across countries. IPD partners with various local data contributors. The markets with the most developed IPD indices are the UK,

---

[2] See www.ipdindex.co.uk.

Table 6.1 Countries benchmarked by IPD by the end of 2006

Country	Index start	Number of properties in the index	Total value of properties (billion €)	Estimated percentage of investment market
Australia	1985	720	45 538	25
Austria	2004	908	7 798	36
Belgium	2005	257	5 342	18
Canada	1984	2 050	47 993	50
Denmark	2000	1 222	12 056	40
Finland[a]	1998	2 830	17 116	61
France	1986	7 518	99 558	62
Germany	1996	2 938	53 847	21
Ireland	1984	331	5 820	82
Italy	2002	840	13 763	24
Japan	2003	835	25 723	10
Netherlands	1995	5 369	45 174	62
New Zealand	1989	281	2 962	
Norway	2000	497	10 817	44
Portugal	2000	587	7 795	53
South Africa	1995	2 478	11 985	60
Spain	2001	549	15 569	53
Sweden	1984	1 027	21 880	34
Switzerland	2002	3 478	29 350	38
UK	1981	12 137	284 622	55

[a] The Finland index is calculated by the Institute for Real Estate Economics KTI and is published by IPD.

France, Germany and the Netherlands. The index for Belgium is recommended for consultative purposes only, and the one for Finland is actually not calculated by IPD, but is IPD-compatible. The IPD Pan-European Property Index measures the combined performance of real estate markets in the 15 countries.

In addition to European countries, Australia, Canada, Japan, South Korea, New Zealand and South Africa are also covered by IPD. Further, the index provider plans to introduce a commercial property index for Hong Kong, with Singapore to follow. Further expansion would include Shanghai and Beijing, as well as a Pan-Asian investment property index similar to one established in Europe. IPD has also launched a Global Property Index. The first release of this index is meant for benchmark reasons only, not as an underlying asset for derivatives. Table 6.1 lists the existing IPD indices by country, with data obtained from IPD.

Most indices are built on an annual format, with the exception of Ireland, Australia and Canada, which are available on a quarterly basis. For the UK and Japan, there are monthly, quarterly and annual indices available.

The size of the portfolios monitored by IPD is largest for the UK indices. Further, the history for the UK indices is much longer than for other countries. The IPD UK All Property Annual index is the flagship index and includes 12 137 properties valued at GB £192 billion by December 2006. IPD estimates that the annual index covers approximately 55 % of the market. It is broken down in subsectors including retail (47 %), office (35 %), industrial (15 %) and others (3 %). The index is significantly weighted towards retail property. The annual index has so far been the reference for derivatives, as it is the most developed and reliable index. A Quarterly Index was launched in May 2006 and captures 67 % of the annual index, with 8273 properties valued at approximately GB £128 billion as of March 2007. This index facilitates derivatives transactions, since transactions will no longer be based upon an annual performance. It is expected that the quarterly index, which matches the funding leg payment frequency of most derivative instruments, replaces the annual index as the new market standard for property derivatives. The same frequency is meant to become standard for other countries covered by IPD.

IPD also produces a monthly index for the UK that, at GB £56 billion, covers less than one-third of the properties contained in the annual version. A monthly index requires monthly capital valuations from data contributors and is thus limited to funds with monthly reporting. Monthly index returns are released on the tenth business day of the following month. The performance of the monthly index is used throughout the year to estimate how the annual index might turn out. However, since the composition between the two is not the same, there is a discrepancy between the annual and monthly index performance.

The index performance is split into capital growth (CG) and income return (IR). Figure 6.2 shows the CG and IR indices for the UK. The total return (TR) index combines both elements and is the default measure for country indices. Furthermore, subindices are available by sector, covering retail, office, and industrial as well as residential properties (see Chapter 16 on sector indices).

The Japanese IPD index is based on the performance of J-REITs and institutional portfolios. In 2006, the index represented 1299 properties with a total capital value of about US$53 billion, representing approximately 10 % of the Japanese investment property market.

The Japanese index does not have full IPD status yet and is mainly for consultative purposes. Rates of return on the index may be restated in the future, with further evolution of the property database for the country. It is predominantly comprised of offices, 61 % of total capital value, with Central Tokyo offices accounting for nearly 36 % of the total index value. Retail and

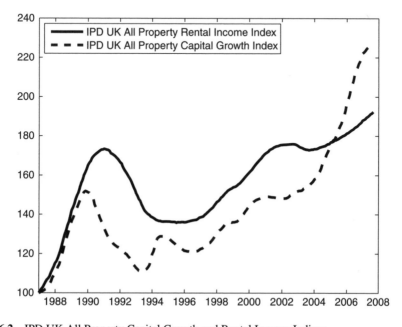

Figure 6.2   IPD UK All Property Capital Growth and Rental Income Indices

residential assets amount to 21 and 17 % of the total index value. The IPD index for South Korea was established in 2007 and is so far also only recommended for consultative purposes.

IPD compiles indices from individual property performance data supplied by institutional investors, funds and property companies, which directly invest in property. The IPD UK index extends back to 1971. It is important to note that the valuation-based indices reflect the accounting practice of institutional investors, since their valuations enter the index. Hence, appraised valuation can deviate from an economic valuation. The valuations used for the calculation of the index are generally the same as those used in balance sheets. However, using a valuation-based index as an underlying asset for a derivative provides a tool that hedges the accounting value of investors.

Index construction

Indices show unleveraged returns on standing investments held through the year. Standing investments are properties held from one valuation period to the next. Any properties bought, sold, under development or subject to major refurbishment during the course of the period are excluded.

The total return (TR) is defined as the annual compounded rate of monthly capital appreciation, net of capital expenditure, plus monthly net income expressed as a percentage of monthly capital employed. Income received is income receivable net of income written off, property management and irrecoverable costs. Therefore annual total returns are calculated in two steps. Returns are first calculated for each individual month and then compounded over the 12 months for which the return is required. For a single monthly period the total return formula is

$$\text{TR}_t = \frac{\text{CV}_t - \text{CV}_{t-1} - C_{\text{exp}_t} + C_{\text{rec}_t} + \text{NI}_t}{\text{CV}_{t-1} + C_{\text{exp}_t}} \tag{6.3}$$

where TR_t is the total return for month t, CV_t is the current valuation at the end of month t, C_{exp_t} is the sum of capital expenditures in t and C_{rec_t} is the sum of capital received from deinvestment. NI_t is the net income in month t, i.e. rental income net of administrative and maintenance costs. The formula assumes that capital expenditures take place at the start of the month, while capital receipts and income are receivable at the end of the month. The same principles apply to the calculation of capital growth (CG) and income return (IR) indices:

$$\text{CG}_t = \frac{\text{CV}_t - \text{CV}_{t-1} - C_{\text{exp}_t} + C_{\text{rec}_t}}{\text{CV}_{t-1} + C_{\text{exp}_t}} \tag{6.4}$$

$$\text{IR}_t = \frac{\text{NI}_t}{\text{CV}_{t-1} + C_{\text{exp}_t}} \tag{6.5}$$

The monthly return forms the basic building block for returns over all other periods. The results are chain-linked into a time-weighted index series; i.e. equal weight is given to each month's return. Quarterly returns are computed by compounding the returns for three consecutive months and annual returns by compounding 12 months of returns. To calculate quarterly and annual returns it is necessary first to construct an index from the monthly values. Starting from a base value of 100, each successive index value is calculated by compounding the preceding index value by the growth rate. The Annual Total Return (ATR) is calculated as the percentage change in the index X_t over the relevant 12 months:

$$\text{ATR}_t = \frac{X_{t+12}}{X_t} - 1 \tag{6.6}$$

If monthly valuations are not available, IPD linearly interpolates between pairs of actual valuations. The method ensures comparability with other assets, which are defined using time-weighted return calculations, and allows more frequent reporting based, for example, on quarterly valuations. The time-weighted method avoids distortions caused by older weighting methods for sales near year-start and purchases near year-end. The IPD indices comply with the Global Investment Performance Standards (GIPS). GIPS require time-weighted returns and do not allow capital-weighted returns. From December 2004, all IPD indices use the time-weighted method of calculating investment performance.

The German IPD/Deutscher Immobilien Index (DIX) is calculated slightly differently, as the valuation method used in Germany tends to smooth the index volatility to a stronger degree than the method used in other countries. In particular, commercial companies traditionally have the value of the buildings they operate from on their books as a cost rather than at current market value. This conservative valuation method is embodied in legislation and is often still practised. However, the trend is to change to an open-market value basis, making the German IPD Index more representative for the physical market.

Constructing a Pan-European index

The methodology to construct the Pan-European index has four main stages. First, the monthly components of total returns on standing investments in each country are derived in the local currency. Then, the components are grossed up, according to the estimated value of the investment market, i.e. the professionally invested funds, in each country. The professionally invested funds include life and pension funds, unitized vehicles, pooled and collective investment funds, traditional estates and charities, quoted property companies and REITs, unquoted property companies and foreign investors. They explicitly exclude small private landlords, owner-occupied property, private equity where investors own the operating business as well as the property, mortgages and property assets of leasing companies, municipal housing. Third, the grossed-up components are converted into a single currency. Finally, the monthly and annual returns are calculated from the combined set of components. IPD plans to extend the index as accurate estimates become available for more countries, e.g. for Austria and Belgium.

6.2.4 FTSE UK Commercial Property Index

The FTSE Group and fund manager MSS Capital launched the FTSE UK Commercial Property Index (FTSEpx) in August 2006 as the first investible UK property index with daily pricing. It is based on the performance of a specially constructed property fund that aims to mirror the UK commercial market. Figure 6.3 displays the index performance.

The FTSEpx is based on the net asset value of a commercial real estate fund, the FTSEpx fund. Within the target sector weightings, aiming to represent the UK commercial real estate market, the fund manager is responsible for the actual composition of the index; i.e. the fund manager decides how best to allocate within a sector. There is a risk that the funds representation objective is conflicting the desire to invest in outperforming property. The index series comprises one main index and three subsector indices.

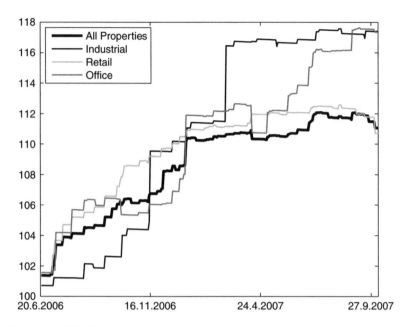

Figure 6.3 The FTSE UK Commercial Property Index (FTSEpx)

For each index, three series are calculated on a daily basis: a Gross Asset Value Total Return Index, a Net Asset Value Total Return Index and a Net Asset Value Capital Return Index, based on the values resulting from the NAV of the FTSEpx fund, net of running costs. The fund comprises direct and indirect property assets, valued by external valuers according to the same principles detailed for the IPD index. Consequently, the FTSEpx faces the same valuation error smoothing issues as the IPD index. The frequency of valuations varies. Around 40 % of the All Property Annual Index is valued once a year in December, 20 % is valued quarterly and 40 % receives a monthly valuation. To be included in the fund, property assets need to meet a number of criteria:

- They need to be available in the open market at the moment of inclusion, or readily tradable.
- Property assets need to enhance the index diversification and representation of assets traded in the open market.
- Direct property assets should not be obsolete, must have alternative value use and they must be substantially let or pre-let.
- Indirect assets may include property unit trusts, limited partnerships and limited liability partnerships, joint ventures, REITs, listed equities, bonds and other assets linked to commercial real estate.

6.2.5 National Council of Real Estate Investment Fiduciaries

The National Council of Real Estate Investment Fiduciaries (NCREIF) is a not-for-profit institutional real estate investment industry association. It was founded for the purpose of promoting real estate as a viable long-term investment for pension plans and other institutional investors. NCREIF collects, processes, validates and disseminates investment and operating information on the risk and return behavior of real estate assets owned by institutional investors. Data include individual commercial properties and properties held in collective investment funds such as Real Estate Investment Trusts (REITs). Besides valuation data, NCREIF's database also contains lease and transaction data. The membership base includes institutional real estate investment managers, institutional investors and certain classes of professional businesses and academics that provide services to institutional investors such as public accountants, pension real estate consultants and appraisers.

Although 17 June 1982 marks the official beginning of the NCREIF organization, the difficult task of uniting a highly competitive industry actually began in the US in the late 1970s. Fourteen investment managers agreed to form an entity to foster research on the real estate asset class. This led to the development of a database consisting of property operating information. NCREIF produces and distributes the NCREIF Property Index (NPI), its flagship index. It is the primary index used by institutional investors to analyze US commercial real estate performance and to benchmark actively managed real estate portfolios. Recently, it has also been used as the underlying instrument for derivatives on commercial property in the US.

The index used to be known as the Russell/NCREIF Property Index, since the Frank Russell Company used to publish the Index (Pagliari *et al.,* 2001). On 1 January 1995, NCREIF assumed full responsibility for the Russell/NCREIF Property Index, including its publication and distribution, and the name changed to the NCREIF Property Index. By the end of 2006, the NPI consisted of 5333 properties with a value of US$247 billion and is the most widely accepted index for commercial real estate in the US. However, it represents only about 5 to 7 % of the commercial property market.

The NPI calculates quarterly returns of properties before deduction of any portfolio management fees, but inclusive of property level management and administration costs. The universe of properties includes investment-grade, nonagricultural and income-producing properties. Only existing properties are included, i.e. there are no development projects. Therefore all properties in the NPI have been acquired, at least in part, on behalf of tax-exempt institutional investors, predominately pension funds. Therefore all properties are held in a fiduciary environment. The composition of the NPI can change over time; i.e. the database is dynamically adjusted each quarter. The index increases in number of properties when data-contributing members add more properties to their portfolios than what is sold or transferred or due to increases in the NCREIF data contributing membership. Properties exit the NPI when assets are sold or otherwise leave the database. All historical data remain in the database and in the index. The NPI consists of both equity and leveraged properties, but the leveraged properties are reported on an unleveraged basis. Therefore the index is completely unleveraged. In addition to the publication of an index based on all properties, NCREIF publishes sector indices (see Table 6.2). Additionally, the NPI also reports total quarterly returns by region, i.e. the East, West, South and Midwest.

Table 6.2 Breakdown of the NCREIF database by property type (market value as of Q2 2007)

Property type	Percentage share
Office	36
Retail	23
Apartment	23
Industrial	16
Hotel	2
Total	100

The NPI total return is the sum of the income return and the capital value return. Capital values may change due to several reasons. First and most obviously, observed changes in market conditions such as occupancy rates, rents, capitalization and interest rates as well as unexpected capital expenditures induce a change in capital value. Further, the capital value may be adjusted due to a new third-party appraisal.

Valuation practices in the US are not as standardized as they are in the UK. To improve the index accuracy, NCREIF provides real estate information standards, i.e. rules for valuation, market value accounting and performance measurement. However, compliance to these standards is not mandatory. Valuations may be performed by internal real estate professionals or by external appraisers. Appraisal companies are often smaller and less-supervised entities than their UK counterparts.

NCREIF requires that properties included in the NPI are valued at least quarterly, either internally or externally, using standard commercial real estate appraisal methodology. Each property must be independently appraised at least once every three years. However, properties held by pension funds typically require annual independent appraisals anyway. Data contributors are required to note whether the appraisal was performed internally or externally. The latter is typically conducted by a Member of the Appraisal Institute (MAI) and is considered to be independent.

While a property may not be eligible to be included in the NPI, it can still be added to the database. Properties that have been sold are removed from the index in the quarter in which the sale takes place, although the historical index data will remain. The basic criteria for a property to be included in the NPI are:

- The property must be at least 60 % occupied when entering the NPI.
- The property type must be either apartment, hotel, industrial, office or retail.
- The property must be owned, partially owned or controlled by a qualified tax-exempt institutional investor or its designated agent.
- The property must be operating, i.e. not under construction or in development, and available for occupancy for more than one year.

The NPI covers only a small fraction of investable properties and is thus considered not to be as representative as its UK counterpart of the IPD.

Index construction

Historical returns date back to the first quarter in 1978. The index is set to 100 points at the end of 1977. Calculations are based on quarterly returns of individual properties, where each property's return is weighted by its market value. The current quarter's return is considered preliminary and subject to adjustment in the subsequent quarter, and previous quarter returns may be slightly adjusted annually as data submission errors are corrected. Index values are calculated for income, capital value and total returns.

A property's net operating income (NOI) measures its income return and is defined as gross rental income plus any other income less operating expenses such as utilities, maintenance, taxes, property management and insurance. The income return (IR) is computed by dividing NOI by the average daily investment in each quarter:

$$IR = \frac{NOI}{BMV + \frac{1}{2}CI - \frac{1}{2}PS - \frac{1}{3}NOI} \tag{6.7}$$

where BMV is the beginning market value, CI are capital improvements and PS are partial sales. The formula takes into consideration any capital improvements and any partial sales that occurred during the period, such as the sale of excess land of the property. The capital value return (CVR), on the other hand, measures the change in market value from one period to the next. A property's value can go up (appreciation) or it can decline (depreciation) depending on market forces. Again, the formula takes into account any capital improvements and any partial sales that occurred during the period. When a property enters the index, the capital return is not impacted until the second quarter of inclusion. Therefore

$$CVR = \frac{(EMV - BMV) + PS - CI}{BMV + \frac{1}{2}CI - \frac{1}{2}PS - \frac{1}{3}NOI} \qquad (6.8)$$

where EMV is the ending market value. Total return is computed by adding the income return and the capital value return. The NPI rate of return calculations underlie the following set of assumptions, which are reflected in the denominator of the formulae:

- NOI is received at the end of each month during the quarter.
- CI occur at mid-quarter.
- PS occur at mid-quarter.

These assumptions make the denominator an estimate of the average investment during the quarter. For example, since it is assumed that CI occur halfway through the quarter, the average investment during the quarter is increased by one half of the amount spent on CI. Similarly, since it is assumed that NOI is received monthly, the cash flow received from the NOI in effect reduces the average investment in the property during the quarter by one-third of NOI.

The NPI formula can be thought of as calculating an internal rate of return for the property each quarter as if the property was purchased at the beginning of the quarter and sold at the end of the quarter, with NOI being received monthly and any capital expenditures and partial sales occurring at mid-quarter. The formula takes into consideration the fact that cash flows occur throughout the quarter. Without the adjustment for NOI in the denominator, Equation (6.8) would be calculated as if all NOI was received at the end of the quarter. This would understate the rate of return. Similarly, if it is assumed that capital expenditures did not occur until the end of the quarter rather than at mid-quarter, the rate of return would be overstated.

This methodology is well accepted in performance measurement and is consistent with what is referred to as the "modified Dietz" formula for measuring investment performance, which considers the average daily investment in an asset. In this case, it is as if the NOI was received on days 30, 60 and 90 of the quarter and capital expenditures and partial sales occur on day 45.

Quarterly returns are first calculated for each individual property using the formula discussed above. These returns are then weighted by the market value of each property, using the average investment calculated in the denominator of the NCREIF formula, to arrive at the market value weighted return for all properties that are included in the index. The NPI can be thought of as a capitalization weighted index as opposed to an equally weighted index. Thus, larger properties in terms of market value have a greater impact on the index than smaller properties.

6.3   TRANSACTION-BASED INDICES

Uncertainties about the ability of appraisal-based indices to reflect commercial property performance accurately raise the question of a potential move towards transaction-based indices. However, transaction-based indices are unlikely to replace appraisal-based indices for the commercial real estate market due to the limited transaction data that are observed. Transaction-based indices are typically used for residential properties, where enough transaction data are available (Gatzlaff and Geltner, 1998).

Here the focus will be on transaction-based indices that have been used, or are likely to be used in the near future, as underlying instruments for property derivatives. Therefore, the universe of indices described is not aimed to be conclusive.

There are some challenges when constructing a transaction-based index. If in every period the same number of objects of the same quality is transacted, it would be easy to construct an index. A simple (weighted) average would provide an accurate index figure. However, data are very heterogeneous over time, and transactions of the same objects are very rare. The goal is to get an index that reflects property price development as purely as possible; i.e., the index should not change just because the sample is different from one period to the next, e.g. just because larger houses have been transacted. It should reflect the pure change in property prices for a property with constant quality.

Two market standard index methods are able to minimize price distortions and thus are suitable for constructing underlying instruments for derivatives (Shiller, 1998): hedonic indices and repeat sales indices, which are described in detail below. In addition to the standard methods, indices can be calculated using *mix adjustment* and *shape fitting*.

For mix adjusted indices, transactions are divided into a series of cells, typically by property type and area. The index is then constructed using a weighted average of the average price within a cell. The more detailed the characteristics of the cells, the better the mix adjustment, but more cells require a larger number of transactions. Depending on the characteristics of the cells, the mix adjustment method can be close to the hedonic method, but the latter is generally considered more robust.

The method of shape fitting starts by converting transaction prices into prices per square foot or square meter. Data from a defined period, e.g. from the past year, is used to construct a probability distribution for the price per square foot in a specific area. A more recent sample of transactions is then fitted as closely as possible to the shape of the distribution, in order to determine the relative quality of recent transaction prices. Once fitted, the shape reveals the price development. The method allows for a daily index to be calculated, and does not need an extensive list of quality attributes. However, the method assumes that the distribution will only change slowly over time.

However, all transaction-based indices have some general shortcomings:

- Transactions in a sample period may not fully reflect the type or regional percentage of the overall market.
- Data may be inconsistent, as characteristics of transacted property may significantly vary from period to period.
- An upward bias could be caused by owners holding on to their properties in a bearish market.
- Calculation methodologies are often complex and regarded as not very transparent.

- As transaction prices do not reflect property yields, it is impossible to calculate total return indices using only transaction data.

Statistical index methods can correct these shortcomings to a certain degree, but there is a limit to the control for heterogeneity.

6.3.1   Hedonic indices

Price indices measure the price change of a good or basket of goods between two dates. The calculation agent of the index needs to make sure that price changes that arise from changes in quality of the transacted objects can be distinguished from pure, constant-quality property price changes. The calculation method needs to standardize properties and represent the price of a typically transacted property, e.g. the median single family home. The need for standardization arises because no two houses are identical and may differ according to a variety of characteristics relating to the physical attributes of the houses themselves or to their locations. Hence, to consider the overall market price only, quality adjustment is required in the index calculation. An index based simply on the arithmetic average is not quality adjusted.

The so-called hedonic method is the most popular statistical method controlling for quality. Hedonic indices are often referred to as constant-quality indices. Both private index providers and statistical government agencies use the hedonic methodology to calculate inflation of complex goods such as cars, personal computers, electronic equipment and houses.

Hedonic indices compare the price of a virtual constant-quality house over time. Quality adjustment means not only standardizing for size and house amenities but also controls for the location of the house. A hedonic index aggregates the price information of a set of transactions by first decomposing property prices into prices of attributes that are valuable to homeowners. Using multiple regression, the price of a single attribute is statistically measured. The dependent variable of the regression is the transaction price; the explanatory variables are described by the valuable attributes of the property. For residential properties, these are, for example, number of rooms, square footage, the distance to a city center and so on. Some attributes are not measurable as a metric but are qualitative, such as whether there is an elevator or a balcony. For these attributes, dummy variables are either zero, if there is no respective attribute, or one, if there is the respective attribute.

The regression coefficients explain the marginal impact of an attribute on the price of the property. For example, a positive coefficient would be expected for square footage, since larger objects typically yield higher prices. The value of the coefficient is the change in price of one additional square foot. Thus the coefficients are the implicit prices of the attributes.

The prices of the decomposed attributes are called hedonic prices. Once hedonic prices are known, the index problem of quality change of transacted objects in a sample period can be solved. The pure price inflation is isolated from price changes that arise from changing attributes and quality of transacted objects. The index is calculated as a standardized, quality-adjusted value of all transactions within a defined period. The method prevents the possibility of short-term changes in the set of properties sold from month to month. A difference in all implicitly valued characteristics of transacted properties in one sample period compared to the previous sample period has therefore no impact on the index movement. Several transformations and robust regression techniques are used to improve the accuracy of a hedonic index.

To be representative, it is critical for the hedonic method to assume that the most important, measurable attributes of the complex good *property* are sufficient to explain the major part of price development (Ferri, 1977; Janssen *et al.*, 2001).

Methodology

There are two basic variations in methodology to construct a hedonic index, the dummy time hedonic (DTH) method and the varying parameter method; see Leishman and Watkins (2002) for a detailed comparison. The drawback of the varying parameter method is that a much larger number of observations is needed. Thus, the DTH method is typically preferred to calculate property indices.

This method is characterized by the fact that neither a past-time weighting (Laspeyres Index family) nor a present-time weighting (Paasche Index family) is applied. The implicit weighting of a DTH index corresponds rather to an average between the base period and the current period, as is the case with the Fisher Index. More precisely, a sample of transactions, including prices and attributes of the properties, is drawn out of the population of all transactions observed in the base and subsequent periods. The method is often referred to as intertemporal.

The time interval between two index points must be chosen such that a sufficiently large number of transactions can be observed to get statistically significant and representative results. A dummy variable is attributed to every period. It takes the value one if the observation falls within that period or else zero. The model thus consists of one single regression equation that includes a number of attributes and transaction periods as explanatory variables. Most variations of this model assume that the impact of every attribute remains constant over time. This assumption may be reasonable in the short to medium term, but in the long term the impact of the attributes can very well shift. For example, the view of a property becomes more valuable, but the age of the building gets less important. Thus, many indices that follow this methodology adjust the parameters after a longer period of time (see Dombrow *et al.*, 1995). For literature on hedonic index calculation methods in general see, for example, Heravi and Silver (2004).

The data set of every observed transaction $j = 1, \ldots, N$ is defined as

$$(p_j^t, D_j^t, x_{j,1}, \ldots, x_{j,k}) \tag{6.9}$$

with p the transaction price and x_k, $k = 1, \ldots, K$, the attributes of the property. The variable D^t indicates the transaction period t. The DTH regression function f describes the relation of price and attributes as

$$\ln p_j^t = f(x_j^t, \beta, D_j^t, \delta) + \epsilon_j^t \tag{6.10}$$

where β are the regression coefficients for the attributes, δ are the regression coefficients for the time periods and ϵ is i.i.d. normally distributed. The function f is often chosen to be a linear, semi-logarithmic, log-linear or Box/Cox (1964) transformation. The following log-linear model is specified:

$$\ln p_j^t = \alpha + \sum_{k=1}^{K} \beta_k^* \ln x_{j,k} + \sum_{t=2}^{T} \delta^t D_j^t + \epsilon_j^t \tag{6.11}$$

with α the intersection constant. It is assumed that the prices of attributes are constant across the sample periods. Hence, the vector of coefficients β^* is time independent.

Once the coefficients of the hedonic regression are calculated, it is straightforward to construct an index. The coefficients of the time period dummy variables δ represent the price changes over the respective periods, keeping the impact of all other coefficients constant (constant quality).

Given the attributes x_j, the estimated vector $\hat{\delta}$ measures the pure, quality adjusted price development of properties. In combination with the estimated vector $\hat{\beta}$, it can be used to estimate the price of an object with any attributes. For example, the mean $\bar{x}_k$ of the attribute x_k over the period 0 to T can be used as the reference quality level. The hedonic price index in the period $t = T$ is defined as

$$I_{0,T} = \frac{f(\bar{x}_k, \hat{\beta}^T)}{f(\bar{x}_k, \hat{\beta}^0)} \qquad (6.12)$$

In the case of the double logarithmic specification, it can be shown that the price changes do not depend on the chosen reference quality level. Thus, the hedonic index is

$$I_{0,T} = \frac{f(\bar{x}_k, \hat{\beta}^T)}{f(\bar{x}_k, \hat{\beta}^0)} = \exp(\hat{\delta}) \qquad (6.13)$$

where $\hat{\delta}$ reflects the estimate of the change of the logarithmic prices of an object while holding the attributes constant. This index calculation method is close to the Toernqvist Index method, which is a theoretically preferred index method (Diewert, 2004).

The results of the hedonic method are efficient in measuring property prices as long as the sample size is sufficiently large. If the sample per period is too small, however, artificial volatility is introduced. The measured standard deviation is larger than the true standard deviation, and typically negative autocorrelation is present in the first lag (see Chapter 7). In sum, the hedonic method, in whatever specific form, is able to construct property indices that are very well suited as underlying instruments for derivatives. It standardizes the heterogeneous asset class of real estate and makes prices comparable. However, the method focuses exclusively on prices. To measure total performance, rents and administration costs must be evaluated in addition.

Alternatively to the hedonic method, when richer data sets are available, repeat sales indices can be constructed.

6.3.2   Repeat sales indices

The repeat sales method provides an alternative to hedonic indices. For an object to be included in the calculation, at least two transaction prices must be known. In contrast to the hedonic method, the attributes of the object do not need to be evaluated, since they are assumed constant for the same object over time.

The main variable used for a repeat sales index calculation is the price change between two arms-length sales of the same house. The two transactions are paired and are considered a *sale pair*. Sale pairs are designed to yield the price change for the same house, while holding the quality and size of each house constant.

These sales pairs are further examined to eliminate outliers that might distort the calculations. Sale prices from non-arms-length transactions, e.g. property transfers between family members, where the recorded price is usually below market value, are generally excluded from the pairing process. In an arms-length transaction, both the buyer and seller act in their best economic interest when agreeing upon a price. Similarly, pairs of sales with very short time intervals between transactions are eliminated because observed price changes for these pairs are not likely to represent market trends.

Further, sales of properties that may have been subject to substantial physical changes between the two transaction dates must be excluded. Also, transactions where the property type designation is changed, e.g. properties originally recorded as single-family homes and subsequently recorded as apartments, are excluded from the index. Furthermore, since a property must have two recorded transactions before it can be included as a repeat sale pair, newly constructed homes should be excluded from the index calculation process until they have been sold at least twice.

Formally, the relation between the two transaction prices is described as

$$\ln \frac{p_z}{p_e} = \sum_{t=1}^{T} \delta^t D^t + \epsilon \tag{6.14}$$

where p_z is the transaction price today, p_e is the transaction price in the past, D^t are the same type of dummy variables as in the hedonic model, δ^t is the rate of change for period t and ϵ is the normally distributed innovation term. The unknown rates of change δ^t are estimated using regression variables. An obvious drawback is that the method ignores a large fraction of all transactions, namely those for which there is no known historic transaction price. Thus, the representativeness of repeat sales indices is often questioned. Clapp and Giacotto (1992) estimate that historic prices are recorded for only 3 % of all properties. Finally, the quality of the resold object may have changed between the sale today and the sale in the past, be it due to renovation or to changed tax rates in the respective area (Case and Shiller, 1987).

Just as for the hedonic indices, repeat sales indices typically represent residential properties. The low number of transactions of commercial properties makes the construction of a reasonable repeat sales index very difficult in that market. Hybrid techniques that combine the hedonic and the repeat sales approaches are able to decrease the impacts of distortions of either method applied individually (Case and Quigley, 1991).

6.3.3   What is a transaction price?

There are multiple prices that can potentially be used in a transaction-based property index. The prices are taken from different points in time of the purchase process. While an early price indication provides more timely data, final prices are more accurate. The following four types of prices are typically taken to construct indices:

- *Asking prices*. The first prices available in the purchase process are the asking prices. With the growth of the internet as a platform for the property market, asking prices are used to create indices from this online marketplace. They may offer a good indication for the market trend, but it is uncertain whether the asking prices are really followed by a transaction based on these prices, and the indices are generally upward biased. Only the supply side is observed which is furthermore easy to manipulate. As filters for outliers are getting better and the number of participants in these platforms increases, viable indices could be created. So far, the author is not aware of such an index being used as an underlying instrument for a property derivative.

- *Mortgage agreed price.* The next available price is the agreed price when a mortgage is offered, providing more transactional evidence than asking prices. However, it is still possible that the transaction will not complete, and prices from cash purchases are generally excluded. Hedonic property indices typically use mortgage agreed prices.
- *Mortgage completion price.* Using the prices after mortgage completion is more accurate but less timely than mortgage agreed prices, given the variable time lags between approval and completion.
- *Final transaction price.* The final transaction price is the one reported to the Land Registry or to an equivalent institution of a given country. These are the most accurate but least timely prices.

6.3.4   Transaction-based rental indices

In the same way as transaction prices, newly agreed rents can be taken to calculate a transaction-based index. Especially for commercial real estate, where rent renewals are much more frequent than sale transactions, rental indices are an attractive underlying instrument. Compared to appraisal-based indices, which are often used to measure the value of commercial properties, rental indices have the advantage of reflecting real market transactions.

To construct a rental index, a hedonic method similar to the one used for price indices could be applied. Instead of referring to a standard average house, the regression equation would measure the rent price of, for example, a square foot of industrial space in a specified region.

However, the problem of rents is that they are often heavily regulated. Also, rental agreements are rarely recorded in a pool as are transaction prices. A price must be disclosed when taking up a mortgage, but a new rental contract by contrast will not be noted by the bank. With the emergence of internet marketplaces, offered rents could be taken instead. However, offered rent prices do not necessarily equal actual price levels, and many offers are not filled.

6.3.5   Halifax house price indices

The Halifax House Price Index (Halifax HPI) is the longest running monthly house price series in the UK and covers the whole country from January 1983. The UK index is derived from the mortgage data of the country's largest mortgage lender, Halifax of the HBOS Group, providing a representative sample of the entire UK market.

The index family includes a number of national indices covering different categories of houses (all, new and existing) and buyers (all, first-time buyers and home-movers). The most commonly used Halifax index is the UK index covering all houses and all buyers. Regional indices for the 12 standard planning regions of the UK are produced on a quarterly basis. Table 6.3 lists the 12 regions of the UK.

Table 6.3   The 12 UK regions covered by the Halifax house price index family

East Anglia	Scotland
East Midlands	South East
Greater London	South West
North	Wales
Northern Ireland	West Midlands
North West	Yorkshire and the Humber

Table 6.4　Attributes of houses used to construct the Halifax House Price Index

Attribute	Measurement
Purchase price	Local currency
Location	Region
Type of property	House, subclassified: detached, semi-detached, terraced, bungalow, flat
Age of the property	Years
Tenure	Freehold, leasehold, feudal
No of rooms	Number of habitable rooms, bedrooms, living rooms, bathrooms, separate toilets
Central heating	None, full, partial
Garage	Number of garages and garage spaces
Garden	Yes or No
Land area if greater than one acre	Acres
Road charge liability	Local currency

The indices calculated are standardized by the hedonic regression method and represent the price of a typically transacted house. The data needed to construct the Halifax house price indices are derived from information on the house attributes listed in Table 6.4.

Those transactions that do not constitute a fully consistent body of attribute data for the purpose of house price analysis are excluded from the indices. These exclusions primarily cover property sales that are not for private occupation and those that are likely to have been sold at prices which may not be at arms-length, such as most council house sales or sales to sitting tenants.

The data refer to mortgage transactions at the time they are approved rather than when they are completed. This may cover some cases that may never proceed to completion, but it has the important advantage that the price information is more up-to-date as an indicator of price movements and is on a more consistent time-base than completions data, given the variable time lags between approval and completion. Only mortgages to finance house purchase are included, while remortgages and further advances are excluded. The sample size is typically as large as 15 000 transactions across the UK per month. Properties transacted at a price above GB £1 million have been included since December 2002 to reflect the increasing number in this market segment.

The monthly indices cover transactions during the full calendar month and the regional quarterly indices cover transactions over the entire quarter. Seasonality prices are varying during the course of the year irrespective of the underlying trend in price movements. For example, prices tend to be higher in the spring and summer months when more people are looking to buy. The Halifax index family also includes a seasonally adjusted series that removes this effect and focuses on the underlying trend in house prices. The seasonal factors are updated monthly.

6.3.6　Nationwide Anglia Building Society House Price Index

Nationwide is the UK's fourth largest mortgage lender and regularly publishes statistics on the housing market in the UK.[3] Their house price index, the Nationwide Anglia Building Society

---

[3] See www.nationwide.co.uk/hpi.

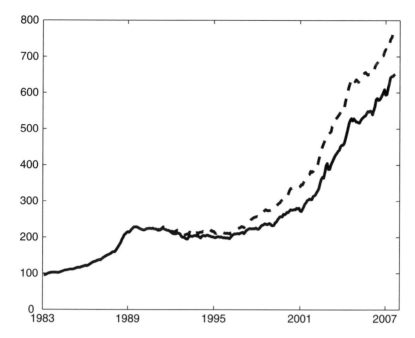

Figure 6.4   Comparison of Halifax HPI and the NAHP Index

House Price (NAHP) Index, is, together with the Halifax HPI, one of the most respected indicators and similarly represents the price development of single-family homes in the UK. It was used as one of the underlying instruments for the London FOX contracts that are described in Chapter 5.

As seen by their respective trajectories in Figure 6.4, the Halifax HPI and NAPH Index broadly follow each other. Discrepancies arise due to different samples and index calculation methods. Nationwide started publishing property price statistics in 1952. The index is published on a monthly basis dating back to 1991.

Like Halifax, Nationwide produces a volume-weighted index of typically transacted properties. Again, only owner-occupied properties that are sold at arms-length are taken into account. Nationwide uses mix-adjustment, yet their methodology is similar to the one of Halifax in that they also use a hedonic regression model. Besides the national all houses index, Nationwide publishes regional indices, indices that are adjusted for inflation or seasonality, indices by housing type and indices by buyer characteristics.

Nationwide bases its index on mortgage approvals but only covers 9 % of the mortgage market, compared to the Halifax HPI that covers about 20 to 25 %. Since the failure of the FOX contracts in 1991, the NAHP Index rarely serves as an underlying instrument for property derivatives (see Chapter 5). The Halifax HPI is considered more representative and covers basically the same market segment. Low market coverage is the main disadvantage of the NAHP Index and probably the reason why the Halifax HPI is today the common underlying index for housing in the UK. Nationwide does, however, publish its data earlier than most other sources, which makes it valuable in determining trends. The NAHP Index is released on the first business day of each month.

6.3.7 S&P/Case–Shiller Indices

The S&P/Case–Shiller home price indices measure residential housing price movements. CSW, the home price research company founded by Case, Shiller and Weiss in 1991 and today known as Fiserv CSW, collects data regarding transactions on residential properties. The indices are based on recorded changes in home values, using a repeat sales pricing technique. The indices, developed by Case and Shiller, use a base value of 100 in the year 2000. Updates to the indices are released to the public on the last Tuesday of every month.

The S&P/Case–Shiller metro area home price indices are designed to be a consistent benchmark of housing prices in the US. Their purpose is to measure the average change in home prices in a particular geographic market. They cover 10 major metropolitan statistical areas (MSAs), displayed in Figure 6.5. Derivatives are planned to be eventually available to 10 further indices, covering the MSAs of Atlanta, Charlotte, Cleveland, Dallas, Detroit, Minneapolis, Phoenix, Portland, Seattle and Tampa. The indices measure changes in housing market prices given a constant level of quality. Changes in the types and sizes of houses or changes in the physical characteristics of houses are specifically excluded from the calculations to avoid incorrectly affecting the index value.

To be eligible for inclusion in the indices, a house must be a single-family home. Apartments are excluded. Houses included in the indices must also have two or more recorded arms-length sale transactions. As a result, newly constructed houses are excluded. Home price data are gathered and after that information becomes publicly available at local recording offices across the country. Available data usually consist of the address for a particular property, the sale date, the sale price and the type of property.

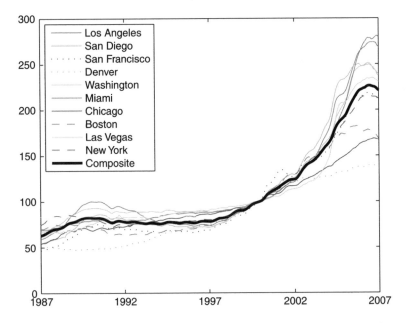

Figure 6.5   The S&P/Case–Shiller indices for 10 metro areas and the US Composite Index

The indices are calculated monthly, using a three-month moving average algorithm; i.e. sale pairs are accumulated in rolling three-month periods, on which the repeat sales methodology is applied. The index point for each reporting month is based on sale pairs found for that month and the preceding two months. For example, the December 2007 index point is based on repeat sales data for October, November and December of 2007. This averaging methodology is used to offset delays that can occur in the flow of sales price data from county deed recorders and to keep sample sizes large enough to create meaningful price change averages.

Each sale pair is aggregated with all other sale pairs found in a particular area to create the corresponding index. The 10 metro area indices are then combined, using a market-weighted average, to create a national composite index.

The indices are designed to reflect the average change in all home prices in a particular geographic market. However, individual home prices are used in these calculations and can fluctuate for a number of reasons. In many of these cases, the change in value of the individual home does not reflect a change in the housing market of that area; it only reflects a change in that individual home. The index methodology addresses these concerns by weighting sale pairs.

Different weights are assigned to different changes in home prices based on their statistical distribution in that geographic region. The goal of this weighting process is to measure changes in the value of the residential real estate market, as opposed to atypical changes in the value of individual homes. Weights are adjusted for factors such as price anomalies, high turnover frequency or the time interval between the first and the second sales.

In particular, to account for sale pairs that include anomalous prices or that measure idiosyncratic price changes, the repeat sales index model employs a robust weighting procedure. This statistical procedure mitigates the influence of sale pairs with extreme price changes. Each sale pair is assigned a weight of one (no down-weighting) or a weight less than one but greater than zero, based on a comparison between the price change for that pair and the average price change for the entire market. The degree to which sale pairs with extreme price changes are down-weighted depends on the magnitude of the absolute difference between the sale pair price change and the market price change. No sale pair is completely eliminated by the robust weighting procedure, i.e. no pair is assigned a zero weight. Only sale pairs with extreme price changes are down-weighted. Although the number of sale pairs that are down-weighted depends on the statistical distribution of price changes across all of the sale pairs, in large metro area markets, typically 85 to 90 % of pairs are assigned a weight of one, 5 to 8 % are assigned a weight between one and one-half, and 5 to 8 % are assigned a weight between one-half and zero.

The S&P/Case–Shiller repeat sales model also includes an interval weighting procedure that accounts for the increased variation in the price changes measured by sale pairs with longer time intervals between transactions. Over longer time intervals, the price changes for individual homes are more likely to be caused by nonmarket factors such as physical changes or idiosyncratic neighborhood effects. More precisely, the model uses a robust interval and value-weighted arithmetic repeat sales algorithm.

The interval weights correct for heteroskedastic, i.e. nonuniform, error variance in the sale pair data. These corrections for heteroskedasticity aim to reduce the error of the estimated index points, but do not bias the index upwards or downwards. Case and Shiller (1987) present a discussion of the heteroskedastic error correction model used in the Case–Shiller repeat sales index model. A more detailed description of interval and value-weighted arithmetic repeat sales indices can be found in, for example, Shiller (1993).

The national composite S&P/Case–Shiller Home Price Index is constructed to track the total value of single-family housing within its constituent metro areas:

$$\text{Index}_{C^t} = \sum_{i=1}^{I} \frac{\text{Index}_i^t \, V_i^0}{\text{Index}_i^0 \, \text{Divisor}} \tag{6.15}$$

where Index_{C^t} is the level of the composite index in period t, Index_i^t is the level of the home price index for metro area i in period t and V_i^0 is the aggregate value of housing stock in metro area i in a specific base period 0. The Divisor is chosen to convert the measure of aggregate housing value into an index number with the same base value as the metro area indices. The composite home price index is analogous to a capitalization-weighted equity index, where the aggregate value of the housing stock represents the total capitalization of all the metro areas included in the composite index.

All index points prior to the base period are estimated simultaneously using the weighted regression model described above. After the base period, the index points are estimated using a chain-weighting procedure in which an index point is conditional on all previous index points, but independent of all subsequent index points. The purpose of the post-base, chain-weighting procedure is to limit revisions to recently estimated index points while maintaining accurate estimates of market trends.

6.3.8   S&P/GRA commercial real estate indices

The Standard & Poor's/Global Real Analytics (S&P/GRA) commercial real estate index family aims to reflect commercial real estate performance by measuring the change in prices by property sector and geographic region. Just as for the S&P/Case–Shiller indices, regional definitions relate to metropolitan statistical areas (MSAs), as determined by the US Office of Management and Budget (OMB), and to property sectors. The indices were first launched as GRA Commercial Real Estate Indices (GRA CREX) in 2006. After Charles Schwab Investment Management took over the real estate research company GRA in January 2007, the indices were relaunched as S&P/GRA Commercial Real Estate Indices in August 2007. The Chicago Mercantile Exchange plans to launch futures and options on the new indices.

GRA has prepared 10 commercial real estate indices, as listed in Table 6.5. The indices track core real estate price movements, excluding certain special property types. All indices are set

Table 6.5   The 10 indices of the S&P/GRA CREX family

Index name	Index type
National	Composite index
Office	Property sector
Warehouse	Property sector
Apartments	Property sector
Retail	Property sector
Northeast	Geographic region
Midwest	Geographic region
Mid-Atlantic South	Geographic region
Pacific West	Geographic region
Desert Mountain West	Geographic region

to a base period of December 2001 at 100 index points. The indices are based on recorded transactions and updated monthly.

The office index includes office properties over 20 000 square feet, and the warehouse index includes warehousing and distribution facilities over 20 000 square feet. The retail index includes regional malls, grocery-drug anchored centers, strip centers, power centers, factory outlets, big box retail, stand-alone retail grocery, drug and pharmacy, auto and hardware stores over 10 000 square feet. Finally, the apartments index includes garden, mid-rise, high-rise, urban and walkup apartments over 20 000 square feet. Mixed-use and special-use properties are generally excluded from the indices.

Index construction

The S&P/GRA CREX indices follow a calculation method which is atypical for transaction-based indices: it uses neither hedonic regression nor the repeat sales technique. The method uses a market capitalization weighting approach, the so-called *base aggregate* approach. This method gives each regional market and sector a weight in the index based on the size and value of its existing stock. The basic elements of the indices are calculated using three-month rolling average prices per square foot. The composite indices are then constructed by a capitalization weighting, using transaction prices and the aggregate values of commercial stock data. Transaction prices for arms-length commercial sales are compiled at the metro group level and are filtered for extreme high and low values, to control for distortions. Derived mean prices are then applied to a weighting factor to calculate aggregate values. The values are summed to create national and regional aggregates, and divided by a base period divisor to generate the current index level. The divisor is also used to adjust stock values without causing discontinuities in the index.

The basic calculation is conducted as

$$\text{Index} = \frac{\Sigma P_i S_i}{\text{divisor}} \tag{6.16}$$

where P_i is the price per square foot of property type and region group i and S_i is the number of square feet of property type i. Commercial stock in square feet used to calculate national, regional and sector level composite indices are updated every five years. Depending on the targeted index, the sum is taken along regions or sectors. The national composite index sums along both vectors.[4]

In a typical month, over 2500 transactions are collected and processed. Data are collected from commercial vendors, brokerage firms, appraisers, mortgage brokers and publicly traded operating companies. Data are reviewed, verified and filtered to retain only arms-length core real estate transactions. The transaction sample is aggregated in rolling three-month periods, to maintain large statistically significant sample sizes and permit statistical precision in mean calculations.

6.3.9 The Residential Property Index (RPX)

The Residential Property Index (RPX) is provided by the research and data firm Radar Logic. Data are gathered from public sources and include all transaction types, be it foreclosure sales, condominiums, new construction or existing single- and multi-family homes.

---

[4] See www.spcrex.standardandpoors.com for a detailed description of the index methodology.

Three RPX values are published daily for 25 US metropolitan statistical areas (MSAs) as well as a composite index, based on one-day, seven-day and 28-day data aggregations. The values include transactions for the respective indicated time frame. Indices represent the price per square foot of actual residential real estate transactions.

The applied shape-fitting methodology differs from traditional transaction-based indices, as it uses a maximum likelihood method to fit price distributions. First, the distribution of transactions, measured per square foot, is specified for each MSA every business day. Further, assuming a power law behavior, the distribution is transformed into a form from which a reliable and representative index can be deduced. Power laws express a relationship between two variables that are related by an exponent and possibly also by a proportionality constant. In the RPX methodology, the frequency of transactions is proportional to the price per square foot raised to a power over a given interval. Seasonal effects are addressed by including data over an entire year to estimate the distribution parameters.[5]

Compared to the S&P/Case–Shiller home price indices, which produce monthly prices and base on repeat sale data only, the RPX appeals by calculating daily prices and by including a broader data range.

6.3.10   Zurich Housing Index (ZWEX)

In Switzerland, the "Informations- und Ausbildungs-Zentrum fuer Immobilien" (IAZI) publishes quarterly hedonic price indices for owner-occupied houses and apartments.[6] Data history goes back to the first quarter of 1980, as Figure 6.6 shows. With the emergence of housing derivatives in Switzerland in 2006, a trustworthy, transparent index that closely tracks the price development of housing was needed. Therefore, the two separate indices (owner-occupied houses and apartments) that represented two aspects of a single uniform investment market were combined to a new housing index, the "Zuercher Wohneigentumsindex" (ZWEX).

The index for residential property in the Canton of Zurich, ZWEX uses data from all real estate transactions where the Zuercher Kantonalbank (ZKB) was involved since 1980, mainly obtained by mortgage financing. By 2006, the data included roughly 17 000 observations, representing an estimated market share of about 40 %. Recently, about 1000 new transactions were observed every year. The index can thus be considered representative for the Canton of Zurich.

The ZWEX is a hedonic index, i.e. it measures quality-adjusted changes of house prices. Variations in quality of traded houses do not impact the index, so pure housing inflation in the canton of Zurich can be tracked.

The ZWEX belongs to the family of dummy time hedonic (DTH) indexes, i.e. the index method assumes constant prices of attributes over time. Ideally for the calculation of such an index, transactions stem from short, partially overlapping time intervals, e.g. from the two most recent quarters. On the other hand, it can be shown empirically that prices of attributes only change slightly over time (Borsani, 2002). Thanks to the use of transactions of multiple periods and not only the very recent ones, the hedonic function can be estimated more precisely. Particularly, for the ZWEX, it is estimated using the last 40 periods. In other words, a ten year

---

[5] For a detailed description of the index methodology see www.radarlogic.com.
[6] See www.iazi.ch/zwex.

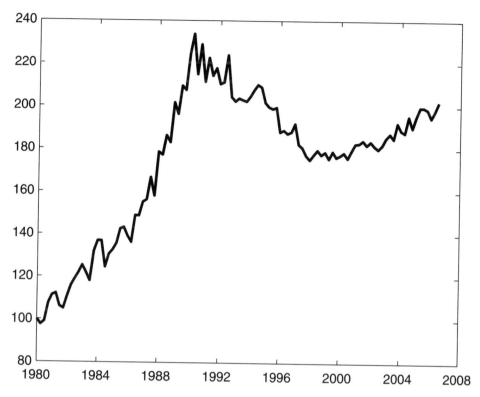

Figure 6.6   The ZWEX Index since 1980

rolling sample of transactions is taken into consideration. The coefficients of that function are estimated using a hedonic ordinary least squares (OLS) regression.[7]

For the ZWEX, the hedonic function seems to possess high precision: 85.1 % of price variations among objects are explained by the chosen attributes. The standard error of the regression is 14 %. To improve the robustness of the estimate, objects with a price deviation of more than 40 % of the estimated price are excluded from the final estimation of the calculation of the index. That criteria excludes about 2 % of all objects. The exclusion of outliers (trimming) is often applied in statistics in order to improve the robustness of results. For example, for the calculation of the LIBOR rate, the highest 25 % and the lowest 25 % of the quotes of the banks participating on the LIBOR panel are excluded.

6.3.11   Further transaction-based underlying indices

The indices described in this chapter so far are the main transaction-based underlying instruments for property derivatives. However, there are further indices that have been used as underlying instruments for a handful of transactions or are considered to be suitable for this purpose. These indices may or may not gain more attention in the future. In 2007, the US

---

[7] For a detailed description of the index methodology see www.zkb.ch/zwex.

investment bank Goldman Sachs says it is willing to facilitate deals on NAR and OFHEO indices in addition to the more popular indices. Further indices are now described briefly.

6.3.12   Conventional Mortgage Home Price Indices

The Conventional Mortgage Home Price Indices (CMHPI) are repeat sales indices calculated quarterly by using data of the American mortgage banks Fannie Mae (FNMA) and Freddie Mac (FHLMC).[8] By 2007, the combined database contains more than 31.6 million of matched pairs. The indices provide a measure of typical price inflation for houses within the US and cover three levels of geographical aggregation: metropolitan statistical areas (MSAs), States and Census Bureau divisions. A national index defined as a weighted average of the nine Census division indices is also published. FNMA and FHLMC jointly developed the CMHPI and began releasing it in the first quarter of 1994. The computation of the index is based on mortgages that were processed by the mortgage banks since January 1975.

6.3.13   Office of Federal Housing Enterprise Oversight

The Office of Federal Housing Enterprise Oversight (OFHEO) is the safety and soundness regulator of FNMA and FHLMC. In 1996, OFHEO began publishing a data series referred to as the OFHEO House Price Index (HPI) on a quarterly basis.[9] OFHEO uses the same joint database of FNMA and FHLMC consisting of repeat sales as a starting point and employs a similar repeat sales method as the CMHPI. As a result, differences between the CMHPI and the OFHEO HPI are extremely small. The sample that is confined to FNMA and FHLMC conforming mortgages is considered to be skewed to the low end of the housing market. The conforming mortgage loan limit was US$417 000 for a single-family home in 2006. To put this limit into perspective, note that the median home price in New York City was around US$450 000 at that time. In California, only about one-sixth of housing is sold with conforming mortgages. In San Francisco, the median price is about US$750 000. OFHEO also uses appraisal data to supplement the samples.

6.3.14   National Association of Realtors

The National Association of Realtors (NAR) produces national and regional house price indices on a monthly basis and indices for MSAs on a quarterly basis.[10] NAR claims to cover 30 to 40 % of all sales in the US.

However, the NAR indices are quoted as median home values in the US; i.e. they do not use repeat sales or hedonic regression methodology. Median values do not address housing performance and may be skewed if the composition of housing stock changes, e.g. if new luxury subdivisions are introduced to an area. Median values simply measure the price at which half of the houses in an area are worth more and half are worth less. As a result, the index not only changes due to movements in home values but also due to movements in the composition of the housing stock.

---

[8] See www.freddiemac.com/finance/cmhpi.
[9] See www.ofheo.gov/HPI.asp.
[10] See www.realtor.org.

6.3.15   The Rexx Index

Rexx Index LLC, a venture of Cushman & Wakefield and Newmark Knight Frank with Rexx's founder Paul Frischer, announced the introduction of new real estate indices for US commercial property derivatives on 29 November 2006. Cushman & Wakefield and Newmark Knight Frank will provide data to be used in the construction of the Rexx Index.

The Rexx indices are constructed using asking and lease rent data, interest rates and inflationary indicators to provide a bottom-up view of the market. The main goal of the index construction method, based on the Frischer–Kranz delta rent model, is to avoid the lag effect of appraisal-based indices and the infrequent data points inherent in transaction-based commercial indices. Rexx will produce, on a quarterly basis, total return and rent indices for 15 US regions as well as four broad-based indices.

6.3.16   Hong Kong: the HKU Real Estate Index Series, the CCI and the RVD Property Price Index

The University of Hong Kong Real Estate Index Series (HKU-REIS) includes four indices, i.e. the All Residential Price Index (HKU-ARPI) and the three subindices Hong Kong Island Residential Price Index (HKU-HRPI), Kowloon Peninsula Residential Price Index (HKU-KRPI) and New Territories Residential Price Index (HKU-NRPI). Figure 6.7 displays the four indices.

The HKU-ARPI is a monthly price index that tracks the changes in the general price level of residential properties in Hong Kong. The index is constructed based on transactions registered with the Hong Kong Land Registry. It covers the entire Hong Kong Special Administrative Region and is a value-weighted average of the subindices for three subregions in Hong Kong.

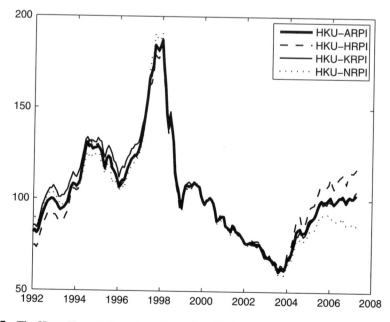

Figure 6.7   The Hong-Kong Indices since September 1991

The weights reflect the market value of the total stock of residential properties in each of the three subregions. The indices were created by Professor K. W. Chau of the University of Hong Kong's Real Estate and Construction Department, using a repeat sales technique.

The Hong Kong Centa-City Index (CCI) is a monthly real estate index also based on property transactions registered with the Hong Kong Land Registry.[11] July 1997 is used as the base period of the index. The index in the base period equals 100. The Department of Management Sciences, Faculty of Business of the City University of Hong Kong maintains the index. Hedonic regression is used to construct the index.

Finally, the Rating and Valuation Department (RVD) of the Hong Kong SAR Government produces a monthly property price index using a mix-adjusted methodology. Just as the other two index providers, the RVD also uses the transaction data of Land Registry.

The three residential indices for Hong Kong correlate closely, despite their different methodologies. However, the HKU Real Estate Index Series is regarded as the most transparent, which could be the critical advantage when investors choose a reference index. The first property derivatives in Hong Kong were based on the HKU Index.

6.3.17   Australia: the RP Data–Rismark Index and the ABS HPI

Australia's largest residential property data and information supplier RP Data and the real estate investment firm Rismark International agreed to develop a series of residential property price indexes in February 2007. The indices should serve as underlying instruments for OTC property derivative contracts. The index method is a rolling hedonic calculation and the indices are published on a monthly and quarterly basis. The series include capital gain and total return indices for houses and home units in each state and territory capital, plus two composite nationwide indices, making a total of 36 separate indices.

RP Data sources sales data under license from all Australian state governments and ultimately collects records on virtually 100 % of all residential transactions executed in the Australian market. The government data are supplemented with information on residential transactions collected from 8000 real estate agents that use RP's software systems, representing over 70 % of all agents in Australia. For research purposes, RP Data–Rismark also calculates repeat sales and median, lower and upper quartile indices.

There are agreements with multiple brokers to use RP Data–Rismark's hedonic indices as the basis for property derivative contracts. However, the Australian Bureau of Statistics House Price Index (ABS HPI) is an alternative to the RP Data–Rismark Index as the underlying index for residential property derivatives. The ABS HPI consists of a series for eight capital cities and their weighted averages and is published quarterly. It is calculated as a Laspeyres index that measures the inflation or deflation in the price of established houses over time.

6.3.18   More indices

A list of underlying indices can never be conclusive. The indices described in this chapter have been considered as underlying instruments to be used for property derivatives. There are other established property indices, such as the French Chambres des Notaires/INSEE Index, the German IMMEX Index or the European INREV indices, which could eventually be used as underlying instruments. In the UK, neither the mix-adjusted house price indices of the

---

[11] See www.centanet.com.

Department for Communities and Local Government (DCLG), of *the Financial Times* and of the property company Rightmove, nor the repeat sales index of the Land Registry, are likely to replace the Halifax indices as underlying instruments for derivatives.

In the US, the race for a benchmark index is still on. In September 2007, Moody's Investor Services started to publish the Moody's/REAL Commercial Property Price indices that use property transaction data collected by Real Capital Analytics (RCA) and a repeat sale methodology developed by the MIT Center for Real Estate (the index was first named The MIT/RCA Index). The indices should serve as underlying instruments for derivatives and thus compete with the commercial indices of NCREIF and the S&P/GRA CREX family. The brokerage firm TFS estimates that Radar Logic's RPX indices will be the main underliers for US housing derivatives, while the NCREIF series will be the indices of choice for US commercial real estate derivatives.

Further, the National University of Singapore aims to launch a series of residential indices by the end of 2007. As the property market gains momentum, many new indices will be constructed.

Part II

Pricing, Hedging and
Risk Management

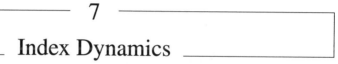

7

Index Dynamics

Fooled by randomness.

Having introduced the property indices that serve as underlying instruments for derivatives, an investigation now follows on how real estate prices and indices actually behave over time. Understanding price and index dynamics is the basis to price and hedge derivatives.

7.1 ECONOMIC DEPENDENCIES AND CYCLES

In contrast to stock prices, real estate prices adapt slowly to changes in the economy and often appear to follow cycles. It is important to understand the reasons for this inert and cyclical behavior. First, the reaction time of property prices is typically slow, as it takes much longer to execute a property transaction than a stock transaction. It thus takes longer for property prices to incorporate new economic information. Second, supply is not very flexible and reacts slowly to a change in demand. It can easily take a few years to construct a new property and have it actually marketed. Further, properties are not only an investment but also a consumption good. People do not make optimal decisions based purely on an investment rationale. Finally, the economic factors that influence property prices, e.g. demand and supply of office space, building activity, or the labor and capital market situation, often exhibit an inert behavior themselves. This interdependence results in cycles in real estate prices and in inertia of price adjustment. The literature shows that not only property prices but also rents and vacancy rates are cyclical at national and regional levels. For a literature overview see Pyhrr *et al.* (1999).

Real estate has multiple links to economic conditions and business cycles. Affordability of housing is typically measured by the price-to-income ratio, which states whether or not housing is within reach of the average buyer. There is, however, no long-run ratio that can be considered fair, mainly because the cost and conditions of a mortgage can change considerably over time. Moreover, price elasticities of demand can vary over time, due to changes in regulatory or tax conditions, or because of demographic developments. Variations attributed to supply include factors such as land scarcity and restrictiveness of zoning laws as well as productivity growth in construction.

Housing cycles in turn can create new economic cycles. Homeowners generally perceive higher house prices as increased wealth. This wealth effect then drives borrowing on collateral, consumption, construction and investment (Catte *et al.*, 2004).

An alternative explanation of property cycles is crowd behavior and mass psychology. Stoken (1993) argues that people are not economic individuals who act in their own rational self-interest. Rather, they are psychological beings who stick to recent experiences of pain and pleasure. Because of this, cycles are created. After a period of prosperity, people become overly optimistic and take excessive risk. The excess is rationalized by the idea that the period of prosperity will continue, and people see less risk than actually exists. As too many people become risk takers, the conditions for a downturn are created. Once it is triggered, a psychology of pessimism is set off and people see more risk than really exists. When too many people become risk averse, economic expansion can start again.

7.2   BUBBLES, PEAKS AND DOWNTURNS

The cyclical nature of real estate prices alone does not explain the peaks and downturns observed in the past. Trends caused by cycles might attract speculators that foster the trend and potentially make the cycle more volatile. It appears that some peaks have been inflated to speculative bubbles. A popular indicator for speculative bubbles is the price-to-rent ratio, which follows from an asset-pricing approach and can be interpreted as the cost of owning versus renting a house.

Over- and undervaluations can be estimated by comparing the prevailing price-to-rent ratio with the one that would comply with the user cost of housing. The latter includes mortgage and tax rates as well as opportunity and holding costs. Table 7.1 lists the estimated valuation discrepancies of 17 OECD countries in 2004 (according to Table III.2. in *OECD Economic Outlook*, 2005).

One of the most prominent examples of a real estate bubble was the price excess observed in Japan that peaked in the early 1990s. The subsequent downturn lasted until 2005 and adversely affected the Japanese economy for years. It destroyed wealth that amounted to 1.6 quadrillion yen, equivalent to about twice the gross domestic product of Japan. Figure 7.1 shows the price development of commercial real estate in large Japanese city areas (Tokyo, Yokohama, Nagoya, Kyoto, Osaka and Kobe) obtained from the Japan Real Estate Institute.

The Organization for Economic Cooperation and Development (OECD) reports 37 large upturn phases in OECD countries between 1970 and 1995; 24 of them ended in downturns that wiped out previous real-term gains by 30 to over 100 % (OECD Economic Outlook, 2005).

Table 7.1   Estimated over- and undervaluations for 17 countries in 2004

Estimated over- and undervaluations in 2004 (%)	
United States	1.8
Japan	−20.5
Germany	−25.8
France	9.3
Italy	−10.9
United Kingdom	32.8
Canada	13.0
Australia	51.8
Denmark	13.1
Finland	−15.6
Ireland	15.4
Netherlands	20.4
New Zealand	7.6
Norway	18.2
Spain	13.4
Sweden	8.0
Switzerland	−9.7

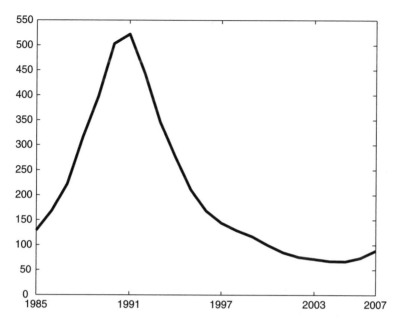

Figure 7.1 Commercial real estate in Japanese cities peaked in 1991 and fell by more than 80 % thereafter

7.2.1 Prediction of downturns

Roehner (2006) finds that price peaks were, historically, roughly symmetrical with respect to their maximum. A so-called soft landing, i.e. an upturn followed by a plateau, has rarely been observed. He describes speculative price peaks as

$$p_t = p^* e^{[-|(t-t^*)/\tau|^\alpha]} \tag{7.1}$$

where p^*, t^* denote the peak price and peak time respectively, and α and τ are two adjustable parameters.

This approach is now applied to an actual example. Currently, market participants fear a price bubble in the UK. Forward prices of the derivatives market clearly point to a downturn in the property cycle. The bearish sentiment is reflected in the prices of swaps that can be used to imply the expected index levels. Figure 7.2 compares the implied forward prices for the IPD index and the estimate according to the above formula. A constant rental income rate of 6.5 % is assumed in order to obtain the capital component from the observed total return forward prices. Further, the historical approximation of $\alpha = 1$ is taken and $\tau = 10$ years is chosen so that the model fits the recent upward trend. It can be seen that implied forward prices comply with the model until 2009. Thereafter, the forward prices imply a further price decrease until 2012, but to a lesser degree than the model predicts. It will be interesting to follow the price development of derivatives and their prediction quality further.

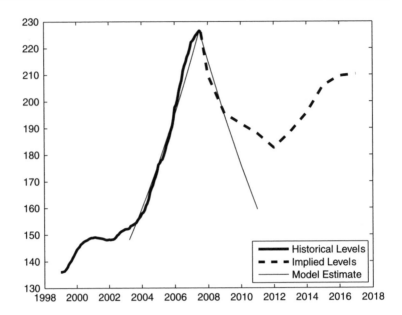

Figure 7.2 Implied forward prices and model prediction

7.3 DEGREE OF RANDOMNESS

The phenomena of cycles and bubbles in real estate prices indicate that property indices follow special dynamics and that their returns are not independently normally distributed (Meyer *et al.* 1997); i.e. future index returns are not entirely random but partly predictable. The degree of randomness is relevant for the suitability of an underlying instrument for derivatives. If the price development of the underlying index is highly predictable, it will be hard to find a party that takes a position against the predicted price. There needs to be a sufficiently high degree of uncertainty in order to attract hedgers.

It is questionable to what extent cyclic characteristics really support a high predictability of prices. Institutional investors say unexpected market development is the main reason for the failure of real estate projects (see Ormorat and Pfnür, 2000). Property derivatives would enable investors to fix market prices in advance, i.e. at the start of an investment project, not only when the construction is finally finished (and the market has potentially changed).

Statistically speaking, cycles are measured by autocorrelation, i.e. serial correlation. Positive autocorrelation means that a positive return is likely to be followed by another positive return and that a negative return is likely to be followed by another negative one, as it typically appears in cycles. On the other hand, negative autocorrelation means that a positive return is likely to be followed by a negative one, and vice versa, indicating a behavior of oscillation. Figure 7.3 illustrates returns that are positively and negatively autocorrelated.

To establish a derivatives market, both buyers and seller must be present simultaneously in a sufficiently large number. It would thus be problematic if expectations are always one-sided only. Autocorrelation, i.e. the fact that future returns are (partly) predictable, could result in such a dominant common opinion. However, even if autocorrelation is present and a trend is thus predictable, market participants can still bet against the consensus of the expected price development, no matter whether prices are generally expected to rise or fall.

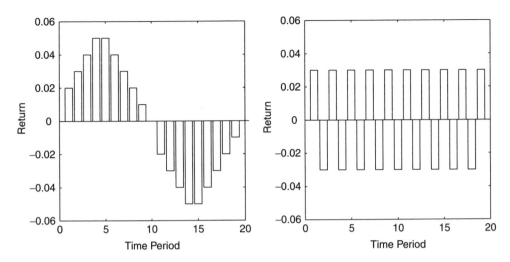

Figure 7.3   Stylized positive (left graph) and negative (right graph) autocorrelated returns

7.3.1   Does autocorrelation allow for arbitrage?

Some market participants consider the real estate market inefficient because they think cycles can be anticipated. However, autocorrelation in the *illiquid* physical real estate market does not mean that there is a "free lunch," and investors cannot necessarily benefit from the predictability implied by cycles. The reason is that investments in physical real estate are time consuming, i.e. create a time-lag, and cause high transaction costs. If transaction costs get lower and transaction speed increases, autocorrelation should partly vanish.

If autocorrelation is present in the base market, price development of properties and their derivatives will disconnect. The reason is that autocorrelation in the price of a *liquid* derivative would actually be an inefficiency that can be arbitraged away, as derivatives can be traded without time-lags and high transaction costs. The derivative would always refer to the *expected* spot price at maturity of the derivative, because any cycle would be anticipated. The discrepancy of spot and derivative price development would decrease the effectiveness of derivatives to hedge physical real estate. Thus, autocorrelation can potentially have a negative impact on the establishment of a derivatives market.

7.4   DYNAMICS OF APPRAISAL-BASED INDICES

In addition to the dynamics of the real estate market itself, the index construction method can cause dynamics on its own. There are several econometric issues related to appraisal-based property indices that arise. Most important, indices that are based on valuations rather than on transactions, such as the IPD indices, generally underestimate the true volatility of the market. There tends to be a smoothing effect in appraisal-based indices for two main reasons. First, not all properties are revalued at the same time and, second, appraised values tend to lag transaction prices when there is a significant change in market conditions. This causes appraisal-based indices to have significant autocorrelation and reduced volatility and to be fairly predictable for one or two periods into the future.

Bond and Hwang (2003) explore the effects of smoothing, non-synchronous appraisal, i.e. the variability of appraisal time points of an individual property and how this may distort the underlying return process, and cross-sectional aggregation. They find that, under certain assumptions, an index based on appraisals follows an autoregressive fractionally integrated moving average (ARFIMA) process, where the AR parameter explains the autocorrelation, the long memory FI parameter explains the level of smoothing and the MA parameter explains the nonsynchronous appraisal problem.

They conduct empirical tests on the IPD and the NCREIF indices and the difference between these indices and their equivalent equity market indices such as FTSE Real Estate (FTSE UK Commercial Property Fund Index) and NAREIT indices respectively. The latter indices do not track properties directly but cover listed property securities that are publicly traded. Their results show that the level of smoothing is far less than assumed in most academic studies, that the nonsynchronous appraisals become a more serious problem for higher frequency returns and that the level of volatility of real estate securities remains much higher than that recovered from an appraisal-based index, even after adjustments for econometric issues and for the leverage inherent in the securities.

Appraisals do in rare cases exactly match true market prices. However, if the valuation errors of individual properties are randomly distributed, these errors should cancel out in a large enough sample. However, if there is a systematic bias towards under- or overvaluation, the index may not be such a good hedge for physical property, i.e. the total returns from the index may not match the generic returns from holding a property portfolio. The issues raised above suggest that appraisals made in one period may be anchored to the valuation in the previous period; i.e. appraisers look first to the most recent valuation and make an adjustment from there and thereby lag the market. Analysis of the IPD Total Return Index from 1987 reveals that one-year autocorrelation is about 37 %, i.e. total returns in one year are significantly correlated with returns in the previous year. In the monthly index, there is a high 86 % autocorrelation observed.

The downward bias in volatility of appraisal-based indices due to smoothing is a well-known problem and has been extensively investigated in the literature (see, for example, Barkham and Geltner, 1994; Blundell and Ward, 1987; Bond and Hwang, 2003; Cho et al., 2003; Geltner et al., 2003). If autocorrelation is the result of smoothing returns from one year to another, the index will be less volatile than the underlying market. During peaks and troughs, prices of property transactions are higher respectively lower than the appraisals reported to the index provider. However, even after adjustment for the smoothing and lag effect, property volatility is still smaller than that of many other assets.

7.4.1 Sticky prices due to owners' regret

Moreover, the behavior of market participants may influence the smoothing effect, for both appraisal-based and even transaction-based indices. Many property managers invest for the long term, and may be able to postpone transactions during market downturns. The result is a low transaction volume in a bear market, reducing the apparent fall in the market. Also, the downward pressure on the private housing market is often reflected in shrinking transaction volumes rather than in a collapse in nominal prices, as owners refrain from selling at a loss. This phenomenon is also called *sticky prices* (Case and Quigley, 2007).Because these low values cannot be observed by appraisers, they are generally slow to mark down properties held in portfolios.

7.4.2 Unsmoothing

If volatility of a property index is smoothed, there are some consequences for derivative investors, as there are for other illiquid asset classes such as hedge funds and private equity. If historical index returns and volatility is used to support investment portfolio allocation decisions, it is important to be aware that the index underestimates true volatility and that actual property returns may have higher risk. If the unadjusted volatility is taken to optimize a portfolio allocation in a simple mean-variance context, property will be overweighted.

Thus, *unsmoothing* is important when performing a portfolio analysis across asset classes, and also in order to compare risk and returns between property and other assets, to identify the exact timing of peaks and troughs in property value cycles and to quantify property investment performance just after turning points in the property market. To unsmooth an appraisal-based index such as the IPD Index, Geltner and Miller propose three types of techniques: zero-autocorrelation techniques, reverse-engineering techniques and transaction price-based regression techniques (see Fisher et al., 2003; Geltner and Miller, 2001). Following Geltner and Miller, the (unobserved) periodic average transaction price levels, $\overline{V}_t$, can be calculates as a function of the observable appraisal-based series, V_t^*:

$$\overline{V}_t = \left[V_t^* - (1-\alpha)V_{t-1}^*\right]/\alpha \tag{7.2}$$

where the adjustment parameter α takes a value between zero and one. The adjustment factor α is often called the signal-to-noise ratio, which is the ratio of the longitudinal variance in market value divided by the sum of that variance plus the cross-sectional variance in the transaction price dispersion (see Quan and Quigley, 1991). Figure 7.4 shows the returns of the original appraisal-based IPD UK All Property TR Index and the correspondingly adjusted returns, assuming an α of 0.2. The latter exhibit clearly higher volatility. There are several further

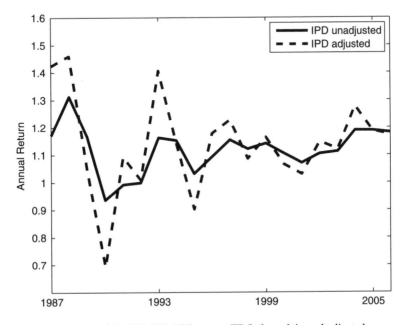

Figure 7.4   Annual returns of the IPD UK All Property TR Index, plain and adjusted

techniques that aim to filter out true noise of the new prices. The impact of unsmoothing and of the adjustment of volatility in the context of portfolio allocation are discussed in Chapter 16.

7.5   DYNAMICS OF TRANSACTION-BASED INDICES

Literature often claims that transaction-based property indices also exhibit autocorrelation (see, for example, Shiller and Weiss, 1999). However, the observed dynamics of a transaction-based property index depend on the applied index methodology. A simple average or median price index could exhibit artificial autocorrelation very well if the average quality of transacted properties changes. For example, the index would rise in a cycle where larger units are traded. A (temporal) trend towards larger houses alone should not influence the price index. An appropriate hedonic methodology is able to adjust for such differences in quality and provides a more accurate picture of true real estate dynamics.

For transaction-based indices, a sufficient sample size for each index point is critical in order to make reasonable estimates of the dynamics. An insufficient sample size could have the following effects. First, a *negative* autocorrelation could arise in the first lag; i.e. the index oscillates around a true value. Just as positive autocorrelation underestimates true volatility, negative autocorrelation overestimates it. The reason for this behavior is that outliers have a much greater impact on a small sample than on a large sample.

Second, if sample size varies over time, i.e. if there is a regime where sample size is large and another regime where sample size is small, volatility also appears to vary over time. Varying volatility, or heteroskedasticity, complicates the pricing and hedging of options on property indices. However, if both heteroskedasticity and variation in sample size is observed, the assumption can be made that they are interrelated. Often, as sample size grows over time due to improved data availability, volatility and negative autocorrelation are simultaneously reduced. A broader data sample implies per se more stable returns, since outliers get a lower weight and are thus diversified away.

When comparing for example the volatility of the ZWEX before and after 1992, as shown in Figure 7.5, a significant change in volatility is observed. According to the index provider,

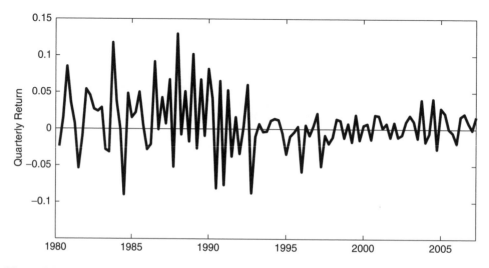

Figure 7.5   The returns of the ZWEX before and after 1992 show two artificially different volatility regimes

the sample size of the ZWEX was drastically increased in 1992. After 1992, when the sample size became sufficiently large, volatility remained quite stable until today.

It should be noted that the S&P/GRA Commercial Real Estate Index family is the only transaction-based measure on commercial real estate that is currently considered as an underlying instrument for derivatives. Due to the heterogeneous nature of individual commercial properties, the distribution of a single commercial real estate price is typically not normal. However, pooling a large sample of transaction prices, on a square foot basis, approximates a normal distribution, making volatility a reasonable risk measure. An individual property is likely to exhibit "fat tail" returns. However, according to the central limit theorem, a large enough pool of such non-normal returns approximates normality. The volatility of the estimated mean return depends on the sample variability and forms the sales population distribution.

Due to the nature of the commercial real estate market, there is a natural lag between the transaction closing date and the data collection month. According to GRA, this lag is about three months on average.

7.6   EMPIRICAL INDEX ANALYSIS

Here the main dynamics for selected indices that are used for property derivatives are tested. Due to the effects mentioned above, lower volatility figures are generally expected for appraisal-based indices than for transaction-based ones. Moreover, while the tested appraisal-based indices all measure total return (except the IPD indices, for which an analysis is also made of the capital growth (CG) and the rental income (RI) indices), the transaction-based indices are pure price indices, i.e. exclusive of rental income. Thus, the long-term drift should be significantly lower for the total return indices. However, the indices cover different market segments, which in turn may have different risk-return characteristics and are thus not comparable directly. Further, positive autocorrelation is generally expected in the appraisal-based indices because of the method's smoothing effects.

The rental income index is expected to exhibit little variation, since rent contracts are typically fixed for a long term and cannot adjust to market conditions quickly. Long contracts are especially typical for office space. However, a high variation in vacancy rates would introduce higher volatility in the rental income index.

Besides drift and volatility, autocorrelation is analyzed with respect to the first lag, as well as at an annual lag. The first lag is not the same time period for all indices, since they are calculated in different frequencies. To indicate whether autocorrelation is significant or not, the Durbin–Watson statistic is used. Durbin–Watson values between 1.6 and 2.4 mean that there is no or only insignificant autocorrelation present. A value lower than 1.6 indicates positive autocorrelation while a value greater than 2.4 indicates negative autocorrelation.

Table 7.2 summarizes the results of the short empirical index analysis. We observe that volatility is generally lower for appraisal-based indices than for transaction-based ones. However, the transaction-based S&P/Case–Shiller Index also shows very low volatility. It is the only transaction-based index that is calculated using the repeat sales method. It can further be seen that autocorrelation in the first lag is typically very high for the appraisal-based indices, but lower on the annual basis. The Durbin–Watson statistic is shown in brackets next to the respective autocorrelation coefficients, all indicating that autocorrelation is significant. Again, the exception of the transaction-based indices is the S&P/Case–Shiller Index with a very high autocorrelation coefficient of 0.93 in the first lag. It appears that the repeat sales method incorporates a stronger smoothing effect than the hedonic method.

Table 7.2 Statistical measures for selected property indices

	Time series	Calculation frequency	Long-term drift (p.a.) (%)	Volatility (Standard deviation) (%)	Autocorrelation, first lag	Autocorrelation, annual
Commercial property indices (appraisal-based)						
IPD UK All Property TR	1987–2007	Monthly	11.56	2.63	0.86 (0.28)	0.37 (1.22)
IPD UK All Property CG	1987–2007	Monthly	4.07	2.73	0.87 (0.26)	0.43 (1.09)
IPD UK All Property IR	1987–2007	Monthly	3.21	2.17	0.92 (0.16)	0.78 (0.42)
NCREIF NPI	1978–2007	Quarterly	10.17	3.38	0.70 (0.60)	0.81 (0.37)
Residential property indices (transaction-based)						
Halifax HPI	1983–2007	Monthly	8.17	4.44	0.44 (1.12)	0.43 (1.14)
NAHP	1991–2007	Monthly	7.84	3.96	0.25 (1.50)	0.64 (0.67)
S&P/Case–Shiller National Composite	1987–2007	Monthly	7.87	2.34	0.93 (0.14)	0.69 (0.60)
ZWEX	1980–2007	Quarterly	2.71	7.71	−0.28 (2.55)	0.33 (1.30)

The ZWEX is the only index that exhibits negative autocorrelation in the first lag. If measured on an annual basis, the sign changes. It should be remembered that sample size is inversely related to frequency (where, in this context, frequency is defined as one year divided by the length of the lag in years); i.e. sample size is larger for longer time-lags. The result strengthens the suspicion that the negative autocorrelation may result from a (too) small sample size.

In summary, positive autocorrelation appears to be a significant component of index returns. These nonrandom index drift components are usually, in an arbitrage-free setting, anticipated in the prices of property derivatives, as will be seen later on.

7.7 DISTRIBUTION OF INDEX RETURNS

The distribution of returns is critical if an asset is analyzed in a mean-variance context, e.g. in the classical portfolio theory of Markowitz (1952), or when it comes to pricing. Most pricing models assume that returns are normally distributed. The reliance on the normal distribution in modern finance is often criticized as a flaw of related models, such as the Black–Scholes (1973) option pricing model or the capital asset pricing model (CAPM) of William Sharpe (1964).

Recent finance theory and practice are particularly concerned with so-called *fat tail* or *heavy tail* distributions, i.e. distortions of the standard normal distribution setup. A fat tail is a property of probability distributions that exhibit excess kurtosis, a measure of the "peakedness" of a distribution. Excess kurtosis means that more of the variance is due to infrequent extreme deviations, as opposed to frequent modest deviations. Thus, the risk of fat tails refers to the fact that observations of a variable are spread in a wider fashion than the normal distribution entails. Ignoring kurtosis risk will cause a model to understate the risk of variables with excess kurtosis.

Figure 7.6 displays the histogram of the monthly returns of the Halifax House Price Index from 1983 to 2007. The solid line represents the corresponding normal distribution. The returns do in fact exhibit excess kurtosis, but the extent is, at 1.09, moderate.

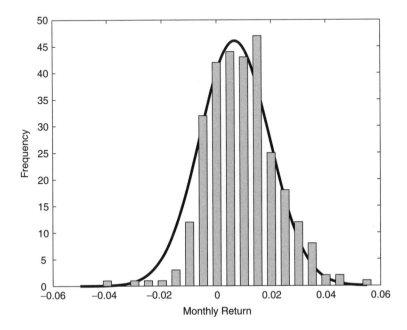

Figure 7.6 The distribution of the Halifax HPI monthly returns

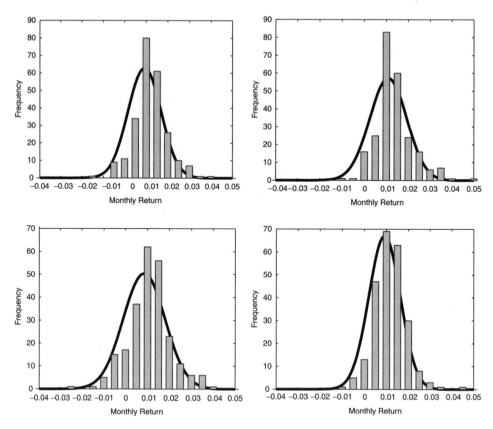

Figure 7.7 The distributions of monthly returns for the IPD All Property and its sector indices: upper left graph, IPD All Property Index; upper right graph, IPD industrial index; lower left graph, IPD Office Index; Lower right graph, IPD Retail Index

Further, Figure 7.7 shows the histograms of the monthly returns of the IPD All Property TR Index and of its sector indices from 1987 to 2007. While the indices for all properties and for the office sector have a modest excess kurtosis of 1.10 and 0.84, the values for the retail and the industrial sector are a bit higher at 1.72 and 2.05 respectively.

To illustrate these values, consider the following example: the occurrence of an event that is more than two standard deviations away from the mean has a probability of 4.55 %, as long as the returns are normally distributed. Using a Student's t-distribution, excess kurtosis of 1.00 is introduced and it is observed that the probability of the same event increases to 7.34 %. For an excess kurtosis of 2.00, the probability becomes 8.56 %. A Student's t-distribution is used with 10 and 7 degrees of freedom d, respectively, as the kurtosis of a t-distribution equals $6/(d-4)$.

It is observed that returns of property indices are not perfectly normally distributed. Consequently, care must be taken with any model that is based on the assumption of a normal distribution, as risk is likely to be underestimated. However, the observed levels of kurtosis are moderate, meaning that the normality assumption is able to provide a reasonable approximation.

8

The Property Spread

Find the missing piece.

Properties have yielded high returns over the past few years. After the period relating to the severe crash in the UK property market, 1990 to 1992, UK properties have almost consistently outperformed cash returns. The excess return has been particularly strong during recent years, due to an environment of relatively low interest rates and a strong performance in the commercial property market. Compared to the risk-free rate of return, measured by the 3-month Treasury Bill, the IPD UK All Property TR Index achieved on average an excess return of 4.66 %. It thus seems natural that the market expects, on average over time, above risk-free returns for properties. Figure 8.1 depicts the annual returns of Treasury Bills and of properties in the UK over the 20 years from 1987 to 2006.

Given this excess return in economically stable periods, why would an investor prefer to invest in cash rather than in properties? Cash has an advantage that can be pivotal: in contrast to an investment in physical properties, Treasury bills can flexibly and almost instantaneously be bought or sold.

8.1 PROPERTY SPREAD OBSERVATIONS

In the UK, property index returns were swapped against LIBOR plus a substantial spread until the end of 2006. However, the spread came down in 2007 and quickly even turned negative. Quotes obtained from market participants that trade swaps on total return property indices differ considerably from prices computed with models based on arbitrage arguments. Buttimer *et al.* (1997) developed a two-state model for pricing a total return swap on a real estate index. Bjork and Clapham (2002) presented an arbitrage-free model that is more general than the Buttimer *et al.* model. Patel and Pereira (2006) then extend the Bjork and Clapham model by including counterparty default risk. However, no pure arbitrage model seems to be able to explain the spreads observed in the market. We call these spreads the *property spreads*.

The missing replication possibility is critical for the existence of the property spread, be it positive or negative. In an equity swap, equity returns are – ignoring counterparty risk – swapped against LIBOR flat, although equities historically also experienced excess returns over LIBOR (see Benartzi and Thaler, 1995). The reason is that the no-arbitrage argument holds in the context of equities. Any trader can sell short equities and invest the proceeds in a LIBOR-returning instrument. It would thus be a "free lunch" to receive a rate higher than LIBOR. This is not true with property derivatives. A property index is a statistic rather than a real asset: the objects that are reflected in the index are typically not for sale; they are held by investors or homeowners for the long-term. The index measures property performance by just observing prices and valuations, not by transacting objects. Traders cannot instantly purchase or even sell short all the properties tracked by a property index.

Since a property derivative cannot be perfectly replicated by trading in the base market, property derivative prices do not necessarily behave in the same way as their underlying

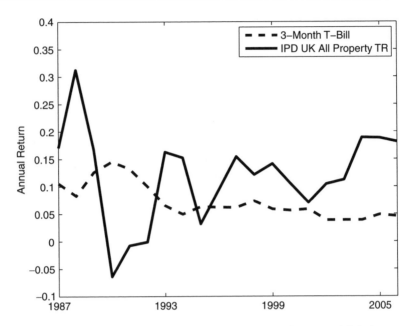

Figure 8.1   Returns of the three-month T-Bill and of the IPD UK All Property TR Index

indices. Even if the index and the derivative do not run in parallel, there is not necessarily an arbitrage opportunity; i.e. the arbitrage argument does not ensure that the index and its derivative are closely tied together. Following from the arbitrage difficulty, the derivative also reflects other factors that influence its price and potentially make the dynamics of the index and its derivative quite different. While volatility of a property index usually underestimates true market volatility (see Chapter 7), volatility of a *derivative* on the very same index is not necessarily lower than the true market volatility. Typically, the price of the derivative fluctuates more than the index itself.

This different behavior of the index and its derivative is illustrated by an example as follows. A five-year certificate on the IPD UK All Property TR Index, such as a typical IPD tracker is considered. The corresponding property swap trades at LIBOR plus a spread of, say, 2 %, reflecting positive market expectations. The spread translates into an annual index adjustment factor for the tracker of minus 2 % every year, in order to get a price at par value. The adjustment factor remains constant for the life of the tracker. The index and the tracker returns, volatilities and correlations are then compared. At maturity, the return of the tracker will by definition of the contract be 2 % lower than that of the index. However, the return of the tracker can still be positive, especially if the index performed better than anticipated in the 2 % spread. To spot the differences in volatility, it needs to be observed how the market develops. Assume that, after one year, the index has decreased by 3 %. In addition, the market is less optimistic about the development of the property market over the remaining four years, and the spread of a corresponding four year swap is at 1 %; i.e. a new tracker with the same four years remaining lifetime as the initial tracker would be priced with an adjustment factor of only 1 %. Consequently, the tracker will trade at a discount of about 4 % (the difference between the contracted rate of 2 % and the prevailing rate of 1 %, times four remaining years). Thus, the tracker has dropped by 3 % (from the index) plus about 4 % (the discount), i.e. by a total of about 7 %. That mechanism repeats itself, upwards and downwards, for the rest of the tracker's

Table 8.1   UK All Property total returns, July 2006 (left) and July 2007 (right)

Maturity	Bid	Offer	Maturity	Bid	Offer
December 2006	775	820	December 2007	−170	−70
December 2007	390	440	December 2008	−400	−300
December 2008	290	360	December 2009	−360	−280
December 2009	250	315	December 2010	−280	−200
December 2010	210	270	December 2015	0	100
December 2015	200	265			

life. The tracker can always trade at a discount or a premium. Obviously, the volatility of the index and that of the tracker is not the same. In this example, the tracker seems to be more volatile than the index itself.

The returns of the index and the one of the derivative do not even have to go in the same direction. While the return of the index reflects the past, derivative prices reflect the future. It follows that the correlation between the index and the derivative does not necessarily equal one and that the two have different correlations with third assets.

8.1.1   Term Structure of Property Spreads

The observed property spreads vary with the maturity of the swap. Table 8.1 and Figure 8.2 show the observed spread levels for different maturities implied by IPD UK All Property

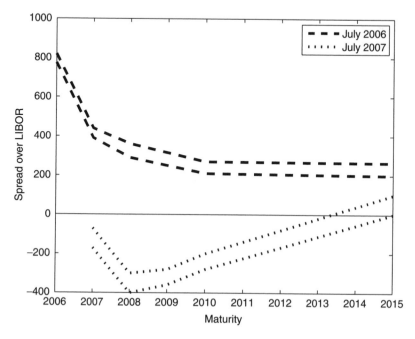

Figure 8.2   The term structure of property spreads: bid and offer spreads over LIBOR for the IPD UK All Property TR Index in July 2006 and in July 2007

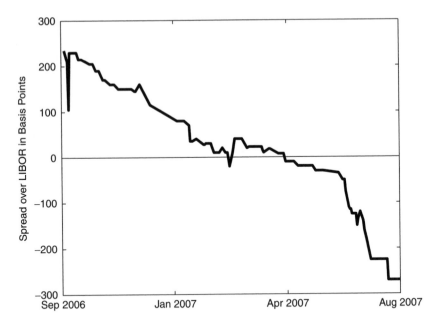

Figure 8.3 The property spread of the December 2010 swap decreased dramatically from September 2006 to August 2007

TR swap contracts in July 2006 and in July 2007. Spread levels can become negative when expectations on property returns are bearish. Figure 8.3 shows the development of the property spread of the December 2010 swap on the IPD UK All Property Index (the spread levels were obtained from TFS, GFI, Merrill Lynch and Bloomberg).

The substantial decrease in property spreads reflects several factors. First, LIBOR experienced a significant increase during that time, offsetting the property spread partially, all other things being equal. In addition, however, the market lowered its property return expectations for 2007 to 2010 significantly. Last but not least, increased hedging demand, due to both lower expected returns on the IPD Index and capacity constraints in this young market, drove the property spreads further down.

The cause for the shape of the term structures of property spreads is not obvious. As liquid and cost-efficient instruments, property derivatives are beneficial to both investors and hedgers. Given the significant transaction cost advantages, it is clear that especially market participants looking for a short-to-medium-term property exposure or hedge can benefit from the use of property derivatives. For long-term investment horizons, the impact of one-off transaction costs is less significant, making a physical purchase or sale a viable alternative to a property swap. Thus the short end of the term structure of property spreads is expected to be more volatile than the long end.

An often heard explanation for the shape of the property spread term structure follows a classical cash-and-carry arbitrage argument. Cash-and-carry arbitrage is a strategy whereby an investor buys the underlying assets, sells short the derivative and holds both positions until maturity. According to the explanation, a property derivative should be priced such that there is no arbitrage opportunity when the derivative is replicated by buying physical properties. In an efficient market, any arbitrage opportunity would be corrected immediately. Thus, when investors are seeking to buy properties, the price of the derivative should reflect the costs that would arise from a physical purchase. These costs comprise the transaction cost of about 7 % and of the annual facility management cost of about 1.5 %. The transaction cost should be amortized over the investment horizon and added to the annual management cost. For example, a five-year investment would induce an annual cost of 1.4 % (7 % divided by 5) plus 1.5 %, totalling 2.9 %. Generally, the longer the investment horizon, the lower the annual total cost. This cash-and-carry approach thus implies an inverse spread curve along maturity. The cash-and-carry argument is an intuitive starting point in explaining the property spread and matches the inverse spread curve that was observed in the market in July 2006. However, it does not help in explaining the curve prevailing in July 2007.

8.1.2 Market Frictions Inhibit Arbitrage

For a stock, cash-and-carry arbitrage works as follows: the fair price of a forward contract must be equal to the price of the underlying stock plus financing costs minus forgone dividends. If this relation does not hold, then cash-and-carry arbitrage can be achieved. If the forward price is higher than the fair value, an arbitrageur can sell the forward contract short, buy the stock and finance the purchase by borrowing. For a forward price lower than the fair value, the arbitrageur would enter a long position in the forward contract, sell the stock short and lend the proceeds to earn interest. However, this second case involves the need to sell the underlying asset short. Short selling is generally not possible for the properties that make up an index; thus it will be hard to perform arbitrage from an "undervalued" property forward contract.

In particular, the simple cash-and-carry argument that implies an inverse term structure of positive property spreads ignores the fact that amortization of transaction costs is not only a problem of investors, but also of hedgers. Suppose a portfolio manager wants to temporarily hedge existing property exposure: he or she would also experience transaction costs and should thus receive LIBOR *minus* a spread. According to the cash-and-carry argument above, the hedger still receives LIBOR *plus* a spread, although he or she has neutralized the property exposure.

The standard arbitrage argument used in modern finance assumes that the market is virtually frictionless, i.e. that the underlying asset can be instantaneously bought or sold at no cost. However, the argument does not hold for property derivatives because the underlying market exhibits many frictions, i.e. because the index and its components cannot be traded continuously and instantly at the prevailing spot price without transaction costs. In particular, the frictions in the physical property market include:

- High transaction costs: practitioners estimate the in and out costs – the so-called "roundtrip costs" – for properties to be between 5 and 7 %, including property taxes.
- Slow transaction process: it is not only costly but also time consuming to trade physical real estate, as the due diligence process, price negotiations and the closing of the contract take a lot of time.
- No short selling: physical properties can typically not be sold short; i.e. one cannot sell a house that he does not own.
- Illiquidity: illiquidity is an inherent characteristic of real estate assets. Every purchase and every sale takes effort to find the buyer with the highest willingness to pay or the seller with the cheapest offer. It is a fact that the property market is not quite transparent and in many regions, or for some sub-sectors, very few comparable transactions can be observed.

Consequently, uncertainty about demand and price for an individual object is high. The result is often a high difference between the prices of bidders and sellers (bid–offer spread), since both sides want to be compensated for the price uncertainty. Fisher *et al.* (2003) note that only in liquid spot markets, transaction prices always reflect true market conditions.

- Cost and utility of physical ownership: the management of buildings require administration costs that do not occur when simply holding a derivative. On the flip side, owning physical properties allows for development and flexibility in the use of properties.

In sum, property returns cannot easily be mimicked. A property derivative, in contrast to physical properties, can be bought and sold almost immediately. Thus, derivatives can make an asset more liquid. However, the lack of frictionless replication possibilities allows market expectations to influence the price of a derivative.

The existence of a property spread can be attributed to the frictions inherent in the property market. If there were no market frictions, perfect replication could be applied and the no-arbitrage argument would make sure that there is no property spread.

Given the frictions, there is an *arbitrage price band* rather than one single arbitrage price for property derivatives. More precisely, the arbitrage price band for a derivative is a function of the price of the underlying instrument and the market frictions. Only if prices are outside this band, arbitrage can be achieved using physical properties. Since it is nearly impossible to trade simultaneously all the properties measured by a property index, the arbitrage band for a property derivative is a *soft* one; i.e. even if some profit is expected after taking transaction costs and time into account, the potential arbitrage would still not be absolutely risk-free. As the frictions have a higher impact for short-term investments than for long-term investments, the arbitrage band is wider on the short end than on the long end. For example, in and out costs of 7 % alone would already justify a bandwidth of 7 % for a one-year contract, and one of 3.5 % for a two-year contract. That is, the one-off transaction costs are disseminated over the life of the contract.

8.2   THE ROLE OF MARKET EXPECTATIONS

In many aspects, property derivatives are comparable to derivatives on other physical assets, e.g. on commodities such as oil or wheat (see Hull, 2000, p.73, on pricing options and forwards on commodities in a Black–Scholes framework).

For commodity derivatives, frictions include the cost of storage. Further, the so-called convenience yield reflects the utility of owning the asset physically. For commodities, this utility is the increased value of a scarce good when demand peaks temporarily and the ability to continue a production process that depends on that good. Correspondingly for properties, there can be a temporal shortage e.g. for office space. This valuable "convenience," which is not captured by an index, may influence derivative prices.

To address these factors, pricing models for derivatives on physical assets typically include variables in addition to the ones of derivative pricing models for financial assets (i.e. equity, interest rates, currencies). Also, Baum *et al.* (1999) consider a parameter that reflects the market price of risk of a nonliquid good. For property derivatives, at least one additional variable must be considered for pricing issues. The observed property spread could naturally be that variable, reflecting the investors' willingness to pay, based on his or her market expectation, within the arbitrage band. In that sense, the property spread reflects the value for making a nontradable asset tradable.

Next, it is of interest what influences the derivative prices within the arbitrage band. We conjecture that the expectations of market participants drive derivative prices and hence the property spread. First, the expectations include the anticipation of autocorrelated dynamics of the underlying indices. Second, the expectations could also reflect the preferences of market participants towards risk. As long as the majority of market participants looks for a long position in properties, the spread is typically positive. In the case where many holders of physical properties want to hedge themselves by taking a short position via derivatives, the property spread can become negative. The possibility to quickly sell property risk is especially valuable in times when everybody wants to reduce exposure. For a more formal consideration of equilibrium pricing in the context of property derivatives, see Geltner and Fisher (2007).

8.3 ESTIMATING THE PROPERTY SPREAD

In a liquid and transparent property derivatives market, market expectations can be extracted by simply looking at the property spread. That spread may in turn be used to price new derivatives. However, if deals are privately traded in an undisclosed over-the-counter (OTC) market, the property spread curve needs to be estimated.

In the absence of derivative prices, historical data of the underlying property index, i.e. the distribution of index returns, are one source of information that must be carefully analyzed in order to make reasonable estimates for future index behavior and property spreads. Moreover, analysts' forecasts can be helpful in estimating the property spreads. In the UK, the consensus forecast of the Investment Property Forum (IPF), a compilation of 20 to 30 different forecasters running back to the end of 1998, may provide some insights into the market expectations up to three years ahead and serves as an indicator for the property spreads. Figure 8.4 compares the

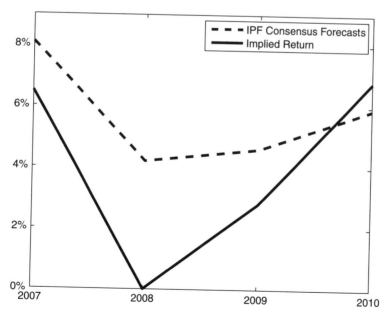

Figure 8.4 IPF consensus forecasts (dashed line) versus implied returns (solid line). Data obtained from Merrill Lynch

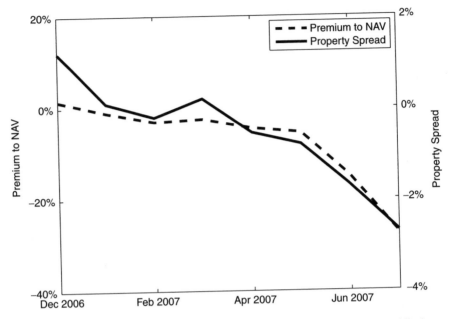

Figure 8.5 Premium to NAV for UK REITs (dashed line) versus property spread (solid line)

consensus forecasts to the property returns implied by the UK derivatives market. A spread lower than the consensus forecasts may indicate that investors demand a higher risk premium. The range of the individual forecasts provides an estimator for the market feeling about the risk and uncertainty of the consensus. In markets where there is no liquid derivatives market, the property spreads can thus be estimated using forecasts. However, forecasts are often considered sticky, i.e. they do not reflect market expectations to the full extent. The *Property Derivatives Handbook* of Merrill Lynch, January 2007, describes the characteristics of forecasts in detail.

Finally, the premiums and discounts to the net asset value (NAV) of REITs reflect market sentiment and provide an estimator for the property spread. Again, the UK market is examined in order to evaluate the estimation power. Figure 8.5 compares the December 2010 property spread to the premium over NAV for UK REITs. The development of the two is actually highly correlated. The premium or discount of REITs is about 10 times the annual property spread, indicating a reasonable discount rate of 10 % for property returns. As the net asset values of REITs enter the IPD Index, a large discrepancy between the premium and the property spread would induce an arbitrage opportunity. This is especially true for the Japanese market, where the IPD Index is based solely on the valuations of the J-REITs. However, when comparing premium to property spreads, attention must be paid to the differences in the structures of REITs and property derivatives, such as leverage, investment horizon and costs.

9

Pricing Property Derivatives in
Established Markets

Every thing has its price.

Trading will only take place in a derivatives market if market participants know, at least approximately, the fair price of the contracts. Under ideal market conditions, supply and demand solve the issue of pricing a contract. The equilibrium price in an established and liquid market is considered true and fair, as it reflects the expectations of the market as a whole. In such an equilibrium, there is no possibility to make a risk-less arbitrage profit.

The underlying indices of property derivatives are not traded assets. This complicates the pricing of property derivatives, as the basic Black–Scholes formula does not apply. In the Black–Scholes model, prices of derivatives do not depend on individual preferences, because any derivative is assumed to be perfectly replicable by an appropriate trading strategy in the underlying asset. Preferences may, however, be reflected in the price of the underlying asset. In other words, it is based on a no-arbitrage argument and does not allow market expectations and preferences to influence the price of the derivative. Since that argument does not hold for property derivatives, a different approach needs to be considered. Other instruments such as weather derivatives face the same issue (see, for example, Mahal, 2001). Pricing standards for weather derivatives do still not exist. Market makers, banks and insurance companies mainly use their individual pricing models, which they do not make publicly available. Just as for weather derivatives, the difficulty of a pricing model for property derivatives is to include the market expectations. These expectations are captured by the property spreads. Standard Black–Scholes or Monte Carlo models must be adjusted to address this issue.

9.1 FORWARD PROPERTY PRICES

The forward price F of a non-dividend-paying financial asset S equals the price of the asset plus the risk-free interest for the term of the contract. This relation holds due to a simple arbitrage argument: a long forward contract can be entered and at the same time the underlying asset can be sold short. Further, the proceeds from the short sale can be invested in a risk-free bond that grows at the risk-free interest rate r. The payoffs at maturity T of the three deals perfectly offset each other (here the transaction costs and the costs for short selling are ignored, as they are typically very low for financial assets). Following that argument, any forward price that is different from $S \times e^{rT}$ would allow for risk-free arbitrage. Clearly, the forward price will equal the spot price at maturity.

Properties, however, cannot easily be traded and sold short. The forward price thus cannot be assumed to be simply a function of the level of the underlying index and the risk-free rate. Here the property spread comes into play, such that the forward price is defined as

$$F_t = \tilde{S}_t e^{(r+p)(T-t)} \tag{9.1}$$

for a given maturity T and an index level $\tilde{S}_t$ at time t. More precisely, t is the date of the most recent index update and T is the date of the last relevant index update before or at maturity. No index information is revealed between two index publication dates and thus the forward price must ceteris paribus stay the same during this time interval. Since property indices are only updated after longer periods, e.g. quarters or years, it is critical to note this matter. The property spread p_T depends on the maturity T, since market expectations and hence the spread level vary with the time horizon. Clearly, according to Equation (9.1), a higher property spread results in higher forward prices.

Also, for a given maturity, the property spread p can change over time as market participants adjust their expectations. Gibson and Schwartz (1990) provide a framework that models the stochastic convenience yield for oil contingent claims in a two-factor model. Accordingly, the model could be applied to model a stochastic property spread. In their model, the convenience yield follows a mean-reverting pattern.

Forward prices that result from observed term structures of property spreads are displayed in Figure 9.1. To put the forward prices in the context of historical prices, the two are linked together. Figure 9.2 shows the historic and forward prices of the IPD UK All Property TR Index in February 2007. Figure 9.3, on the other hand, shows the historic and forward prices of the Halifax House Price Index. Since the overall time horizon is very long, a log-scale is used to illustrate the index growth over time. Please note that, in the long run, a total return index (such as the IPD TR Index) grows at a higher rate than a price index (such as the Halifax HPI), since the former includes rental income.

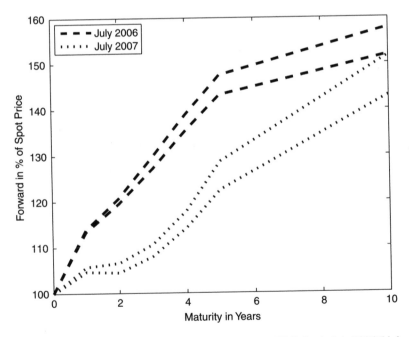

Figure 9.1   Forward prices (bid offer) of the IPD UK All Property TR Index in July 2006 (higher curves) and in July 2007 (lower curves)

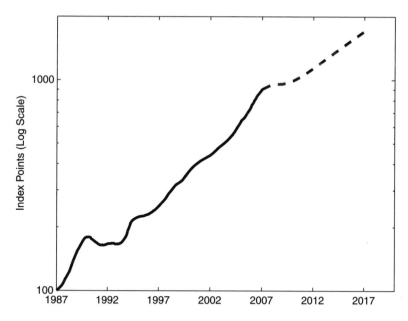

Figure 9.2 Historic and forward prices of the IPD UK All Property TR Index in July 2007 (log-scale)

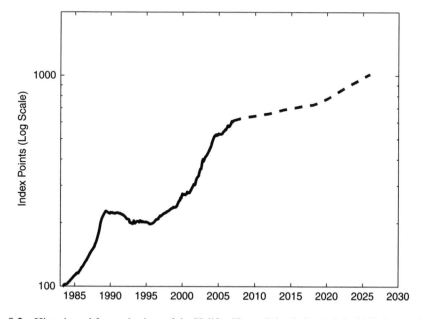

Figure 9.3 Historic and forward prices of the Halifax House Price Index in July 2007 (log-scale)

9.2 PRICING OPTIONS ON PROPERTY INDICES

Several parameters are required to price options properly on property indices. The parameters that are needed in general to price options are described in Chapter 2. In particular, the value of the underlying index, the strike price, the maturity and the interest rate are directly observable or set by definition of the option contract. However, the drift rate and the volatility of the index need to be estimated.

In a market where property swaps are liquidly traded, the corresponding observed forward price curve is the best estimate for the future drift rate; i.e. the property spread p needs to be included in addition to the traditional parameters.

The spread accounts for several issues relevant for property derivatives. As it reflects market expectations, it implicitly accounts for any inert or cyclic behavior that can be anticipated. To price European-style options that can only be executed at maturity, it is sufficient to adjust the drift parameter in the Black–Scholes formula by p. There is no need to include a further autoregressive term. In analogy to the pricing of options on commodity futures, Black's model (1976) can be applied. The argument of that model is that futures or forwards contracts can be used to replicate the option payoff.

9.2.1 Hedging with forwards and futures

The lack of replication possibilities with the underlying index itself potentially causes a problem when pricing contingent claims on a property index. To price a claim in a Black–Scholes framework, there is one crucial condition that must be fulfilled: the claim must be replicable, i.e. there must be some sort of liquid instrument on the underlying index that can be used to hedge the contingent claim.

Although the market for underlying properties will probably never be liquid enough to replicate a contingent claim on an index, the market for forward contracts can very well become liquid, as long as there are enough risk sellers and risk takers. In turn, forward and futures contracts can and will be used to replicate options on property indices.

For now, it is assumed that a liquid forward, futures or swap market exists (a swap is in fact just a series of forward contracts, and can thus be used as a hedging instrument as well). Suppose that these instruments can be used to replicate contingent claims without friction. This assumption will be relaxed in Chapter 12, where property derivatives are priced in incomplete markets.

It is now important to note that it is not necessary for the index to follow a random walk. As seen earlier, autocorrelation and other distortions are present in many property indices. However, if derivatives markets are efficient, i.e. if there are no risk-less arbitrage opportunities, the price of a forward contract will follow a random walk.

If returns of the forward contracts are normally distributed, it is sufficient to consider their drift and volatility when pricing contingent claims. Normally distributed returns is a further requirement when pricing contingent claims in a Black–Scholes framework.

To derive option prices in the Black–Scholes framework, the mentioned characteristics of properties and of forward contracts on properties are considered and the price process of the forward price F on the (untraded) property index $\tilde{S}$ is defined as

$$\frac{\mathrm{d}F}{F} = \sigma \, \mathrm{d}W \tag{9.2}$$

where σ is the volatility of the forward contract and W is a standard Brownian motion. In accordance with Black's model, the price of a European call option on a forward contract reads

$$C(F_t, t) = e^{-r(T-t)}\left[F_t\Phi(d_1) - K\Phi(d_2)\right] \tag{9.3}$$

where

$$d_1 = \frac{\text{Ln}(\tilde{F}_t/K) + (\sigma^2/2)(T-t)}{\sigma\sqrt{T-t}}$$

and

$$d_2 = \tilde{d}_1 - \sigma\sqrt{T-t}$$

and K is the exercise price and Φ represents the cumulative probability distribution. The risk-free interest rate r as well as the forward price F can be directly observed. As long as no implied volatility is observable, volatility σ must be estimated, e.g. as described in Chapter 7.

Substituting Equation (9.1) into (9.3), the option price is obtained in terms of the prevailing index level $\tilde{S}$ as

$$C(\tilde{S}_t, t) = \tilde{S}_t e^{p(T-t)}\Phi(\tilde{d}_1) - Ke^{-r(T-t)}\Phi(\tilde{d}_2) \tag{9.4}$$

where

$$\tilde{d}_1 = \frac{\text{Ln}(\tilde{S}_t/K) + [r + p + (\sigma^2/2)](T-t)}{\sigma\sqrt{T-t}}$$

and

$$\tilde{d}_2 = \tilde{d}_1 - \sigma\sqrt{T-t}$$

9.2.2 Volatility

Besides the drift, the second parameter that needs to be estimated to price options is volatility. Volatility cannot be implied from prices of linear claims such as forwards, futures and swaps, but only from nonlinear claims such as options. However, as long as only very few options exist in the market, it is nearly impossible to extract a reasonable implied volatility level from the observed option prices. The historical standard deviation of index returns is typically not a good indicator. It is in fact the volatility of the forward or futures prices that is relevant to price option, since these instruments are used for replication. The underlying index typically exhibits lower volatility than its forward prices because of several reasons:

- Property indices are often smoothed, as described in Chapter 7.
- The index exhibits autocorrelation, meaning that the standard deviation underestimates true volatility.
- A change in market expectations influences forward prices, even if the index is unchanged.

Thus care should be taken to estimate the volatility to price options. If no volatility can be implied from traded options, measuring historical volatility of forward prices provides the best estimate for the volatility to be used in option pricing.

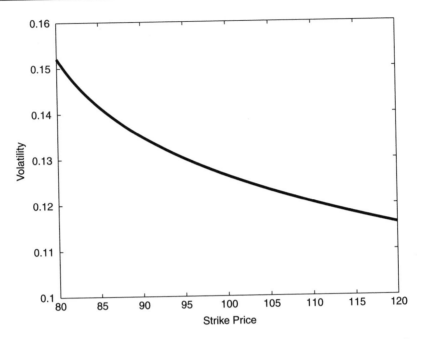

Figure 9.4   A typical, stylized volatility smile for stock options. The smile is in fact a calibration of volatility to fit into the Black–Scholes framework

9.2.3   The assumption of constant parameters

The Black–Scholes model as well as Black's model assume that interest rates, drift rates and volatility are constant. In reality, however, this is not the case. Still, the pricing models are widely used as they allow easy price calculations that result in reasonable price levels. In fact, the models became the standard pricing approach for derivatives. The models' shortcomings with respect to the assumption of constant parameters are addressed by defining the input parameters such that they fit to the model. The most prominent example is the so-called *volatility smile*. Depending on the strike price (and maturity), a corresponding volatility level is taken from a curve that describes volatility levels along strike prices. Figure 9.4 shows an illustrative example of such a volatility curve. Since that curve resembles a smile, it is often referred to as the volatility smile. Similar relations and curves exist for interest and drift rates. Using these curves, the model can and commonly is applied to price almost any kind of option. A volatility curve is not yet observable in the property derivatives market, as there are very few quoted option prices. However, the example of the volatility smile describes well how an assumption of the Black–Scholes model can be relaxed in practice.

9.2.4   Jumps in the diffusion process

In standard finance literature, pricing and hedging of options is based on the assumption that the prices of the underlying assets follow a geometric Brownian motion. However, empirical studies show that, in reaction to significant new information, prices can exhibit jumps. Classical pricing models might thus induce mispricings, as price evolution in reality is more complex than a geometric Brownian motion.

Options on property indices are no exception. In particular, the low frequency of index publication leads a priori to discrete price changes. The question is which changes can be considered continuous, i.e. could be generated by running a Brownian motion, and which changes are jumps. Between the publications of two index points, prices of futures and swaps develop according to the expectations of market participants. The participants continuously receive new information about the property market, about interest rates and about the economy in general, causing them to adjust their expectations. Although only the index level at maturity is relevant for the payoff of a European-style option, index publications before maturity can provide significant instant new information that may result in changed expectations and thus in price jumps for futures and swaps.

As options are replicated using futures and swaps, jumps in their prices introduce a further hedging challenge. In the Black–Scholes framework, dynamic replication assumes continuous Brownian price diffusion, but real prices can move discontinuously, making accurate replication difficult. These observations have led to an extensive literature that incorporates jump diffusion into the Black–Scholes model.

Merton (1976) was the first to extend the Black–Scholes model to include jumps. The introduction of jumps implies that option prices are no longer determined by the no-arbitrage argument alone. Merton addressed this pricing problem by assuming that jump risk was not systematic. Another early approach that includes price jumps was provided by Cox and Ross (1976). They consider a simple jump-type process from a single source of randomness with a fixed jump amplitude. There are many further models featuring a combination of diffusion and jump processes, e.g. the ones of Jarrow and Rosenfeld (1984), of Ball and Torous (1985), of Ahn (1992), of Mercurio and Runggaldier (1993), of Amin (1993) or of Bellamy and Jeanblanc (2000). However, none of them is widely used in practice. Black–Scholes still provide the commonly applied framework for option pricing on all sorts of underlying instruments, although option traders adapt the model by varying its input parameters.

The described approach to price options on a property index assumes that a liquid market for forward, futures or swap contracts exists. As long as this is not the case, the pricing of property derivatives cannot be based on standard no-arbitrage pricing: this is mainly a consequence of a lack of replicability, as there are no property derivatives available that could be used for a hedge. There are uncertainties with respect to pricing and hedging that are inherent in every market that is just emerging. The measurement and management of risk is thus a sensible task and of the utmost importance.

10

Measuring and Managing Risk

No risk – no fun.

So far, a pricing framework has been presented for property derivatives that is based on the assumption that at least one contract on the underlying asset, e.g. a property swap, is liquidly tradable. In other words, it is assumed that any claim can be replicated by the contracts that exist in the market. However, in most countries there are very few or almost no trades in property derivatives. This means that claims cannot easily be replicated in the market and that a bank that issues property derivatives needs to think about how to handle its property risk. A property index has some special characteristics that need to be considered when its risk is measured. Generally, a hedger must be aware that the frequency of index calculation is low (monthly, quarterly or annually) and that there is a lack of risk indicators as long as contracts on the index are not liquidly tradable.

The low calculation frequency and the lack of risk indicators complicate the risk management. The low calculation frequency implies relatively large jumps in the underlying asset, exposing the hedger of a contingent claim to so-called *gamma risk* (see Chapter 2 for details on gamma risk). In addition, the lack of risk indicators, such as the implied forward rate or volatility, make it harder to find appropriate pricing and hedging parameters, as the hedger must rely on historical data or estimates.

10.1 MARKET DEVELOPMENT AND LIQUIDITY

In Chapter 9, it was assumed that the market for futures, forwards or swap contracts is liquid. This is not the same as assuming that the market for the underlying properties is liquid. Although the market for physical properties is (and probably always will be) inherently illiquid, a liquid derivative market can develop. Derivatives on inflation are a good example of this phenomenon.

By liquid is meant that it is possible to buy or (short) sell instantaneously any notional amount of an asset or contract at the prevailing market price. In a liquid market, bid-offer spreads are small and there is an active secondary market, meaning that an investor can unwind his or her position at any time at low cost. In order to identify and measure risk for the emerging property derivatives market, a distinction is made between two stages of market development:

- *Early stage*. Property index contracts cannot be traded in the market and property risk cannot be easily transferred to third parties. Property derivatives cannot be hedged in a reasonable time frame. Deals are only closed occasionally.
- *Mature stage*. Property index contracts can be traded at all times, either directly in the market or through risk transfer to third parties. Property exposure can be reduced by offsetting deals and contingent claims can be replicated in a reasonable time frame.

10.2 EARLY AND MATURE STAGES

At a mature stage, property exposure can be traded liquidly and risk can be hedged in the market. Thus, intermediaries such as banks can apply the common risk management for liquid markets. At an early stage, however, there is no liquid market and intermediaries need to handle property exposure in an alternative way. Here the focus is on risk management strategies at the early stage and three strategies are described that can be followed by a bank trading property derivatives. The first and the second of these strategies imply no direct market risk for the intermediary, while the third requires risk management.

10.2.1 Strategy 1: back-to-back matching

A derivative market typically starts with a contract between two counterparties who agree to swap well-defined payments that depend on an underlying instrument. To bring the counterparties together and to match their needs and desires, an intermediary such as a bank usually steps in.

Although the intermediary mostly acts as the counterparty for both clients, he or she might not want to take the risk of the underlying property index. The intermediary matches the payoffs, maturities and principal amounts of both clients and does not allow the contract to be redeemed before maturity to avoid being exposed to market risk. Counterparty default risk remains with the intermediary who charges a premium for that risk. In the case of default, market risk becomes relevant again in order to define the loss-given default.

As long as intermediaries are not willing to take on market risk, derivatives contracts are in effect matched bargain trades between a buyer and a seller. Pricing of the derivatives is therefore determined through bilateral negotiations. This process of bringing buyers and sellers together is commonly known as back-to-back matching.

This strategy is the simplest but also most inflexible approach of developing a market. Obviously, it is hard to find two counterparties that have exactly opposite views and agree on all terms. Mostly, a back-to-back matched contract is the result of a compromise. Many deals that would take place in a liquid market therefore just do not happen in an illiquid market. One big issue is the desire for secondary trading, i.e. the possibility to sell the contract or part of it back at any time before maturity.

Intermediaries will typically maintain this limited offer as long as they are not comfortable assuming risk that they cannot offload immediately. For property derivatives in the UK market, this procedure lasted until 2005, when intermediaries started to temporarily assume some property market risk.

10.2.2 Strategy 2: auctions and public exchanges

Often, it is very difficult for a bank to find discrete back-to-back order matches. An auction framework can be considered in order to help establish the market.

There are various examples of how derivatives are traded in an auction framework. Goldman Sachs and Deutsche Bank launched an auction platform to trade economic derivatives in 2002. Further, International Securities Exchange (ISE) established a platform based on the Rexx commercial real estate property indices in 2007.

Both examples use a so-called universal Dutch auction framework that intends to pool and maximize liquidity for a given interest in the offered contracts. It is a closed system, i.e. premiums paid in are used to fund all payouts of filled orders. Prices are calculated to meet the equilibrium. Auctions are typically held one day prior to the publication of the underlying index that defines the payoff and last for one hour. The contracts typically take the form of standard OTC derivatives, where the intermediary is counterparty to all bidders.

A typical auction process works as follows. The intermediary determines the auction contract details (e.g. strikes, maturities, etc.) in advance of the auction, based on customer demand. It also sets initial prices by seed orders and provides some minimum liquidity. During the auction period when market participants start to bid, forward prices, probabilities and volatilities can be implied from quoted prices. Until the auction closes, orders may be modified at any time. The orders are filled objectively based on the limit price submitted by the participating long and short bidders. The orders submitted during the auction period create equilibrium prices and are executed at this equilibrium price at auction close. The equilibrium price is usually called the *market clearing price*. Such a pricing solution is said to be liquidity optimizing and prices are determined solely by submitted orders. The mechanism provides combinatorial, market-driven pricing and liquidity (many-to-many matching). To be fair and unbiased, however, an auction must have a large enough number of participants.

A contract subject to an auction is, for example, a one-year at-the-money call option on a quarterly quoted property index. An auction would take place, for example, at an exchange every quarter, i.e. periodically before the publication of the latest index level. Liquidity is considerably increased by compressing the orders from one-quarter into one hour. Thus auctions potentially work more efficiently than continuous market making. Auctions have been applied to property derivatives in several attempts. e.g. at the Chicago Mercantile Exchange (CME Auction), at the International Securities Exchange (ISE), on the platform of Goldman Sachs and Deutsche for economic derivatives auctions and on those of the spread betting firms IG Index and City Index.

The mechanism of a public exchange is similar to an auction. Market participants can bid and offer for a contract by using a limit price. However, there is no market clearing price at the end of a bidding period, but a trade is executed as soon as a bid and an offer price match. The disadvantage of a public exchange in a young market is that it can take a long time until a trade actually matches. This is currently experienced at the Chicago Mercantile Exchange (CME), where property derivatives were introduced in May 2006. Applying a periodical auction instead of permanent quoting in a public market would concentrate the trading volume.

While traditional market making in a public exchange (i.e. the bank constantly quotes a bid and an ask price) implies that other market participants such as investors and hedgers are price takers, an auction framework provides a market-driven price for risk. The prices of the contracts are based on relative demand. The auction pricing mechanism, if set up properly, can be considered transparent and fair.

10.2.3 Strategy 3: warehousing and market making

Eventually, as more and more contracts are transacted, banks anticipate growth in the market of property derivatives and start to take the associated real estate risk on their proprietary trading account, until they find a (partly) offsetting counterdeal. This procedure of temporal exposure to market risk is called *warehousing*. By following a warehousing approach, banks are able to permanently make a market for real estate derivatives and provide a flexible contract design for customers.

If the intermediary expects the market to become liquid, taking warehoused risk temporarily is usually seen as a necessary effort to help the market take off. However, the net exposure of the intermediary will hardly be nil; i.e. there will be a residual net position for the intermediary.

This net position can potentially be large, especially in the early stage of market development. The intermediary thus needs to allocate costly risk capital for the net market risk that is taken. Depending on the (in-)ability to balance long and short exposure, the cost for not being able to completely hedge during the early stage can be considerable.

Each trade changes the warehoused exposure of the intermediary. Again, the question of market liquidity arises. In a liquid derivatives market, the intermediary could act simply as a market maker and always keep the position neutral, if necessary by quoting slightly dumped prices. In an illiquid market, however, the possibility of offsetting positions is limited, and potentially only very heavy price dumping could result in the desired offsetting transaction. Such heavy price dumping is likely to result in a loss for the market maker.

At a more mature stage, when the market is finally liquid, intermediaries will act as market makers. Issuers typically act as market makers for the derivative securities they launched themselves. Market making implies an obligation to the issuer to always quote binding bid and offer prices during trading hours and under normal market conditions. This means that investors can buy or get out of their investments very flexibly. As soon as a client order matches the quote of the market maker, the order is executed. Often, the issuer is committed to keep the bid-offer spread narrow, e.g. below 1 % of the price. Market makers still warehouse market risk typically for a short time, but have better possibilities to offset their risky position than in a very embryonic market. Generally speaking, the narrower the spread and the larger the offered size at prevailing prices, the more liquid and mature is the market.

10.2.4 Subsidies in an embryonic market

When managing a trading book for property derivatives, the net warehoused position of all outstanding contracts must be measured and put in the context of the risk appetite of the intermediary and of the risk limit that must not be exceeded; i.e. transactions must be coordinated in such a way that the risk of the net position always remains controllable. The better the coordination of transactions, the smaller is the ratio of the residual net position to the total outstanding position.

As long as the market for property derivatives is embryonic, such coordination is necessary in order to manage risk. Thus, it is likely that demand cannot always be met to a client's full satisfaction. Conflicts of requested contracts with the intermediary's exposure (net position) may arise.

Coordination also means limitation of size per contract. Suppose the intermediary, typically a bank, offers a security that is linked to a property index for public subscription. At the start of the subscription period, the bank does not know the final demanded size. If demand exceeds the bank's risk appetite or limits, the bank must limit subscription size as well. Fair and equal treatment of clients and reputation risks must be taken care of in that case. Also, consistent pricing must be maintained for different derivative products over time, in order to build lasting credibility and confidence in the market. Coordination and limitation only becomes obsolete when the market gets full liquidity, i.e. when the bank is able to hedge any exposure in the market.

In the early stage, the bank should not focus only on profits and losses that arise from trading derivative contracts. The establishment of the market and the limitation of risk are more important at that stage. The focus on risk requires measurability of all outstanding contracts and of the overall net position.

As long as property derivatives cannot be replicated, i.e. hedged, the measurement and management of risk is of the utmost importance. A bank that warehouses risk can try to promote products that best offset the risks contained in its trading book. If the bank is not able to sell such products, the applied pricing is generally not in line with market expectations and needs to be reviewed.

Taking all risks and associated (regulatory and economic) costs into account, property derivatives are unlikely to be highly profitable if a bank tries to build up a market, i.e. in the early stage. Once markets are liquid, however, the impact and cost of warehoused risks drops since a trader or market maker does not need to bear the risks but can hedge his or her position at any time.

From an economic viewpoint, it can make sense for a bank not to charge all risk associated costs in the early stage. Assume that property derivatives provide benefits to market participants as long as they are priced at levels that would prevail in an established market. The total benefit, or total utility, derived from a property derivative market by participants is denoted by u. All costs of risks associated with property derivatives in the illiquid early stage, on the other hand, are summed in c. These costs shrink to c' when the market becomes liquid. Consequently, if

$$c > u > c' \tag{10.1}$$

it is necessary to subsidize contracts in the early stage by at least $c - u$ so that trades can take place and the market can develop. Without that subsidy, nobody would participate and buy or sell property contracts, since the utility derived is lower than the price paid.

Once the market has developed and costs have dropped from c to c', the bank can charge margins up to $u - c'$ and participants still close deals with the bank. At that stage, the deals will become more profitable for the bank.

The main driver of costs in a embryonic market is the cost of required regulatory capital, which drops dramatically once a market becomes liquid, as will be seen later on. Thus, the bank needs to avoid running into the trap of charging full costs from the very beginning. It should subsidize the market, where meaningful, in an early stage with a strategic long-term view. A subsidy could typically come in the form of cheap risk capital that is allocated to illiquid property index risks.

In sum, risk management should be distinguished on at least two periods, an early stage (corresponding to the illiquid buildup period) and a mature stage (corresponding to an established and liquid derivatives market).

To evaluate profitability, another aspect is of relevance. Besides the unhedged net exposure, it can be expected that a part of the full exposure can be hedged, be it through offsetting contracts or through risk transfer to a third party. Profitability of property derivatives trading will thus depend on both the risk-return characteristics of the remaining net position and the generated commissions and bid-offer spreads on all positions. The exposure that is offset does not require risk capital.

Warehousing requires thorough risk measurement and risk management. Next a bank's most popular risk measure, value-at-risk, will be described in the context of property risk. Further, risk management will be addressed in the next chapter in the context of hedging in an incomplete market.

10.3 PROPERTY VALUE-AT-RISK

Both the importance of risk measurement and the possibilities of risk management have increased dramatically in recent years. Banks need to measure and manage their portfolio market risk. They could simply do so by using historical volatility as a risk metric to measure how often a loss occurs. The problem with doing this is that it would provide a retrospective indication of risk. The historical volatility would illustrate how risky the portfolio had been over, for example, the previous 100 days. It would say nothing about how much market risk the portfolio is taking today.

For institutions to manage risk, they must know about risks while they are being taken. If a trader mishedges a portfolio, the bank needs to find out before a loss is incurred. Value-at-risk (VaR) gives institutions the ability to do so. Unlike retrospective risk metrics, such as historical volatility, VaR is prospective. It quantifies market risk while it is being taken.

VaR is a single statistical measure of losses and is widely used by banks. It is a risk metric that describes probabilistically the market downside risk of a trading portfolio. Losses greater than the VaR are suffered only with a specified small probability, called the confidence level. An intuitive illustrative definition of VaR is: "We are 99.9 % certain not to lose more than US$ 1 million over a time horizon of ten business days due to our exposure to the equity market."

The VaR concept is based on a distribution of future price changes of the risky assets under consideration. During the late 1980s and early 1990s, a number of institutions implemented VaR measures to support capital allocation or market risk limits. In 1996, the Basel Committee on Banking Supervision implemented market risk capital requirements for banks. According to the Basel Amendment, financial institutions should maintain eligible capital against their market VaR in addition to the conventional capital requirements for credit risk. The first Basel requirements were based upon a crude VaR measure, but the Committee also approved, as an alternative, the use of banks' own proprietary VaR measures in certain circumstances. Today, refined methods in accordance with Basel II apply. In addition, the Securities and Exchange Commission (SEC) allows the use of VaR in order to report market risk exposure.

A few papers have investigated the theoretical merits of VaR (e.g. Artzner *et al.* (1999) analyze the fundamental requirements of a risk measure). Kaplanski and Kroll (2002) describe the merits of VaR as a decision-making measure in comparison with other risk measures. They conclude that VaR is at least as good as other risk measures for decision-making purposes. However, for non-normal distributions, there are alternatives that are considered superior to the VaR criterion. In the normal case, the mean-VaR criterion (with a constant reference point) as well as the well-known mean-variance criterion are optimal. Under the normality assumption, minimizing variance is equivalent to minimizing VaR.

The VaR measure defines the regulatory required capital-at-risk (CaR). This risk capital must be maintained as equity. It is costly to the bank, since a return is required on equity; i.e. CaR directly results in costs for risks that are taken by and remain in the bank. The goal of risk management for property derivatives must thus be, even if subsidized at an early stage, to use as little capital-at-risk (CaR) as possible. VaR and CaR consequently serve the actual steering of the bank's risk appetite and limits.

In the context of property risks, the industry talks about the property value-at-risk (PVaR). Since property risk is much less transparent and measurable than most other market risks, regulators ask themselves how to use a PVaR in measuring capital adequacy for financial institutions. PVaR would be a measure of exposure to property value fluctuations, i.e. property risk, but it seems to be difficult to define and to implement.

There is limited regulatory agreement on benchmark measures, on the sensitivity of actual properties to benchmarks, on reasonable time horizons and on appropriate confidence levels. Financial institutions are exposed to property risk through occupied buildings they own, through direct and indirect property investments, through loan collateral of mortgages and, eventually, through property derivatives. Measurement of exposure to property risk of direct property investments may be especially difficult, given complex lease arrangements and the individual behavior of borrowers, tenants or landlords. There is to date limited disclosure of PVaR for both financial and nonfinancial companies. There are both theoretical and practical issues in providing and verifying disclosure of property derivatives portfolios. The definition and use of PVaR must and will be further developed in the near future.

10.3.1   Definition of value-at-risk

Value-at-risk is typically applied to liquid trading portfolios. A liquid trading portfolio can reasonably be marked to market on a regular basis. VaR considers a portfolio's or asset's performance over a specific time horizon, called the VaR horizon. The VaR horizon for a liquid portfolio is typically 10 business days. Further, VaR is measured in a particular currency, e.g. US$, called the base currency. The confidence level is for most applications in financial risk management either 0.990, 0.995 or 0.999, i.e. the probability that a loss exceeds VaR during the VaR horizon is 1.0, 0.5 or 0.1 % respectively. The summarized, single VaR number is a function of both the portfolio's current value and its random value at the end of the VaR horizon. VaR depends on the confidence level, the time horizon and the dynamics of the portfolio or asset under consideration.

When applied to illiquid assets, however, VaR is typically specified differently. For example, the VaR horizon for a derivative on an illiquid asset can be as long as its full term to maturity. Also, the confidence level is typically specified to be more conservative than for liquid assets.

A random variable with density function $f(X)$ and cumulative distribution $F(X)$ is denoted by X. The quantile X_P of X is the maximum value of X for which there is a probability of P to be below this value under $F(X)$. The definition of X_P is thus

$$\text{Prob}(X \leq X_P) = P \tag{10.2}$$

The value-at-risk at a $1 - \hat{P}$ confidence level, VaR$_{\hat{P}}$, is defined as the loss below some reference target over a given period of time, where there exists a confidence level of $1 - \hat{P}$ of incurring this loss or a smaller one. The reference target, denoted $\eta F(X)$, can be, for example, the expected mean of X, a constant such as the risk-free rate or zero. The official Basel Amendment recommends calculating the VaR as the potential loss below the current value (Basel Committee, 1996).

Time is measured in business days, current time being zero. Further, the portfolio's current market value is known. Its market value after one business day is unknown; i.e. it is a random variable. Thus a probability distribution, such as the normal distribution, needs to be ascribed to that variable. With VaR, a portfolio's market risk can be summarized by reporting some parameter of this distribution. In this example, a ten-day VaR of US$ 1 million at the 99.9 % confidence level means that there is a probably of 0.1 % to experience an absolute loss (reference point is zero) higher than US$ 1 million below today's value within the next ten days. In terms of the quantile function, VaR$_{\hat{P}}$ can be written as

$$\text{VaR}_{\hat{P}} = \eta F(X) - X_{\hat{P}} \tag{10.3}$$

The VaR calculation involves two primary steps. First, the forward distribution of the portfolio's returns at the specified time horizon needs to be derived. Second, the first $\hat{P}$ % of this distribution needs to be calculated. Figure 10.1 illustrates this process.

For liquidly traded assets, banking regulation requires that the VaR is calculated as a 99 % quantile of loss over a two-week horizon (10 business days). In the next step, the risk measure

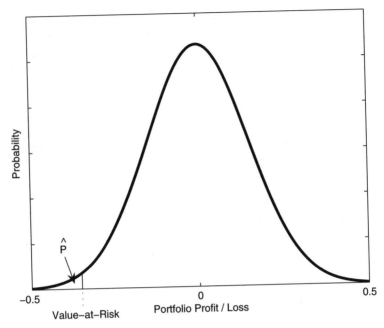

Figure 10.1 Distribution of the portfolio value after a specified time horizon. $\hat{P}$ then defines the value-at-risk

VaR determines how much capital financial intermediaries must hold as equity, so-called capital-at-risk (CaR). Generally, the required CaR equals the VaR. The CaR is a capital unit for one unit of risk and has a linear required return or cost. For financial intermediaries such as banks, the required return is either regulated (Basel II) or benchmarked against the market. Thus this cost is assumed as given. While the CaR and its cost is small for liquid assets, it is typically much larger for illiquid assets, often impacting the pricing of the latter substantially.

From a risk perspective, market liquidity and the corresponding time to hedge play a decisive role. For risk management issues, banks often measure the VaR at a confidence level of 99.9 % on a ten-day horizon. For illiquid assets, however, the confidence level is often set at 99.5 % and the time horizon equals the full time to maturity of the contract.

The confidence level of the VaR or CaR is often defined such that the measured risk corresponds to at least an A-rating. The time horizon typically equals the hedge horizon for a contract. The hedge horizon is the time needed to unwind the asset position under consideration. Obviously, illiquid positions are estimated to need more time to be absorbed by the thin market. To achieve an A-rating, a time horizon of one year, for example, results in a confidence level of about 99.9 %.

Figure 10.2 shows the VaR for various hedge horizons. A short horizon of ten days applies for liquid assets, while a five-year horizon would apply for a five-year contract on an illiquid asset that is not hedgable. The figure illustrates that the VaR depends heavily on the hedge horizon. The asset that underlies the contract is assumed to follow a standard Brownian motion.

For property derivatives, the applied VaR method depends on the stage of liquidity. In the early stage, where contracts must be assumed to be "held-to-maturity," an *unrestricted* VaR should be chosen; i.e. the hedge horizon should be set equal to the time to maturity of the

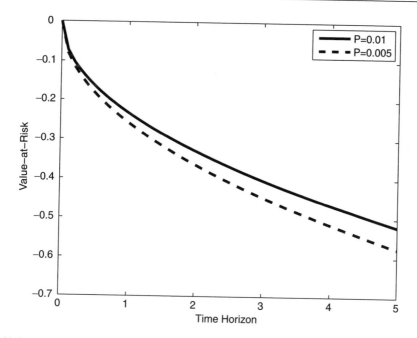

Figure 10.2 VaR depends on the specified hedge horizon. The graph illustrates this relation for the 99.0 and 99.5 % confidence levels. A volatility of 0.1 and zero drift are assumed

contract under consideration. This assumption implicitly assumes that it is not possible to hedge the contract during its life and that correspondingly capital-at-risk must be allocated. In the mature stage, on the other hand, a ten-day horizon is appropriate, since it can be assumed that an offsetting hedging transaction can be executed within that time.

The costs of the VaR and CaR can be substantial and strain the pricing of derivatives at an early stage. However, there are several ways to reduce the VaR.

- Trading a new derivative that offsets the risk of an existing one. That new derivative would have the same underlying asset but the opposite sign for the bank's payoff.
- Putting limits such as caps and floors on the derivative contracts. The VaR measures rare events as extreme, so-called *tail risk*. Since limits actually simply cut off the tails of the payoff distribution, the VaR will typically be reduced.
- Building liquidity. The sooner the market gets liquid, the quicker a bank can switch from a conservative VaR method to a more aggressive one, as the hedge horizon gets shorter.
- Hedging with assets that mimic the payoff of the contract under consideration can also reduce the VaR. However, as long as the hedging assets do not perfectly replicate the payoff, there will always be a tracker error.

Hedging in an incomplete market setting will be investigated further, as it is provides the possibility to reduce a bank's risk, i.e. the variance of profits and losses of a trading book. Before that, there will be a discussion on how a property index can be decomposed and what assets can be used for a hedge.

11

Decomposing a Property Index

Bricks in the wall.

Widely applied methods to price contingent claims are based upon a no-arbitrage and self-financing trading strategy, in which the payoff at maturity is replicated and the initial endowment required for the strategy is regarded as the fair price of the claim. In this approach, it is assumed that the underlying instruments are traded without frictions at any time, divisible into any unit, and short sales are allowed.

The same reasons that motivate the introduction of property derivatives make replication difficult. It is hardly possible in practice to trade the constituents of a property index, i.e. individual buildings and spaces, liquidly. These assets are usually indivisible and not traded in small units. Moreover, trading real estate causes typically large transaction costs and taxes, further inhibiting liquidity. Finally, the market price of physical properties is not frequently observed. A dynamic hedging strategy using the physical properties that constitute the index is regarded as impossible for property derivatives.

However, as derivatives on property indices become more and popular, there is a growing interest of what explains the indices' dynamics. If a property index can be decomposed into factors, some of which are traded assets, then the index can at least in part be mimicked. First, the general drivers of property prices are described, before focusing on the explanatory factors that are actually tradable and thus applicable in a hedging strategy.

11.1 GENERAL EXPLANATORY FACTORS

Fluctuations in property prices are mainly driven by macroeconomic factors. However, empirical evidence suggests that the housing market has its own distinct dynamics. According to Zhu (2003), almost three-fifths of the overall variation in residential property returns can, on average, be explained by price changes in the housing market itself; i.e. the cyclical behavior of the property market, as described in Chapter 7, partly explains future returns. According to Zhu, the other factors that explain the variation in property returns are gross domestic product (GDP), interest rates, bank credit and equity returns. Further, population growth and real income per capita have a significant impact on property prices. While interest rates and bank credit reflect the cost of homeownership, population growth influences demand and income per capita relates to affordability.

However, the importance of individual factors differs substantially across countries. Zhu mentions various reasons such as demographic dynamics, constraints on land availability, local land planning systems, housing financing systems, subsidies and differences in transaction costs and taxes. The duration of the mortgage rates also varies across countries. The mortgages of some countries are mainly based on short-term interest rates, making house prices generally more responsive to short-term interest rates. Examples include Australia, Finland, Germany, Ireland, Italy, Spain and the United Kingdom. By contrast, the majority of mortgage financing is tied to long-term interest rates in Canada, Denmark, France, the Netherlands, Sweden and the United States (see *OECD Economic Outlook*, 2005; Borio, 1995).

Further, the nature of the penalties on early repayment plays a significant role on whether households are willing and able to refinance their mortgage debts when interest rates fall. In the US, refinancing is more popular than in other countries, not only because of smaller penalties but also due to innovations in mortgage securitization (Deep and Domanski, 2002).

Moreover, collateral valuation practices have significant implications for credit supply. Valuation methods that are very sensitive to market values, in combination with high loan-to-value ratios, would generate a boom in credit supply when property prices rise and a credit crunch when prices fall (see Borio *et al.*, 2001; Turbulence in asset markets, 2002). Finally, lower transaction costs may stimulate turnover and enhance the responsiveness of housing markets to macroeconomic shocks.

All of these factors are local and specific to each market, leading to cross-country differences in housing price movements and in the relative importance of various factors.

The link of property prices to interest rates is probably the most obvious one. Interest rates directly influence financing cost, i.e. the terms of mortgages. With lower interest rates, financing is cheaper and consequently investors and homeowners are willing to pay more for a property. From an investment perspective, lower bond yields mean lower opportunity cost for real estate investments, making properties more attractive and driving their prices up. Clearly, property prices are expected to be inversely related to interest rates.

Unlike residential property, commercial property is typically a pure investment asset and not simultaneously a consumption good. Its value is mainly determined by the expected future rental income and calculated as discounted cash flows. During an economic downturn, reduced business activity results in lower demand for commercial property. Consequently, vacancy rates rise and rental rates as well as property prices fall. Compared with a residential property, commercial property prices tend to be more responsive to macroeconomic conditions.

Zhu (2003) finds that the dynamics of commercial property prices are less autonomous than those of residential property prices, but more responsive to the other explanatory variables. For example, the influence of the bank credit factor is more important in explaining commercial property prices. Commercial property prices are usually closely connected with borrowers' financial positions, as buildings are systematically used as collateral. The availability of additional credit for higher real estate values drives prices further upward. On the other hand, falling values strain the financial position of borrowers and push prices downward, as banks lend more restrictively.

Both residential and commercial property prices are responsive to stock price returns. Stock holdings and housing are the two largest portfolio components of household wealth in developed countries. Price movements in one component is likely to influence the investment decision on the other one. The resulting reallocation of portfolios will affect prices. The so-called wealth effect predicts that an increase in stock prices, by increasing the value of household wealth, will allow households to expand their investment in housing, driving property prices upwards.

The connection between stock and house prices is supported by empirical evidence. Zhu finds a clear pattern in a lead–lag relationship between stock and house prices in 12 developed countries. He finds that property prices lag stock prices about six quarters on average. In particular, the lead–lag correlation peaks at a stock lead time between three to nine quarters for 11 of the 12 analyzed countries, the exception being Germany with 16 quarters lead time for stocks versus properties. Borio and McGuire (2004) also document a tendency for house prices to fall about a year after equity prices have peaked.

11.2 TRADABLE EXPLANATORY FACTORS

To hedge a property index with correlated assets, however, only liquidly tradable factors that explain index returns are of concern. The goal is to find out how a property index relates to these assets. Several empirical researches suggest that there are securities that correlate with property prices. Liang *et al.* (1998) examine the ability of existing futures contracts to hedge the returns of Real Estate Investment Trusts (REITs). The results from various hedging strategies suggest that existing futures contracts provide the means to partly hedge REIT returns.

Empirical analysis also suggests that there are traded assets that potentially provide a hedge to property indices that underlie derivatives (see, for example, Englund *et al.*, 2002; Flavin and Yamashita, 2002). They include mortgage-backed securities, REITs, listed property companies and funds, equities, short and long interest rates as well as credit spreads. The availability of these assets, however, differs from country to country.

The development of real estate vehicles that invest in very specific property types allows a better selection of explanatory variables. In the US, there are REITs that invest purely in one commercial property sector, making the REIT a proxy for that sector. Moreover, the securitization of commercial mortgage-backed assets has become very popular in both Europe and the US. The focus of real estate vehicles on a specific property type provides appropriate opportunities to hedge derivatives on commercial property sector indices.

Decomposition is applied for many financial indices. For example, parallels can be drawn from other illiquid asset classes, where banks try to mimic returns. Such procedures became popular in 2006, when Goldman Sachs and Merrill Lynch rolled out investment products that are designed to provide hedge fund returns. They use a set of algorithms to analyze and assess the various explanatory factor exposures. The goal is to provide a product that mimics the characteristics of hedge funds as closely as possible, but avoids their drawbacks of high costs and illiquidity. Similar methods could be applied to property indices, which have the same drawbacks, in the future.

11.3 EXAMPLE: THE HALIFAX HPI

An analysis of tradable assets that correlate with the Halifax House Price Index (HPI), a hedonic residential property index measuring house price development in the United Kingdom (see Chapter 6), is conducted.

The traded assets that are commonly referred to when a property index is decomposed are used. First, to reflect the long- or short-term interest rates, the UK Citigroup Bond Index (CGBI) and the interest rate on the three-month UK Treasury Bill is taken. Second, the national stock market index FTSE100 is used to address wealth effects associated with equity investments. The credit spread, measured by the difference between the UK prime rate and the Treasury Bill, further addresses the cost of ownership. Finally, the UK European Public Real Estate Association (EPRA) Index covers the listed real estate vehicles.

Using these explanatory variables, an ordinary least square (OLS) regression is run on the seasonally adjusted Halifax HPI, where the index is log-transformed. The regression uses quarterly data points and runs from the first quarter of 1991 to the first quarter of 2007.

Table 11.1 Variables that explain the Halifax HPI

Variable	Coefficient	Time-lag	Significance (%)
Halifax HPI	0.65	−1	>99%
Real estate vehicles (UK EPRA Index)	0.07	−2	>99%
Short interest rates (UK T-Bill)	−0.79	0	>99%
Credit (prime rate − T-Bill)	−1.97	0	>95%

Besides the autoregressive term, a positive relation is obtained of the Halifax HPI to the bond index CGBI, to the FTSE100 Index and to the EPRA Index. The relation to the interest rate on the Treasury Bill and to the credit spread, both of which are measured in percent, is negative. It is further observed that the relation to the CGBI is lagged by one quarter and the relation to the FTSE100 and to the EPRA is lagged by two quarters. These results are as expected from the above interpretation of the factors.

However, multicollinearity is observed between the explanatory variables; i.e. a high degree of linear correlation exists amongst two or more explanatory variables in the regression equation. Multicollinearity makes it difficult to separate the effects of them on the dependent variable. In particular, the CGBI is highly inversly correlated with the interest rate on the Treasury Bill. Further, the EPRA Index is significantly correlated with the FTSE100 Index.

As the variables CGBI and FTSE100 have a significance level below 90%, they are eliminated from the regression equation. This solves the multicollinearity issue and raises the significance of the remaining variables. The remaining factors are all highly significant, as listed in Table 11.1. The adjusted coefficient of determination R^2 is at 66%, meaning that the regression explains two-thirds of the variation in the Halifax HPI.

The regression equation is

$$\Delta \log(I_t) = c + \beta_1 \Delta \log(I_{t-1}) + \beta_2 \Delta \log(E_{t-2}) + \beta_3 \Delta T_t + \beta_4 \Delta C_t + \varepsilon_{t+1} \qquad (11.1)$$

where c is a constant, I is the Halifax HPI, E is the EPRA Index, T is the interest rate on the Treasury Bill and C is the credit spread. The regression coefficients are β_i and ε is the noise term. The distribution of the noise term indicates the goodness of the regression model. Ideally, it would be i.i.d. standard normally distributed. In fact, the noise term does not exhibit significant autocorrelation, indicating that the model is not biased systematically over time (the Durbin–Watson statistic of 2.13 means that there is no or only insignificant autocorrelation present). This regression equation is used to price and hedge property derivatives on the Halifax HPI in the next chapter.

For the future, the increasing integration between the property and the capital market could have several effects that have an impact on the decomposition of property indices. It could dampen the real estate cycles and thus weaken the autocorrelation observed in property indices. Moreover, further development of funding vehicles such as REITs and mortgage securities make the financing of properties more flexible. However, market discipline gets more important, and controls are needed to avoid aggressive and speculative investments. Publicly observable prices of real estate vehicles reflect the concerns of market participants faster, enabling the market to detect price imbalances earlier. As more and new vehicles are traded and property price behavior changes, the decomposition of property indices must be re-evaluated.

12

Pricing and Hedging in Incomplete Markets

To hedge or not to hedge.

Hedging analysis yields implications for market completeness. The well-known Black–Scholes framework provides prices and hedging strategies based on the assumption of complete and liquid markets. As described in Chapter 9, the framework can be used for property derivatives if there exists a liquid market of property forwards or futures. However, if such a market does not exist, a different approach must be chosen.

If a combination of existing assets is able to replicate changes in property indices perfectly, then the introduction of new securities on the indices would be redundant. Putting aside transaction costs, anyone wishing to buy or sell property risk and return could do so synthetically by trading existing instruments. If, on the other hand, empirical evidence finds that currently traded securities do not effectively reflect property prices, the analysis would motivate the introduction of property derivatives, making the market more complete.

In reality, many derivatives on liquidly traded assets exist although they are theoretically redundant. The reason is that replicating an option requires continuous trading in the underlying asset and in a risk-free security. As this is not practical for most investors, they prefer to simply buy an option and leave the hedging to the bank. Derivatives on nontraded instruments such as property indices have the additional motivation of missing redundancy of the underlying asset.

Most proposed pricing models for property derivatives are based upon the no-arbitrage argument using a replicating strategy, which implies that the physical property or the property index itself can be traded at any time, at full market value, by any small unit without any trading cost (see, for example, Buttimer *et al.*, 1997). In reality, however, properties are usually indivisible and not traded in small units. Transaction costs and taxes are large, and liquidity is very thin.

Replicating strategies using the properties that constitute the underlying index should be regarded as impossible. However, as suggested in the previous chapter, there are traded securities that correlate with property indices. These securities can be used to mimic the returns of property indices.

12.1 HEDGING ANALYSIS

Hedging refers to a trading strategy that generally *reduces* portfolio risk. *Replicating*, on the other hand, refers to a strategy that completely *eliminates* portfolio risk, i.e. allows a perfect hedge.

The value of many derivatives is typically not derived from a liquidly traded asset as in the classical replication setting, but rather from a random variable that is not traded in a liquid market. Examples include derivatives on inflation, temperature or rainfall. Nonetheless, an attempt is made to apply a hedge as good as possible using traded assets. This is usually referred to as the possibility of hedging with correlated assets.

As banks start to trade property derivatives, they bear the risk of the positions they warehouse. If there is at least one asset that highly correlates with the index that underlies the derivatives, the bank can partly hedge changes in the index level and consequently reduce its risk position.

Correlated assets are traded assets whose price processes are closely related, but not identical, to the price process of the underlying asset of the derivative. The usual argument in favor of their use is that a sufficiently well correlated asset should do almost as well as the underlying asset itself, if it were a traded asset.

12.1.1 Hedging assets

In the context of property derivatives, think of the following situation. A claim is written on a house price index that tracks owner-occupied housing in a given region. An intermediary can obviously not buy and sell all the houses, or even a fraction of these houses, that constitute the index. Further, it is assumed that there is no liquid market for contracts, e.g. futures, on the index itself. However, there are some other assets, such as interest rate, real estate or credit instruments, that reflect some dynamics of the residential housing market. These assets are traded in a liquid market without frictions. In fact, explanatory regression variables can, as long as they do not lead or lag the property index returns they explain, be used to hedge derivatives on the index. The basic idea is that the price process of the index and the one of the variables is sufficiently similar to justify the use of the latter as a *hedging asset*.

Since prefect replication of a claim written on a property index is not possible by only trading in hedging assets, it is natural to ask how small the hedging error can be made. One way to quantify the hedging error is by considering its variance, which subsequently is to be minimized. This leads to the well-known concept of the variance-optimal martingale measure, which is closely related to the notion of the minimal martingale measure (see Föllmer and Schweizer, 1991).

An investigation follows on how hedging assets are optimally applied and, subsequently, the impact of a hedge on the pricing of property derivatives.

12.1.2 Discrete time setting

Most dynamic hedging strategies, such as the well-known delta hedging approach, address the price change of a derivative for a change in the underlying instrument over an infinitesimal time period. The delta hedge concept assumes a continuous movement of prices, and provides the optimal hedge ratio only for a small move in the underlying instrument. After such a move, the delta must be adjusted.

Property indices are typically calculated on a monthly, quarterly or annual basis. The smallest possible change in the index thus occurs only at low frequency. At the time a new index point is published, the price of a derivative on the index might jump and incorporate the new information quickly; i.e. there is not a continuous but an abrupt price development.

To mitigate the problem of low frequency, a discrete time setting is considered. Since it is known that no move in the index will happen until the next release date, there is not really much interest in infinitesimal price moves. Instead, there is concern with the price changes that can be expected when the new index point is released.

Low frequency complicates the hedging concept. If a nonlinear portfolio of derivatives is considered, an abrupt change in the underlying asset potentially reduces the hedge efficiency, in the same way as the Black–Scholes concept no longer provides a perfect hedging strategy in discrete time. The risk of price jumps with regard to the nonlinearity of a derivative is commonly referred to as *gamma risk*.

12.1.3   Optimal hedge ratios

A simple replacement of a nontraded underlying instrument by a hedging asset is not the optimal hedging strategy. Ederington (1979) shows that the regression coefficient of a hedging asset with respect to the underlying index is the adjustment factor that minimizes risk, using an example where a spot asset is hedged using a futures contract. The regression's coefficient of determination R^2 represents the percentage of risk that is eliminated by holding the hedging asset. Ultimately it is R^2 that indicates how effective a hedge is when risk, measured as variance of the hedging error, is to be minimized. In accordance with the reasoning of Johnson (1960) and Stein (1961), Ederington (1979) argues for an optimal hedge ratio in a mean-variance context. A hedger uses hedging assets for the same risk-return reasons as an investor who optimizes his or her portfolio in a mean-variance context.

The specific characteristics of property derivatives are addressed by setting the following framework. Let $\tilde{S}$ be a property index that is not traded directly but serves as an underlying instrument for derivative claims. Further, there are hedging assets S_j that can be traded liquidly. Throughout this chapter, the expectations $E[\cdot]$ refer to the objective probability; i.e. the expectations are based on observations.

There are two main differences to the traditional delta hedging concept:

- Index returns are only observed infrequently.
- Only hedging assets can be traded, but not the underlying index itself.

Consider a bank that is engaged in issuing, trading and warehousing property derivatives and thus holds a corresponding derivatives portfolio. The trader can engage in hedging positions by trading the hedging assets S_j that are correlated with the underlying index $\tilde{S}$. The objective of this hedging analysis is to minimize variance of the combined portfolio by choosing the hedging weights ϕ optimally. We start by looking at a portfolio that only includes linear claims, i.e. the gamma risk of the trader's portfolio is assumed to be zero. The optimal hedge ratios in the hedging assets, i.e. the weights that minimize the variance of the combined portfolio, are obtained as

$$\phi_j^* = -\beta_j \Delta + \lambda_j X_{S_j S_j}^{-1} E[\delta S_j] \tag{12.1}$$

where β_j is the regression coefficient of asset S_j in a multiple regression including all hedging assets as explanatory variables and the property index $\tilde{S}$ as a dependent variable. The aggregated option delta of the portfolio is denoted Δ and linearizes the relation between the hedging assets S_j and the index $\tilde{S}$. This linear relation allows the use of linear regression coefficients. The second term of Equation (12.1) represents the shadow price of the hedge, i.e. the monetary cost to the trader of investing in the hedging asset S_j.

To refine the hedge, the aim next is to minimize the variance of the hedging error under the consideration of the gamma risk that represents the curvature of the portfolio. Gamma can, just as delta, be additively aggregated in a portfolio of derivatives that is based on the same index. Gamma is given for the overall portfolio by Γ. While call and put options both have a positive gamma, it is zero for linear contracts. The gamma-adjusted hedge positions in the hedging assets S_j are given as

$$\phi_j^* = -\beta_j \Delta - \Gamma \frac{X_{\tilde{S}\tilde{S}}}{2} X_{S_j S_j}^{-1} X_{\tilde{S}^2 S_j} + \lambda_j X_{S_j S_j}^{-1} E[\delta S_j] \tag{12.2}$$

where the second term adjusts for the curvature of the derivatives portfolio.

If hedging assets as well as options on the hedging assets can be used, delta and gamma can be treated separately. Two hedge portfolios are built, one for the delta hedge and one for the gamma hedge. While delta addresses the linear relation between the derivatives portfolio and the underlying instrument, gamma accounts for the curvature in the derivatives portfolio. For a detailed description of how the hedge ratios are derived, refer to the Appendix.

12.1.4 Remaining risk

For every hedging strategy, it is natural to ask how much risk can be hedged and how much risk remains with the trader. The more effective a hedge, the smaller is the remaining risk in terms of variance of the combined portfolio. To illustrate the hedge effectiveness, we first look at a situation where one hedging asset is available and then turn to a situation with two hedging assets. The variance of the hedging error is plotted as a function of the correlation between the hedging assets and the underlying index.

The parabola shown in Figure 12.1 reveals that risk cannot be reduced if there is zero correlation, but can be eliminated completely if the correlation is either one or minus one. The graph assumes that the optimal hedge position is applied. The variance of the hedging error is in fact reduced by a factor $(1 - \rho^2) \le 1$, with ρ being the correlation coefficient.

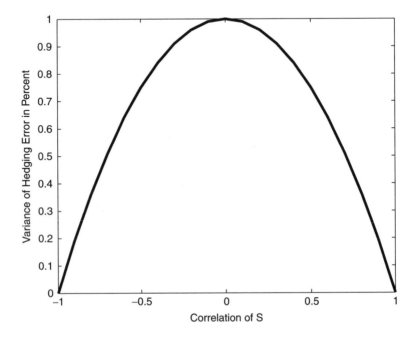

Figure 12.1   Variance of the hedging error when using one hedging asset

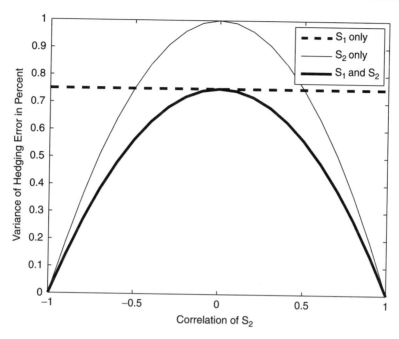

Figure 12.2   Variance of the hedging error when using two hedging assets

Next the impact of using a second hedging asset is illustrated. Suppose that one of the hedging assets, S_1, is correlated with the underlying index $\tilde{S}$ by ρ_1 equal to 0.5. A second hedging asset, S_2, is now added, which is correlated with $\tilde{S}$ by a correlation coefficient ρ_2 that lies somewhere between -1 and 1. The following hedging strategies are compared:

(a) hedging with S_1 only;
(b) hedging with S_2 only;
(c) hedging with S_1 and S_2.

Figure 12.2 compares the three hedging strategies. The horizontal line represents strategy (a), where only the hedging asset S_1 is applied. This line touches the parabola that represents the hedging strategy (c) at the maximum, i.e. where $\rho_2 = 0$, and intersects the parabola of strategy (b), where $\rho_2 = \rho_1 = 0.5$. It is observed that using both hedging assets, i.e. following strategy (c) is able to reduce risk further compared to hedging with only one hedging asset. Assuming the two assets are independent, the variance of the hedging error is reduced by the factor $(1 - \rho_1^2)(1 - \rho_2^2)$.

The approach of using hedging assets can be extended to an arbitrary number of hedging assets following multiple regression. If there is a large number of liquid hedging assets available in the market, with sufficiently significant correlations to $\tilde{S}$, the portfolio risk can be reduced further. Statistically, the greater the number of hedging assets used in the regression, the higher is the coefficient of determination R^2. However, simple R^2 ignores the fact that multiple hedging assets introduce a risk of multicollinearity, i.e. that hedging assets are not completely independent. To mitigate this issue, the assets are selected such that *adjusted R^2* is maximized. This criterion adjusts for degrees of freedom, and in this way hedging assets are only added to the hedge portfolio if they contribute in a significant way. This methodology tries to achieve the simultaneous goals of selecting a portfolio that has a small number of hedging assets but also effectively hedges the property index. With potentially fewer assets, the transaction and monitoring costs are also reduced for our hedge portfolio. Up to five hedging assets are commonly used to hedge a portfolio using the adjusted R^2 criteria.

The risk that cannot be eliminated using hedging assets is refered to as *intrinsic risk*. This intrinsic risk is orthogonal to the returns of all hedging assets and can be isolated for the portfolio and for each claim.

In the next step, for each new derivative that is priced, the incremental intrinsic risk needs to be considered in the context of the intrinsic risk that already exists in the trading portfolio. If the incremental risk offsets existing risk, issuing the new derivative is beneficial to the bank. A portfolio position that favors a new deal is commonly referred to as having an *axe to grind* for this deal.

12.2   PRICING WITHOUT A PERFECT HEDGE

When pricing a property derivative in an incomplete market setting, two basic issues need to be addressed.

First, the property spread p needs to be estimated in order to obtain a price as if the contract was traded in an established market. The estimation of the property spread allows forward prices to be obtained as if the markets were complete. As described in Chapter 8, either consensus forecasts or the premiums and discounts to the net asset value of REITs can be used to estimate the property spread. However, if such information is not available, a regression model can be used to obtain an estimation of future index returns. Figure 12.3 shows the estimated

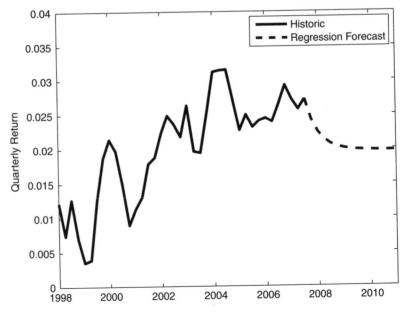

Figure 12.3   Estimated quarterly returns using the regression model

quarterly returns for the Halifax HPI using the regression Equation (11.1). In particular, the autoregressive term, i.e. the fact that property indices are inert, as well as the lagged variables influence the estimated returns. Constant interest rates and credit spreads are assumed, as well as a 5 % annual growth rate for the EPRA Index. As the returns of the HPI are autocorrelated, the estimated returns converge only gradually to their long-term mean. The corresponding estimated property spread can be obtained using

$$I_T^{\text{estim}} = I_0 e^{(r+p)T}.$$
(12.3)

The second issue when pricing derivatives in incomplete markets relates to the fact that there is no perfect hedge. A term needs to be added that addresses the risk premium a trader requires when taking risk he or she cannot hedge. Assume that the bank already has a portfolio of derivatives on a property index $\tilde{S}$. If the bank now issues a new contract, the trader needs to consider the effect of the new contract on the portfolio's risk, not only the risk of the new contract in isolation.

Depending on the composition of the existing trading portfolio, an additional claim can add or offset risk. If the bank has an "axe to grind," it has an incentive to look actively for risk-offsetting deals.

When a new derivative is to be traded, the *incremental* risk that is added or withdrawn from the trader's portfolio is relevant to price the claim. The price of a derivative contract is written as

$$\tilde{H} = H(\tilde{S}, K, \sigma, r, p, T) + \kappa \, \text{sign}(\Delta R)\sqrt{|\Delta R|}$$
(12.4)

where

$$\Delta R = \text{var}_{n+1}^* - \text{var}_n^*$$
(12.5)

is the difference in portfolio variance given optimal hedging positions with and without the new derivative. H is the derivative price as if markets were complete and κ is the price for the incremental intrinsic risk $\sqrt{|\Delta R|}$ that is added or withdrawn from the portfolio.

The problem of charging a premium for incremental risk is pricing instability. The impact on the portfolio risk and thus on the price of a new contract depends on the composition of the existing trading portfolio. Thus, the same contract can have different prices if launched from different trading portfolios, all other variables being equal. The price of incremental risk becomes negative if the new contract unloads existing risk exposure. Using correlated assets to hedge the portfolio exposure, risk is reduced to its intrinsic part, and pricing becomes more stable than it would be without hedging.

Pricing instability is neither in the interest of clients nor of banks and intermediaries. Budgeting and planning new launches will help to keep prices stable. Ideally, the long and short positions in a portfolio would completely offset each other. This equilibrium would indicate that the intermediary perfectly manages its risk position and that the pricing is in line with demand and supply.

12.2.1 The price for intrinsic risk

If a derivative cannot be hedged perfectly because the market is still in its infancy, the issuing bank will charge a price for the risk it cannot hedge. To do this, the bank needs to set its preferences towards various kinds of risk.

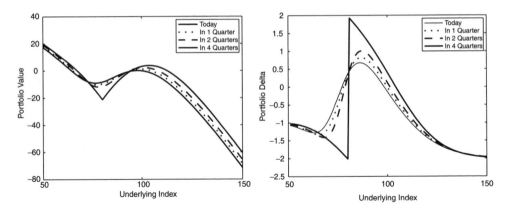

Figure 12.4 Profit and loss of the nonlinear trading portfolio (left graph) and its option delta (right graph)

There are several risk measures that can be applied when risk is warehoused. On the one hand, the bank typically wants to stabilize returns, i.e. targets to reduce the variability of profits and losses. Thus, a bank could charge a premium for the variance of the hedging error, as described by κ in Equation (12.4).

On the other hand, the bank is concerned with the risk that would hurt it seriously, which is typically measured by the value-at-risk (VaR), as described in Chapter 10. In effect, a higher VaR requires more regulatory capital. For an illiquid market, required capital is even more costly than for a liquid market, since it typically takes much more time to unload risk positions from the trading portfolio.

As regulatory capital is not free, the risk premium should at least incorporate the cost of required regulatory capital. Depending on the risk appetite of the bank, it can charge an additional premium for taking the risk of uncertain profits and losses.

For a portfolio containing options, minimizing the variance of the hedging error is not equivalent to reducing the VaR. For example, the VaR of selling a call option is significantly higher than the one of buying it. While the bank can only lose the premium in the latter case, the potential loss of a short call position is unlimited. In contrast, the variance of the hedging error of a short position is not necessarily higher than for a long position. Thus, to find the right price, a bank must set its preferences towards the different risk measures.

12.3 EXAMPLE: HEDGING A TRADING PORTFOLIO

The hedging approach is illustrated by the following example. Assume that a trading portfolio consists of short two five-year call options with a strike price at 100 index points, short three three-year put options with a strike price at 120 index points and long four one-year put options with a strike price at 80 index points. All these claims are based on a quarterly index $\tilde{S}$ that stands at 100 index points, has a volatility of 10 % p.a. and an estimated drift rate equal to the risk-free interest rate of 5 % p.a.

Figure 12.4 shows the profit and loss of the trading portfolio along $\tilde{S}$ as of today and its evolution over the next four quarters. Also, the corresponding option delta of the portfolio is

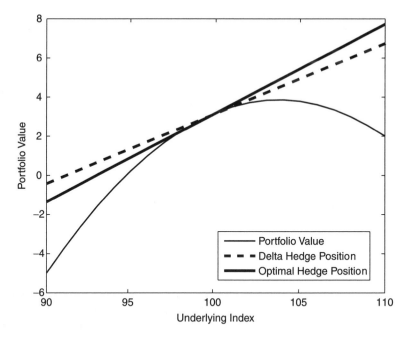

Figure 12.5   Gamma-adjusted hedge ratio versus traditional delta hedge ratio

displayed. It can be observed that the delta changes considerably with changes in the underlying index. As there are only quarterly index observations, the risk of a change in delta can be significant and will adversely affect the hedge effectiveness.

First we assume that the portfolio can be hedged by trading directly in the index $\tilde{S}$. In particular, we compare the hedge effectiveness of the discrete time hedging strategy as described above with a traditional delta hedging strategy. We apply the gamma-adjusted hedge ratios as defined in Equation (12.2). Figure 12.5 illustrates the two hedging strategies.

The gamma-adjusted hedge ratio does not eliminate the hedging errors that arise due to the portfolio nonlinearity. Gamma risk could only be eliminated if liquidly traded options on the underlying index are available. However, the adjusted hedge ratio allows the portfolio curvature to be incorporated such that the variance of the hedging error is minimized. Compared to the traditional delta hedging approach, the variance of the hedging error is reduced by 8.3 % in this example.

Next a more practical setting is presented where the trader cannot buy or sell the index itself, but is able to trade in hedging assets. It is assumed that there are two assets that significantly correlate with the property index. In particular, the Halifax HPI is considered as the underlying index and the variables of the regression are those performed in the previous chapter. Of these variables, the short interest rate and the credit spread can be used as hedging assets, as they do not exhibit a time-lag when explaining property index returns. The EPRA Index does not serve as a hedging asset, as the upcoming index return only correlates to an EPRA Index return with a lag. For simplicity, it is assumed that the expected excess returns of the two hedging assets is zero.

Table 12.1   The risk reduction due to hedging

Variance of hedging error	Without hedge	With hedge	Change (%)
Linear claim	0.046	0.030	−34.61
Five-year call option 100	0.652	0.549	−15.88
Three-year put option 120	2.001	1.878	−6.14
One-year put option 80	85.153	85.148	−0.01
Portfolio	0.007	0.006	−10.24
Value-at-risk			
Linear claim	−0.039	−0.033	−15.12
Five-year call option 100	−0.151	−0.130	−14.08
Three-year put option 120	−0.359	−0.351	−2.08
One-year put option 80	−2.329	−2.329	−0.00
Portfolio	0.005	0.006	+19.02

Again, the hedge ratios defined in Equation (12.2) are used. Moreover, the investigation concerns not only the impact on the variance of the hedging error but also on the value-at-risk. Table 12.1 shows the impact of the hedging strategy on the two risk measures for a one-quarter hedge horizon, simulated over the historic returns from 1990 to 2007. In particular, considertion is given to the options of this example in isolation and on the portfolio that combines the options.

It can be seen that the impact of the hedge on the two risk measures is not equivalent. The two reasons are that the portfolio is not linear and that the returns are not normally distributed. In some cases, the impact on the two risk measures can even be conflicting, as in the case of the option portfolio; i.e. the trader can apply a hedge that minimizes the variance of the hedging error, but needs at the same time to bear a higher value-at-risk. The trade-off with respect to the optimization of the two risk measures introduces a further challenge for the risk management of a property derivatives portfolio.

12.4   RISK TRANSFER

In an illiquid market, it potentially makes sense to transfer some risk from the issuing bank to a third party, e.g. a reinsurer or a hedge fund. Banks underlie regulatory capital requirements that are costly. Third parties may not have to bear these costs. Moreover, due to a low correlation to traditional asset classes, property risk is welcome to many professional portfolios. When a bank wants to transfer risk from its trading portfolio to a third party, it typically needs to pay a premium.

The insurance seller requires this premium for taking property risk. As the premium often implies an expected excess return, it becomes clear why hedge funds are interested in risk transfer deals. From the bank's perspective, the transfer of risk to a third party can help to reduce the VaR that defines the bank's regulatory required capital. As long as the premium is smaller than the bank's costs of required capital, plus a term depending on the bank's risk appetite, risk transfer can benefit both the bank and the insurance seller. Risk transfer includes finding a counterparty better able to absorb the transferred risk, mitigating risk-appetite and reducing regulatory cost.

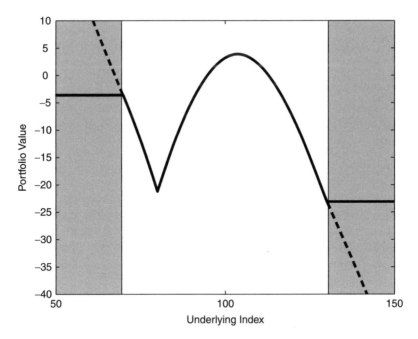

Figure 12.6 Transfer of portfolio tail risk

The transfer can be structured as a simple profit and loss sharing, as a transfer through derivative contracts or as a transfer of loss tranches, respectively, of tail risk. The terms of the transfer framework are typically updated periodically, in line with the development of the market. Figure 12.6 illustrates the transfer of tail risk for the example described above. For a given hedge horizon, the bank transfers the profits and losses that arise in the event of an extreme index movement above 130 % or below 70 % of the initial level to a third party. By limiting these extreme losses, the bank can reduce the VaR and save regulatory capital.

Part III
Applications

13

Range of Applications

Real estate is everywhere.

Areas of applications for property derivatives are numerous. Over the last few years, more and more professionals engaged with the new instruments. Property derivatives offer many benefits to property funds, insurance companies, pension and life funds, speculators, hedge funds or any asset manager with a view on the real estate market. Institutional investors and property companies can either hedge their property risk, gain real estate exposure or optimize their portfolio composition through, for example, simply entering a swap on a property index.

Moreover, developers, builders, home suppliers, occupiers, banks, mortgage lenders and governmental agencies can manage their real estate risk better using property derivatives. A property developer or contractor, for example, can start a housing project without worrying whether prices will fall sharply by the time it is completed. Financial firms such as mortgage lenders, on the other hand, can use property derivatives to insure their mortgage portfolio against collateral risk, especially in the subprime market segment where loan-to-value ratios and default risk are high. Finally, even retail investors can broaden their asset allocation and get diversification benefits by buying a structured product on a property index.

The fact that there are many potential users alone does not imply a need for a property derivatives market, if there is no need to transfer risks. However, the allocation of real estate risk is by far not optimal for most participants in most economies. The majority of market participants is either under- or overexposed to properties, be it to a specific sector or to a geographical region. That provides a strong rationale for instruments that allow property exposure to be shifted.

Investors, primarily institutional, take the long side of derivative contracts as a means of diversifying their portfolios. The short side, on the other hand, should be taken by owners of region- or sector-specific real estate, including managers of property portfolios, developers, corporations, farmers as well as individual homeowners.

Virtually any business whose profits or losses are related to any area of the real estate or housing industry could use property derivatives to manage their risks better. Most of the applications would either be more costly and time-consuming or not be possible at all without the use of property derivatives. Case, Shiller and Weiss (1993) describe an investor's motivation as follows:

> The establishment of real estate futures and options contracts might be described as having the effect of spectacularly lowering transactions costs for trading real estate. The modern theory of the transaction costs [...] stresses the importance of traders with superior or inside information: dealers must announce bid-asked spreads wide enough that they are not routinely "picked off" by more informed traders. Baskets of corporate stocks and other financial assets are inherently subject to lower bid-asked spreads than are individual assets because there is less informed trading about the aggregates. The same would be true about the baskets of real estate on which the index is used to settle real estate futures and options contracts is based. Those who invest in real estate would be spared the concern that they are buying lemons, they can thereby forego the enormous costs and risks associated with buying individual properties.

13.1   PROFESSIONAL INVESTERS AND BUSINESSES

In recent years, investors began to analyze real estate along risk-return criteria that are common for most other asset classes. That made real estate comparable to equities and bonds. Still, directly held properties play an isolated role in financial planning for many market participants, be it corporate or private investors. In contrast, equity and bond portfolios are constantly optimized using the latest fashion finance methods. Reasons for the special treatment of real estate are that investment instruments for properties are rare, and benchmark data are often available only very limitedly.

The lack of data results from the fact that the property market is very illiquid, and it makes the property market nontransparent. Illiquidity and nontransparency are caught in a kind of vicious circle. A lot of effort is needed to collect reliable data and to create benchmark indices that can be applied as underlyings for liquidly traded property derivatives.

In the absence of property derivatives, access to both direct commercial and residential real estate investment is a difficult proposition for the average investor. Reasons for this include:

- High barriers to entry. Individual commercial properties can easily exceed GB £100 million in value, which is out of reach for most investors.
- High transaction costs. Taxes, legal fees and agent provisions leave little room for short-term investment horizons.
- Limited liquidity. It takes a long time (often many months) to buy and sell buildings.
- Idiosyncratic risks. The risk specific to individual property investments (e.g. a key tenant leaving) suggests the importance of diversification, which is even more capital intense.

To mitigate some of these barriers it is possible for the average investor to invest in real estate funds, trusts or companies. However, such vehicles offer their own challenges. For example, often the interests of the investor and the portfolio manager are not aligned. As will be seen later on, listed real estate vehicles rarely provide true exposure to property risk and return.

For the average investor, property derivatives would alleviate many of the problems and concerns with investment into direct real estate. Without the use of derivatives, it is hard to invest in a diversified portfolio of real estate without incurring enormous transaction costs. If investors cannot invest in a widely diversified portfolio of real estate, they cannot invest in a truly diversified portfolio. Consequently, the presumed diversification that is supposed to be practiced by all investors according to modern financial theory cannot happen. Property derivatives also avoid transaction costs associated with property transactions, including stamp duty, land tax and conveyance. Transaction costs are about 0.5 % for derivatives, compared to 5 to 7 % for physical transactions (according to Tullett Prebon and DTZ).

However, derivatives are also an elegant way to enable investors and speculators to reflect a view on the property market by trading properties synthetically, while reducing implementation time significantly. They allow investors to short sell a position without first buying it and, of course, to take on long exposure with no cash investment. Further, they enable property owners for the first time to actually hedge their property exposure.

13.2   THE PRIVATE HOUSING MARKET

That is not the end of the story. Nonprofessionals such as mortgage borrowers, homeowners and building savers could benefit from property derivatives: while homeowners and mortgage borrowers can (at least partially) unload their lumpy property risk, building savers can anticipate house price appreciation.

Homeowners naturally assume risk associated with general movement in house prices. Individuals expecting to move to a new area also face house price risk. For example, individuals relocating between jobs might be concerned about rising prices of homes in their new area of residence. Anticipating price moves of a new home, an individual could enter a hedge position to mitigate unexpected price increases. In addition to the anticipatory hedge, retail investors wishing to diversify their portfolio might also be interested in a long position that gains with an increase in house prices. The potential for buying and selling house price risk is substantial. In the US, by the end of 2005, the value of residential homes equaled $21.6 trillion, comparable in size to the $17.0 trillion in domestic equities and $25.3 in fixed income assets, according to the US Federal Reserve Statistics. In addition to the magnitude of the market, house price volatility has been considerable. Quarterly changes of more than 8 % (annualized) have been observed in US aggregate house prices in 1 out of 10 quarters in the last 20 years. This even masks the severe volatility in regional prices such as the 28 % (annualized) increase in Seattle house prices in the late 1990s and the 12 % (annualized) decrease in Houston house prices in the mid 1980s (see Case et al., 1993).

So far, most property derivatives currently in the market are structured as total return swaps and exchange-traded futures referenced to a property index. Under standardized swap terms, the buyer periodically pays LIBOR plus a spread in return for the annual return on the property index. A total return swap includes both price change and net cash flow of the properties contained in the underlying index. The amounts paid and received are calculated on an agreed notional amount. Conversely, a seller pays away the return on the index and receives LIBOR plus a spread. The spread is chosen such that the value at initiation of the swap is zero. Maturities usually range from three to five years with quarterly interest payments and annual property index payments. Banks intermediate buyers and sellers by matching trades and facilitating transactions (e.g. through standardization and by assuming counterparty risk). However, swaps and futures are not suitable instruments for many market participants, especially for retail investors and homeowners who are engaged in the owner-occupied residential market.

Institutional investors have dominated the market for property derivatives so far. However, the applications for private individuals including retail investors, homeowners, mortgage borrowers and building savers need to be investigated more intensely. The market for residential properties is huge and risks are not optimally allocated. Innovative use of property derivatives could create a great improvement in general welfare.

14

Investing in Real Estate

Making a difficult asset class easy.

Real estate has become an increasingly important component of efficient mixed-asset portfolios. The asset class of real estate meets the investment criteria of sufficient size, competitive risk and return characteristics as well as diversification benefits. At the end of 2002, development economy assets consisted of US$ 48 trillion in residential properties, US$ 14 trillion in commercial properties, US$ 20 trillion in equities, US$ 20 trillion in government bonds and US$ 13 trillion in corporate bonds. That makes real estate by far the largest asset class with 54 % of total stocks, bonds, and real estate assets, as shown in Figure 14.1 (according to UBS Real Estate Reserach (2003), Global Industry analsys (2006), Datamonitor (2006), DTZ Research (2006) and *The Economist*).

The worldwide *investable* real estate universe, however, is estimated to be worth only US$ 6.2 trillion. Investable real estate refers to properties held by investors such as institutions, funds, property companies and private individuals, which are let out for a rental income. The *noninvestable* real estate market, mainly residential and privately held commercial properties, accounts for the lion's share of the asset class as a whole.

In the United States, for example, the value of all domestic commercial properties was estimated at US$ 6.7 trillion at the end of June 2006, more than a third of the global commercial real estate market (see *Commercial Real Estate*, 2006). The class of owner-occupied residential housing, on the other hand, accounted for almost four times that value.

In Europe, the Investment Property Databank (IPD) estimates the size of the European real estate investment market to be €1242 billion, based on collected reportings. The total size of the European commercial real estate market, however, is significantly higher than the investment market due to the substantial amount of commercial property that is not investable, held mainly by corporations and governments.

To give an idea of what the total size might be, the proportions in the UK, where reliable data are available, are taken to estimate the European market. The UK's investable property market was €462.5 billion at the end of 2005 while the total UK commercial real estate market was estimated at €1148 billion, resulting in a multiple of about 2.5 times. Based on this measure, the value of the total European commercial real estate market is estimated to be about €3100 billion. European *listed* property companies accounted for only €118 billion in market capitalization in June 2006, a fraction of roughly 4 % of the overall commercial real estate pie, according to the FTSE EPRA/NAREIT Global Real Estate Index Series.

Recent record levels of direct investment in European commercial real estate should create both the diversity of investors and the liquidity required to generate more trading volume throughout Europe. Both insurance companies and pension funds are increasingly willing to invest outside their domestic markets, especially via indirect property funds. The French market is opening up to international investors. In Germany, given the rate of change in ownership, trading volumes grew further in 2007. The worldwide increase of net capital flows into the real estate sector, the rise of cross-border real estate activities, the growth and greater variety of

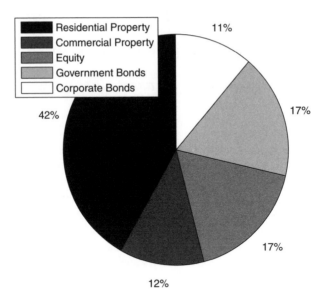

Figure 14.1   Global real estate market compared to equities and bonds

investment vehicles and the much improved market and performance data are all contributing to the trend of increasing real estate investment.

Generally, real estate investments experienced a revival in recent years. It is today widely recognized as a legitimate asset class. Many corporate and public pension funds have initiated or raised their allocations to the real estate asset class. Much of this capital is committed as long-term investment. In December 2003, 70 % of respondents to a global UBS survey answered that institutional investors' allocation to real estate should be at least 11 % (see UBS Global Real Estate Survey Results, 2003). The real estate industry has gained credibility thanks to greater transparency, the development of performance benchmarks such as IPD in Europe or NCREIF in the US, and the proliferation of Real Estate Investment Trusts (REITs) and other real estate investment vehicles.

14.1   PROPERTIES OF PROPERTY

Real estate investments are seen as an integral part of the asset allocation for many institutional investors such as pension funds. Increasing sophistication of private investors and their appreciation of diversification benefits has also led to broader asset allocations. The reasons typically mentioned why someone should invest in real estate are as follows:

- Favorable risk-return characteristics
- Diversification benefits due to low correlation with other asset classes
- Stability and consistency of income
- Retaining purchasing power to housing

The asset class can provide investors with exceptional risk-return characteristics. Figure 14.2 shows property performance (IPD UK All Property TR Index) as well as the total return indices

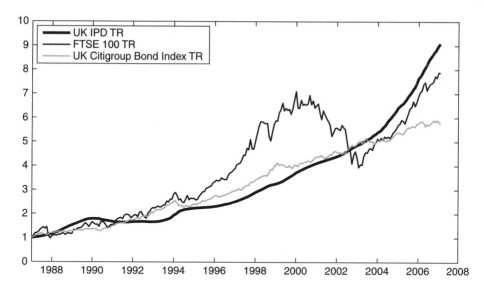

Figure 14.2   IPD UK All Properties TR Index, FTSE 100 TR Index and the UK Citigroup Bond Index (data obtained from Datastream and IPD)

for UK equities (FTSE 100 TR Index) and UK bonds (UK CGBI). Figure 14.3 shows the annual returns of the IPD Index and compares them to those of equities and bonds. Risk and returns for real estate investments are typically between those of equity and bonds in the long run. However, as Figure 14.4 shows, over time, returns of bonds and real estate converge much faster to their long-term mean than those of equities. This reflects the greater risk involved with equity investments.

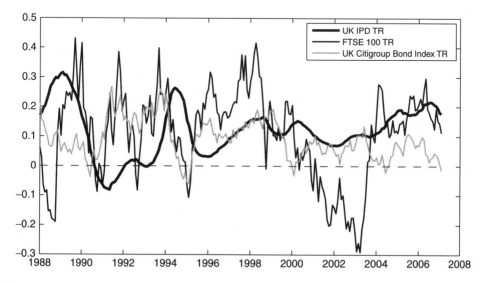

Figure 14.3   Annual returns for IPD UK All Properties TR Index, FTSE 100 TR Index and the UK Citigroup Bond Index

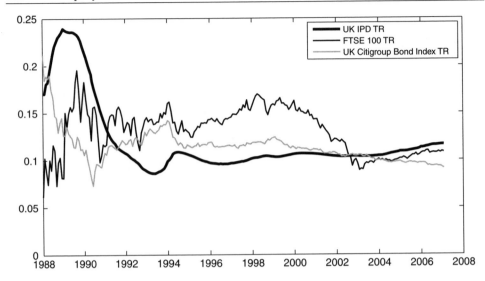

Figure 14.4   Annualized returns and their convergence to long-term mean returns for stocks, bonds and properties. The 20-year observation period starts in January 1987

The combination of relatively low volatility, regular income and the potential for capital appreciation lends itself to adding property to a diversified portfolio. However, care must be taken with property volatility when comparing it to volatilities of other assets such as equities. It is important to note that many indices such as the ones from IPD are based on valuations rather than on transaction prices, which tend to underestimate the true volatility of the market. However, even after making adjustments for valuation "smoothing," property volatility is still lower than that of equity, as shown in the following section.

14.1.1   Making volatility comparable

In order to analyze property in a portfolio context, a property index cannot simply be taken and included in a theoretical portfolio context. As seen in Chapter 6, property indices suffer from smoothing and inertia, and do not truly and timely reflect property performance and volatility. Also, as seen in Chapter 8, an investment instrument on a property index does not track the index one-to-one, but is influenced by other market variables that drive the property spread.

To make a property index comparable to investable assets such as stocks and bonds, the index needs to be adjusted. This adjustment process is usually known as "unsmoothing." Unsmoothing is not always needed but is important in doing portfolio analysis across asset classes. Here, the standard deviation of the IPD Index is adjusted by a factor based on a simple zero autocorrelation technique. In particular, annual returns are corrected for the first-order autoregression coefficient. For annual returns, that correction is regarded as sufficient (see Geltner and Miller, 2001). Volatility is adjusted by multiplying it by the factor

$$\xi = \frac{1}{1 - \text{AR}(1)} \qquad (14.1)$$

Table 14.1 Risk and return on an annual basis. The UK IPD All Property TR Index is used for properties, the FTSE 100 TR Index for equities, the UK CGBI Index for bonds and the three-month Treasury Bill for cash

1987 – 2007	Return(%)	Volatility(%)	Return/risk ratio
Equities	12.1 %	16.1 %	0.75
Bonds	9.5 %	7.6 %	1.24
Cash	7.3 %	3.2 %	2.24
Properties	11.9 %	8.4 %	1.42
Properties adjusted	11.9 %	**14.1 %**	0.84

where AR(1) is the first-order autoregression coefficient of annual returns. Typically, the long-term mean is assumed to equal the unadjusted appraisal-based mean. This must be true as long as there is no long-term bias in the mean, i.e. if the "smoothed" index eventually reflects a realistic level and does not completely drift away from reality. In the following portfolio analysis, the adjusted, more realistic volatility is always used. Table 14.1 displays the risk-return ratios of the asset classes, including the adjustment for properties.

14.1.2 Diversification benefits

If property is added to a portfolio, portfolio risk can be reduced considerably for any given return. A strong diversification effect arises from the typically low correlation of property to traditional asset classes, meaning that property often performs well in times when other assets perform poorly, and vice versa. Property has historically provided significant diversification benefits due to its low correlation to equities and bonds. Table 14.2 shows correlations between equities, bonds, cash and property in the UK.

Derivatives based on property indices provide property exposure that has a correlation similar to that of direct property investments. Lower correlation results in a higher allocation in a mixed-asset portfolio, as diversification benefits are larger. The improvement of the efficient frontier when adding property to a portfolio in a simple mean-variance context is considerable (see Markowitz, 1952). Figure 14.5 shows this effect. The efficient frontier shows the maximum level of expected return that can be achieved for a given level of risk.

Especially for investors with higher return targets, property can reduce associated portfolio risk dramatically. For example, a target of 10 % expected return without property is only

Table 14.2 Correlations between asset classes in the UK. These are taken between the IPD UK All Property Index, the FTSE 100 Index, the CGBI Bond Index and the three-month Treasury Bill

1970 – 2004	Equities	Bonds	Cash	Properties
Equities	1.00	0.29	0.21	0.16
Bonds		1.00	0.41	−0.27
Cash			1.00	−0.44
Properties				1.00

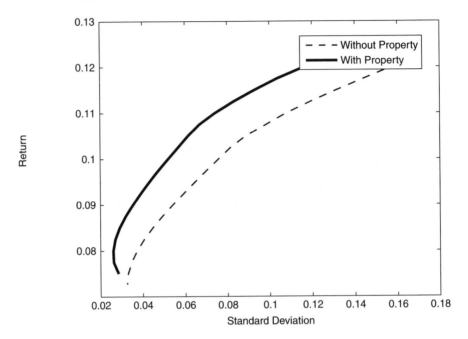

Figure 14.5 The effect of adding real estate into a portfolio: improvement of the efficient frontier. Adjusted property volatility is used, as described above

achievable with a risk of 7.6 % (in terms of volatility). Including property, the risk can be reduced to 5.2 % while keeping the expected return target; i.e. risk is reduced by almost a third. To put it another way, the investor needs to expect an annual loss only with 2.7 % probability, instead of 9.4 % when no properties are included. Figure 14.6 shows the optimal allocation of a portfolio that invests in equity, bonds, cash and property. For a target return of 10 %, the optimal, risk-minimizing proportion to be invested in property amounts to 29.9 %.

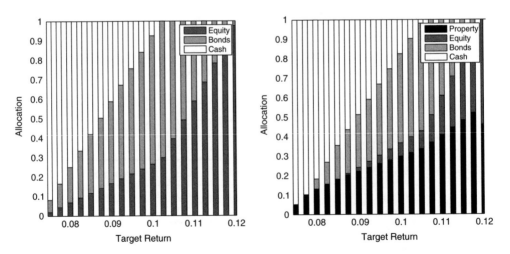

Figure 14.6 Risk-minimizing allocation for a given target return, with and without property

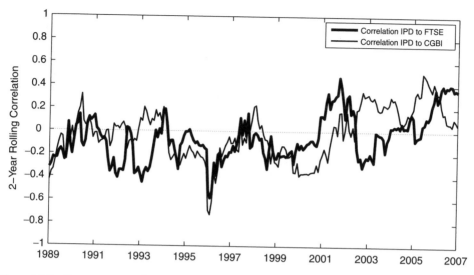

Figure 14.7 Correlations of the IPD Index versus the FTSE 100 Index and the CGBI rolling over time

However, correlation can change over time. Depending on the economic conditions and cycles, asset classes tend to move in parallel to a stronger or weaker degree. Worldwide equity markets, for example, tend to move together when there are extreme price moves. Measured correlation heavily depends on the chosen time period. Correlations turn unfavorably high at the time when low correlation would provide the greatest benefit. The question thus arises of whether correlations of properties to other asset classes are reasonably stable over time. Only constantly low correlations provide truly substantial diversification benefits. Figure 14.7 shows the two-year correlations of the IPD Index versus the FTSE 100 Index and the CGBI. Correlations turn both negative and positive, but are generally low. They almost never leave the range of −0.5 to +0.5, indicating true diversification effects. Depending on the investment horizon, investors should look at short- or long-term correlations. There are also techniques that give higher weight to more recent correlations and lower weight to correlations that are further away in the past. Portfolio allocation under stochastic correlation is being investigated by, for example, Buraschi, *et al.* (2006).

14.1.3 So what inhibits investors from investing in real estate?

Although the benefits of investing in real estate are convincing, there are some obstacles that inhibit investors from doing so. The mean-variance approach shown above does not illuminate the whole picture. Several reasons are relevant and must be taken into account when property risk is evaluated:

- Heterogeneity
- Bad divisibility and thus hard to diversify within the asset class
- Lack of fungibility
- Lack of a public marketplace
- Lack of transparency in the market

These reasons can be summed up by the notion of illiquidity. The asset class of real estate is much more illiquid compared to equities and bonds. Illiquidity is caused by many factors such as the heterogeneous nature of real estate, the lack of transparency, regulation, taxation, emotional relation to an object and so on. Few transactions in turn result in low transparency, as transaction information is rare.

Illiquidity is not reflected in transacted or appraised prices. The transacted price only tells the outcome of the negotiations, but not how long it took to close the deal and how difficult it was to find a buyer. During that time, the holder not only bears the costs to find a buyer but also the opportunity costs of the capital that is locked in the property. Traditional securities, on the other hand, can usually be sold almost immediately. Illiquidity makes it hard, especially in a market downturn when only few transactions take place, to quickly implement a new market view. The risk of illiquidity must be taken into account when including direct property into a portfolio, in order not to underestimate the involved risks. However, indirect investment vehicles and property derivatives solve, at least partially, the problem of illiquidity, as will be seen next.

14.2   PROPERTY DERIVATIVES AND INDIRECT INVESTMENT VEHICLES

An investor willing to allocate part of his or her funds into the asset class of real estate can invest in indirect investment vehicles, besides the classical direct investment. These vehicles in turn invest directly or again indirectly in properties. Table 14.3 lists the universe of real estate investment forms.

The illiquid nature of the base market is probably the main driver for the emergence of indirect real estate investment vehicles. According to the AME Capital analysis of global real estate securities market in January 2007, the worldwide market capitalization was just above GB£ 1 trillion, i.e. GB£ 1 009 148 232 132, with GB£ 426 551 494 205 or about 42 % in the form of Real Estate Investment Trusts (REITs). Figure 14.8 shows listed real estate investment vehicles by region.

However, less than 10 % of worldwide commercial property is investable through indirect property vehicles. The rest is owned by individuals or families, financial institutions, pension funds or by businesses themselves. Generally, properties are not optimally allocated, and property derivatives could be the instruments needed to do that.

Demand for indirect vehicles have been growing strongly since 2003. Especially structured vehicles such as REITs are booming. REITs are public vehicles that invest predominately in real estate and are tax exempt if they distribute almost all of their income to shareholders.

Table 14.3   The investment universe for property

	Property investments	
Indirect investment vehicles	Direct investments	Property derivatives
Trusts and REITs	Sole ownership	Swaps
Real estate companies	Partnership	Forwards and futures
Real estate funds		Options
Mortgage-backed securities		Structured products
Real estate private equity		
Real estate certificates		

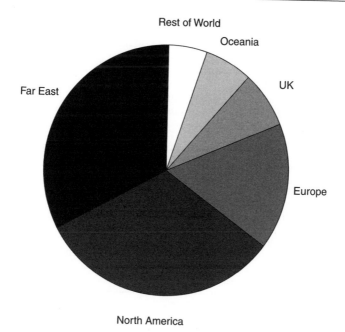

Figure 14.8   Global listed indirect investment vehicles by region, based on market capitalization (data obtained from AME Capital)

However, publicly traded investment vehicles rarely trade exactly at their intrinsic net asset value (NAV). In bullish markets, they often trade at a premium to the NAV, meaning that investors are willing to pay more than the real value of the objects contained in the vehicle. Premiums can well be justified. The investor benefits from much better liquidity, flexibility and diversification when investing in an indirect vehicle compared to a direct investment.

Real estate funds have some fundamental differences and peculiarities to real estate companies. In Switzerland, for example, funds can be redeemed at the NAV, i.e. the investor can not only sell shares of the fund on an exchange but can also redeem them to the fund management. That right to redeem at the NAV provides some protection to the investor, since a discount to the NAV would be eliminated by arbitrage. Funds mainly trade at a premium over the NAV and redemption is rare, since a higher price can be achieved by selling the shares on the exchange.

Funds are generally regulated more strictly than listed real estate companies. Funds are typically obliged to distribute most of the generated cash flow and are very limited in terms of debt level, in terms of investments in businesses other than real estate and in terms of a minimal number of objects. *Real estate companies*, on the other hand, only need to comply with the general company law and have no additional restrictions. They are often involved in activities that are related to real estate investment, such as development, property management or construction.

From a taxation perspective, *real estate trusts* often have advantages compared to real estate companies or funds. The main incentive to set up a REIT is favorable taxation. There are other types of trusts that are exclusively offered to tax-exempt institutions such as pension funds and can thus be tax-treated in the same way as their owners.

Table 14.4   Indirect investment vehicles versus direct investment

---

Advantages of indirect investment vehicles

Improved liquidity
Sector and/or geography specific exposure possible
Possibility to earn alpha versus the benchmark
Investment flexibility
Possibility to leverage

Disadvantages of indirect investment vehicles

Limited overall liquidity in many vehicles
Long cash position before investing, diluting returns
Simultaneous selling when investors exit
Stamp duty and other property taxes
Lack of transparency in the investment strategy
Cost of managing direct properties plus fund performance fee
Returns subject to equity market dynamics
Interest rate exposure due to leverage

Real estate private equity vehicles often invest in special properties such as hotels, hospitals, public venues and so on. The character of their risk and return often differs considerably from other real estate investments, since the properties are very closely linked to a specific business.

Real estate certificates typically track an index that contains real estate funds or companies (e.g. the FTSE EPRA/NAREIT Indices, the FTSE Real Estate Index or the PHLX Housing Sector Index). Thus they are derivatives on indirect investment vehicles. As such, they are broadly diversified. Certificates with fixed maturities and open-end are common, and dividends are either distributed, reinvested or discounted and deducted from the issue price. Unlike for real estate funds or companies, the investor is exposed to the counterparty risk of the certificates' issuer.

Finally, *mortgage backed securities* (MBS) offer a way to assume real estate exposure. However, MBS more generally resemble a fixed income investment than a property investment, and real estate risk is not the only driver of defaults, but also the quality of the mortgage borrower. MBS are further exposed to interest rate and prepayment risk. Also, payoffs are asymmetric: while the downside risk of a mortgage buyer goes hand in hand with the value of the collateral (the property), the upside is limited to the promised interest and principal payments. Thus, an investor cannot participate in a strong boom of the property market, but is only compensated by potentially fewer defaults.

Table 14.4 lists the primary advantages and disadvantages of the indirect real estate investment vehicles. Besides traditional real estate funds and real estate companies, REITs become more and more important and their expansion deserves a short description.

14.2.1   Real estate investment trusts

REITs were introduced in 1960 in the US to promote investment in real estate. However, it took more than 30 years until the modern REIT era made its debut. In the early 1990s, professional real estate owners and operators began taking their real estate companies public. Since then, the number of REITs as well as their capitalization and trading volumes have grown rapidly.

Table 14.5   The REIT universe: countries with REITs or REIT-like structures (from data obtained from the European Public Real Estate Association (EPRA) Global REIT Survey, August 2007)

Australia	Malaysia
Belgium	Mexico
Brazil	Netherlands
Bulgaria	New Zealand
Canada	Pakistan
Chile	Puerto Rico
Costa Rica	Singapore
Dubai	South Africa
France	South Korea
Germany	Spain
Greece	Taiwan
Hong Kong	Thailand
Israel	Turkey
Italy	United Kingdom
Japan	United States
Lithuania	

In the US, in order to classify as REIT, at least 75 % of the revenue has to stem from real estate investments. Further, 90 % of income must be distributed to investors as dividends.

Similar structures exist today in 31 countries worldwide. In France, for example, a REIT-like structure is adopted by a vehicle called Les Sociétés Immobilliéres d'Investissements Cotées (SIIC). Companies have to distribute 85 % of their income within one year and 50 % of their capital gains within two years. The corresponding vehicles are called J-REITs in Japan and Listed Property Trusts (LPTs) in Australia. The UK and Germany introduced REITs as of 1 January 2007. Companies have indicated that they are likely to convert to REIT status when legislation allows them to do so. Pakistan has had a draft legislation in place since 2006. Most market participants expect that the highest level of activity will be in the Far East, with Singapore competing with Hong Kong to provide REIT structures for portfolios located in mainland China. With the worldwide introduction of these attractive vehicles, most firms are likely to switch their portfolios into REITs, due to their tax advantages.

All these vehicles allow pooled investment in income-producing property assets through a tax-transparent structure, with most or all of their net income paid out to investors. They are typically subject to very stringent disclosure requirements. In turn, taxes are usually paid only on the dividends rather than at the corporate level. The increasing number of countries adopting REITs and REIT-like structures makes it easier for investors to access international real estate markets in a more efficient way. Table 14.5 lists the countries where REITs or REIT-like structures exist.

14.2.2   True real estate exposure?

The correlation between real estate indices and listed property vehicles is surprisingly low. In the UK, the IPD All Property Index and the FTSE EPRA/NAREIT Index that tracks listed vehicles correlate by only 0.11, as shown in Table 14.6. Since listed property vehicles such as

Table 14.6 Correlations between asset classes in the UK, including listed properties. These are taken between the IPD UK All Property Index, the FTSE 100 Index, the CGBI Bond Index, the three-month Treasury-Bill and the FSTE EPRA/NAREIT UK Index

1970–2004	Equities	Bonds	Cash	Properties	Listed Properties
Equities	1.00	0.29	0.21	0.16	0.53
Bonds		1.00	0.41	−0.27	0.14
Cash			1.00	−0.44	0.13
Properties				1.00	0.11
Listed properties					1.00

REITs have exclusively real estate as their assets, their returns might be expected to correlate strongly to the IPD Index. However, there are significant differences in sector weighting and geographical makeup. Moreover, investors are entitled to get the dividend, but cannot directly influence the sale of properties to realize capital gains. They must rely on the management, which in turn is restricted to behave conservatively by the vehicle's guidelines.

An investment into a listed real estate vehicle is not the same as investing in a property index in many aspects. As Table 14.6 shows, listed vehicles react to changes in the broader equities markets, while a property index is generally very much uncorrelated to equities. Figures 14.9 and 14.10 compare the commercial property indices of the UK and US with the listed counterparts, i.e. the indices of listed vehicles. The vehicles seem to be more volatile than the indices. However, the index underestimates true volatility, as mentioned earlier. Still,

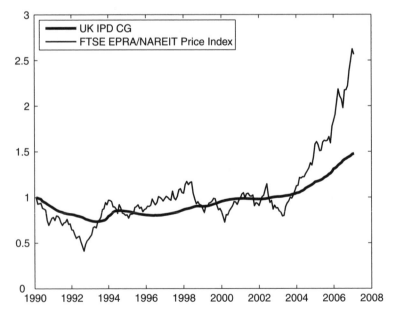

Figure 14.9 UK FTSE ERPA/NAREIT versus UK IPD All Property Index

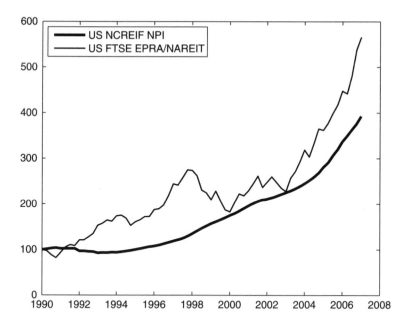

Figure 14.10   Indirect investment vehicles and property derivatives: US FTSE EPRA/NAREIT versus US NCREIF NPI

listed vehicles are riskier because they have leverage, are less well diversified and are exposed to management risk.

Property indices are generally less sensitive to a change in interest rates than shares of real estate companies or funds. The reason why real estate companies and funds react to interest rates is twofold: first, funds and companies typically pay high and stable periodic cash flows. These cash flows are generated by rents, and many vehicles such as REITs are required to pay out the main part of these rents as dividends. From an investor's perspective, funds and companies thus resemble a fixed-income investment, rather than a real estate engagement. To value the investment, the typically stable income stream is discounted at a rate that directly depends on prevailing interest rates. This view of investors is reflected in the price of the investment or in the premium or discount to the net asset value (NAV). The premium and thus the price of the fund or company typically shrinks when interest rates start to rise and vice versa. The idea of discounting future income is clearly reflected by the market, since the income component is dominant. Second, real estate funds and companies are often leveraged through the use of mortgages. This also enhances the sensitivity to interest rates. A property derivative that tracks an unleveraged price index, on the other hand, pays the index level at maturity; thus the expected index level is the dominant factor rather than any change in interest rates.

In sum, returns of indirect vehicles are, statistically speaking, not significantly related to those of direct real estate investments measured by a property index. Reasons include the equity character of indirect vehicles, which is reflected in the price of the vehicle. Also, indirect vehicles often react more sensitively to interest rate changes than indices do, due to their fixed-income character and leverage. In the very long run, however, if properly adjusted for leverage, direct and indirect investment performance must converge in the absence of arbitrage.

14.3   INVESTING IN REAL ESTATE WITH PROPERTY DERIVATIVES

Studies and optimized role model portfolios of institutional investors show that in an efficient portfolio, the asset class real estate should have a much higher weight than in the status quo. Large investors who have the means to directly invest in a large number of properties typically allocate about 15 to 30 % in that class. That share is easily justified in most portfolio contexts. However, smaller investors often do not have the possibility to do so. Given the limited availability of investable instruments for the asset class real estate, property derivatives offer an attractive, flexible and quick way to enter into the asset class.

Derivatives open up new investment opportunities. They make it possible to diversify a property portfolio or to gain exposure to international property markets without an investment in physical property. Also, property funds can synthetically invest in sectors of the market to which they would not normally gain exposure due to price or size constraints. With a property derivative, an investor gets passive property exposure, i.e. property beta, either for a single real estate market or for a basket of sectors or countries. Passive investments are common in the stock and bond market, in the form of Exchange Traded Funds (ETFs) or index certificates. The advantage of a passive investment is the absence of idiosyncratic risk, i.e. the advantage of getting a very well diversified exposure while being cost efficient. With derivatives, this investment possibility is for the first time introduced into the asset class of real estate. Table 14.7 lists the market and specific performances of the different forms of property investments.

The most common instrument of a property derivative is the total return swap, where one counterparty agrees to exchange with another the performance of a property index for a fixed or floating interest on a given notional amount. The property return leg reflects the net rental income plus capital growth of properties and is usually paid annually. The fixed or floating leg, on the other hand, is structured in the same way as for a normal interest rate swap and is a function of the interest rate yield curve.

Like most swaps, property swaps are unfunded instruments where no physical sale or purchase of property occurs, no notional amount is exchanged and the value at day one is zero. An investor can use swaps to get synthetic exposure to property risk and returns, instead of directly buying properties or investing in property funds or companies. If the property index rallies, the property return receiving counterparty (the *swap receiver*) gets the net difference between the index total return and the fixed or floating rate, including the property spread (see Chapter 8 on property spreads). If the property index rises by less than the fixed or floating rate, the swap receiver pays the net difference. The loss of a swap is almost unlimited. Unfunded swaps allow a high leverage and are capital efficient since no principal must be paid upfront. They are highly customizable, but require in turn a large minimum size and an extended documentation. They are generally offered to institutional clients only.

Table 14.7   What you get from property investments

	Market performance	Specific performance
Direct investment	Property beta	Property alpha
Listed REITs/funds/companies	Property-equity beta	Management alpha
Derivatives	Property beta	

Table 14.8 Property derivatives solve many problems of traditional investment vehicles

---

Advantages of derivatives versus indirect investment vehicles

---

Synthetic exposure is cheaper than physical investment
Cash bridge/efficient management of the cash balance
Better diversification effects than other indirect investments
Well diversified within the asset class of properties
Tax and legal advantages for cross-border investments
Possibility of unwinding quickly, i.e. flexibility
Enables shorting and tactical allocation
Possibility of leverage

Besides swaps, there are many other derivative instruments that allow participation in the property market. Structured products and notes already allow investments for very small sizes, and the maximum loss is defined upfront. In turn, they allow less leverage than unfunded swaps. Using the form of structured products, banks target retail as well as institutional clients. Capital-protected products are very popular among investors. The protection is usually financed either by the income component of the underlying property index or by giving up some of the upside participation. Structured products without capital protection typically simply track the total return of a property index. At maturity, the investor receives a one-for-one participation in the upside and downside of the index return, subject to an annual adjustment that depends on the property spread. Property notes that track a short position are also offered. They benefit from negative performance, but they lose principal if the index increases. However, only a few structured products have been launched so far, as market participants are currently mainly institutional investors engaging in swaps.

Table 14.8 lists advantages of property derivatives versus traditional indirect investment vehicles. For derivatives, costs are lower than for indirect vehicles and are known in advance, whereas the vehicle costs are only known when they are sold. Moreover, property derivatives offer a permanent 100 % exposure to property, while investment vehicles can and often do hold a large part of their capital in cash. Tax advantages include the avoidance of corporate tax that indirect vehicles need to pay. In many European countries, they can get as high as 30 to 37 %. Further, real estate specific taxes are not due in most jurisdictions and, depending on a country's tax treatment and the domicile of issuance, a withholding tax is not raised.

14.3.1 What performance can be expected from a property derivative?

Figure 14.11 compares the historical rate of total return on the annual IPD UK Index with the returns implied by the forward curve in July 2007. Compared to actual rates of return over the last 20 years, which were on average 11.9 %, the implied returns for 2007 to 2016 were low at around 5 %. Therefore investors can take a view on the direction of the commercial real estate market relative to this level by either going long, i.e. electing to receive the IPD index and pay about 5 %, or short, i.e. electing to receive about 5 % and pay the rate of return on the IPD index. Instead of paying the 5 % fix, the investor could chose to pay LIBOR plus a spread. The implied level can be interpreted as the market expectation for future returns.

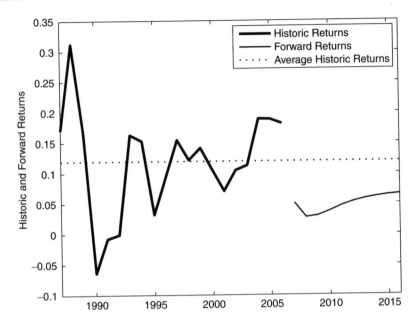

Figure 14.11 IPD actual, average and forward returns

Property derivatives offer an alternative way of indirect investment into property, as well as a mechanism for managing existing exposures in both direct and indirect markets. They enable strategic and tactical management of property market risk by gaining or reducing exposure without dealing in the physical asset or through indirect vehicles. Exposure can relate to the market as a whole, to individual property sectors or to the relative performance of one sector against another.

In summary, real estate is a growing and global asset class, which offers attractive returns and low volatility. There is currently no ideal vehicle to invest dynamically in real estate. Property derivatives offer a cost-effective way of gaining property beta exposure.

15

Hedging Real Estate Exposure

Catch me when I fall.

Derivatives are often seen as speculative high-risk instruments, as large losses can occur where they are not used properly. Originally, however, derivatives emerged due to hedging needs. Still, hedging has one of the most important roles of derivatives.

Hedging is the full or partial reduction of an asset's price risk by entering a contract that offsets the risk. The existence of market participants in need of a hedge is a fundamental condition for the establishment and success of a derivatives market. In the absence of that need, it is hard to close contracts between counterparties, since demand and supply of risk and return is likely to be out of balance.

There are two basic types of a hedge, a short hedge and a long hedge. The short hedge reduces risk for current property owners, while the long hedge anticipates prices for future owners.

A hedger can reduce the property exposure and lock in the asset value. Besides property owners, builders, mortgage lenders and other market participants that are exposed to property risk can benefit from the hedging possibility. For example, a developer would recoup a part of the losses when the housing market plummeted if he or she had entered a short future contract or a put option on a property index.

When hedging with a derivative that is based on an index, property beta, i.e. the systematic risk of the region or sector that the index refers to, is hedged. This is why an index-hedge is often referred to as a beta-hedge. A full hedge, or insurance, on the other hand, would not only eliminate the systematic risk but also the specific risk of the building to be hedged. However, insuring specific risk is costly, since the insurer charges a premium for the issues of moral hazard and adverse selection. The advantage of a beta-hedge is cost efficiency and ease of handling, since taking an index as reference is objective and not subject to moral hazard or adverse selection. However, hedging property beta exposure means that the hedger retains specific risk.

Moral hazard refers to the possibility that the transfer of risk to an insurer changes the insured's behavior. For example, a person whose house is insured against price depreciation may be less vigilant in keeping the house in good order than somebody who is not insured. Adverse selection refers to a process in which bad selection occurs due to information asymmetries between the insured and the insurer. A person who knows about a bad feature of his or her house, of which the insurer is not informed, is more likely to buy insurance.

Since it is possible to enter into a contract that refers to either the all property index or to a specific property sector index, market participants have the choice over which property beta they would like to hedge. For example, an investor who has a direct investment in the office sector can decide whether to hedge the all property beta or the office sector beta. Moreover, it is possible to go one step further and enter into contracts by subsectors and geography, e.g. London city offices.

A hedge can be implemented over specific time periods. As liquidity develops in the market, it is possible to break the risk up into different horizons, i.e. hedge different property market maturities. For example, to protect against property exposure for 12 months in two years time, a property investor could sell a three-year maturity swap and buy a two-year swap. Alternatively, it is also possible to hedge this position with a forward by selling (shorting) a three-year forward and buying (going long) the two year.

Hedging activity can be distinguished by routine hedging and selective hedging. Routine hedging is a strategy that tries to insure a risk position on a regular basis. The goal is to minimize shortfall risk constantly. When hedging selectively, on the other hand, the asset manager insures risks for sectors or assets where he or she expects a negative price development over a selected period of time. The goal is not a complete risk immunization but rather the avoidance of a loss given an anticipated adverse scenario.

Hedging does not necessary refer to derivatives. Other instruments or strategies can take the role of hedging, e.g. insurance policies. For real estate however, the instruments to hedge an existing portfolio are rare. Mostly, the only way to reduce exposure is to sell physical properties.

Derivative markets are driven by speculators and hedgers, and if both groups develop a serious interest in the instrument, volumes can even become larger than in the underlying market. While speculators need price volatility, hedgers need to be confident that they can rely on the index to hedge their position.

Derivatives based on property market indices limit the investor's ability to do this, because the index is not itself investable. A long position in property cannot be perfectly matched by a short position in a derivative because it is not possible to buy the index, but only the derivative on the index. As seen in Chapter 8, the derivative does not behave in exactly the same way as the index. This introduces basis risk during the contract's live and makes the hedge less attractive. At maturity, however, the hedger is sure what payoff is given, directly depending on the index level.

15.1 SHORT HEDGE

Property portfolio managers have a desire to hedge both capital value and rental income. Capital value is exposed to price risk; i.e. a loss occurs if property prices fall and are realized in case of a sale. Future rental income, on the other hand, is probably the most important success factor of a real estate portfolio that focuses on rental apartments and offices. Hedging rent price levels against an unexpected decline is thus of great benefit to holders of rental buildings or developers who build rental apartments. A strategy that insures property owners against adverse price or rent level changes is called a short hedge, since the hedger enters a short position to offset exposure. Offsetting risk via derivatives allows the manager to hedge the property portfolio for a specific period, but he or she retains ownership in the long term.

In a short hedge, it is generally not possible to insure the specific risk of an individual object or portfolio through a property derivative. Derivatives typically refer to a broad property index, not to single buildings. The advantage of an index-hedge is that the incentive problem typically referred to as moral hazard does not arise; i.e. if an investor could insure the rental income of specific buildings, he or she would have no more incentive to optimally rent out the apartments and to maintain them. Hedging through a derivative avoids misalignment of incentives and is thus much cheaper than an insurance contract, which is typically subject to moral hazard and consequently charges a premium for that misalignment (see Thomas, 1996). On the flip side, the investor has to keep the tracking error, i.e. the specific risk and reward (see Case *et al.*, 1993).

15.1.1 Property portfolio managers

Assume that a manager of a commercial property portfolio is bearish on the overall property market for the next two years. It would be almost impossible and very costly to sell all properties today and build up the portfolio again in two years. By entering a swap, the manager converts property returns into a cash flow consisting of LIBOR plus a spread. He retains the risks and management costs pertaining to individual properties in the portfolio and, as a result, any income returns and capital gain from the property portfolio in excess of the market returns measured by the index. If portfolio returns are less than the index returns, the hedger must make good the difference. However, the manager is not exposed to any systematic market risk on which he or she has a negative view. At maturity of the swap contract, the portfolio returns to its original position.

Suppose that another manager is looking to reduce exposure generally and wants to lock-in current valuation for a part of the portfolio. The long-term solution to reduce exposure is the sale of direct properties but this can be a lengthy process. Thus, a bridge hedge could be constructed using property derivatives. In order to get a hedge in the short term, the manager enters a total return swap whereby the manger pays the total return index in exchange for LIBOR plus a spread. Depending on the property portfolio, the all property index or a sector index such as office, retail or industrial can be applied.

To be effective, the hedge transaction must be based on an index that is a good proxy for the portfolio to be hedged. The richer the available index family, the more suitable the hedging applications and, consequently, the more transactions will take place.

15.1.2 Developers, builders and corporations

Developers can also greatly benefit by using property derivatives. They can hedge speculative developments in various ways. Suppose a developer acquires some land in order to build a condominium on it. The development and building period takes about three years. The return and profitability calculations are based of course on the assumptions made at the start of the development period. In other words, the project is profitable as long as prices and rents do not drop significantly. Using property derivatives, either on a price or a rent index, the developer can avoid such an adverse scenario and lock-in the levels that are expected at the beginning of the development period. The hedge should be based on the respective regional subindex.

The traditional rent guarantee contracts are also a kind of property derivative. A developer or construction company usually provides the rent guarantee contract, which is in fact a put option, to a landowner for facilitating construction of a building on the land. The owner pays a premium to buy the put option. In turn, the developer pays the shortage of rent if it falls under a predetermined level. By providing rent guarantee contracts, the developer assumes the risk of declining rental income during the development or building period. To offset the risk of these contracts, the developer can enter a short position in a derivative on the corresponding rental income index. In this way, both the owner and the developer fixed the rent level from the very beginning of the building period.

Corporations that have buildings for operations, but do not want to be engaged in the real estate market strategically, are further potential candidates for a short hedge. Using property derivatives, they can efficiently protect themselves against a market downturn while retaining control of the physical buildings. Corporate applications are described in detail in Chapter 17.

Finally, for investors who must hold regulatory capital against direct property assets, a hedge through a property derivative can free up capital that in turn can be invested elsewhere. However, the regulator must allow property derivatives for hedge accounting when required capital is to be reduced.

15.1.3   Mortgage lenders and collateralized mortgage obligations

Further, derivatives have the potential to be used for tactical and hedging reasons by mortgage lenders and managers of mortgage-backed securities such as collateralized mortgage obligations (CMOs). A CMO manager could, in order to mitigate the impact of scenarios where collateral value declines, sell property risk by short selling a derivative on a property price index. In the scenario where the value of the index declines, the structure would receive a payment to offset the losses on the CMO portfolio. Given this hedge, it may be possible for rating agencies, bond investors and banks to accept higher leverage. In turn, however, when property prices rise, the hedger will either forego some of the performance or, if hedged with a put option, the premium paid.

The 2007 crisis in the US subprime mortgage market reveals the risk of declining house prices to mortgage lenders. Property derivatives on housing indices would have been a suitable instrument to hedge this risk. Figure 15.1 illustrates the inverse relationship of house prices, measured by the S&P Case–Shiller Index, and the subprime foreclosure rates.

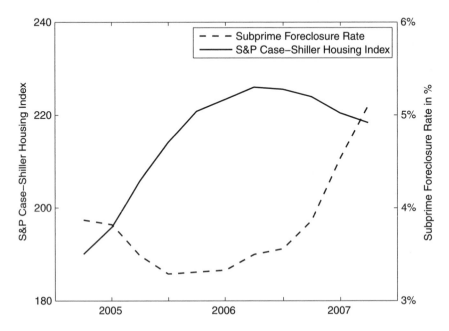

Figure 15.1   S&P Case–Shiller Index and subprime foreclosures in the US

15.1.4   Owner-occupiers

Besides professional property holders, owner-occupiers can benefit from a short hedge. For example, Goldman Sachs issued put warrants on the UK Halifax Average House Price Index in 2004. These warrants were targeted at UK owner-occupiers. A resident who owns UK residential property, say a GB £250 000 house, may be concerned that house prices fall over the coming two years. He or she does not wish to sell the property, but rather to hedge out the risk of a declining property market by purchasing put warrants on the UK Average House Price. If the index falls, the value appreciation in the put warrants offsets, at least in part, the lower value of the house. Again, such a hedge carries the risk that the value of an individual house will not rise and fall to exactly the same extent as the index. To determine how many put warrants are required for a hedge, the current value of the house is divided by the index level. If house prices rise over the term of the hedge, the homeowner gains value on the house but loses the premium of the put that expires worthless. If house prices fall, he or she loses in value on the house and gains value on the put, net of the premium.

Instead of plain warrants, a similar house price hedge can also be implemented by a mortgage that is linked to a property index. Index-linked mortgages are described in detail in Chapter 19.

15.2   LONG HEDGE

Besides the hedgers mentioned so far, there are market participants that would suffer from a price or rent level increase. Somebody who is potentially going to need additional office space in the future, for example, would be able to lock in current rent levels by entering a long position in a derivative on the corresponding rental index. This is thus called a *long hedge*. Expenses can be planned much more accurate by when such price fluctuations are hedged. Long hedges are standard, e.g. in the airline industry, where operators buy futures on oil or kerosene in order to lock in prices.

As a slightly different application, the tenure of rent and lease contracts can be considered. The levels of rents and leases typically depend on the tenure of the contract; i.e. there is a term structure of rent and lease prices, typically for office space. A tenant that only can get a short-term lease contract but wants to lock in prices for a longer period of time can avoid a rise in rents by entering a swap where he or she receives short-term and pays long-term lease levels.

A long hedge is often used in *anticipatory hedging*. If an investor or company knows that a transaction will take place in the future, e.g. the purchase of new retail stores to expand distribution channels, the company might want to ensure that it will get the stores at a price that is no greater than today's level. Anticipatory hedging can also take place in the form of a short hedge, e.g. for a builder who will sell condominium apartments after a three-year construction period, but wants to lock in the sales prices of today.

A cross-hedge is a hedge where the asset to be hedged and the underlying instrument are not exactly the same. While a short hedge is a cross-hedge by nature, i.e. a broad index is used to hedge an individual property or property portfolio, using an index in a long hedge can very well be perfectly suitable. Suppose that a company wants to acquire an office building in central London in a couple of years. It does not know which exact building it is going to buy, but it wants to hedge against a general price appreciation for offices in central London. Thus, a London office index is exactly the right measure to use for such a hedge.

Finally, savings that are linked to property prices is a further example of a long hedge. Indexed buildings savings are described in Chapter 18.

15.3   HEDGE EFFICIENCY AND BASIS RISK

Most hedging strategies attempt to eliminate price risk by trying to fix the price of an asset or portfolio at a future date. If the change in the asset price during the life of the hedge is exactly equal in magnitude and opposite in sign to the change in the hedging instrument, a perfect hedge is obtained. If not, the hedge is risky. This type of risk is called *basis risk*. The difference between the asset price and the price of the hedging instrument is the basis. During a hedging period, the basis may widen or shrink with advantageous or harmful results to hedgers.

A hedge involves two types of basis risk, cross-hedge basis risk and time basis risk. The former is introduced when, for example, the price of a property or a property portfolio is not perfectly correlated with the hedging instrument. While the former refers to the fact that the derivative does not perfectly match the portfolio that is hedged, the latter describes the time difference between the hedge horizon and the maturity of the contract. If the maturity can be chosen arbitrarily by the hedger, the time basis risk is nil. Figure 15.2 illustrates the cross-hedge and time-related basis risks.

For a short hedge with a property derivative, the cross-hedge basis risk arises in two steps. First, the price development of the derivative is not necessarily equal to the evolvement of the index. Second, the index will not exactly track the property portfolio that is hedged. Suppose a UK asset manager hedges his or her commercial real estate portfolio with the IPD UK All

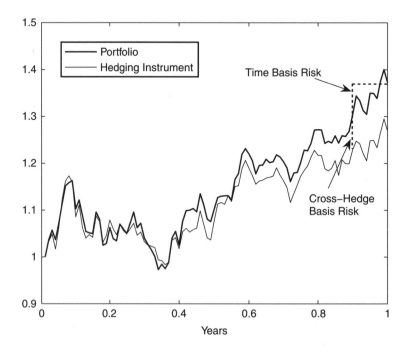

Figure 15.2   Cross-hedge and time-related basis risks

Property Index. The index obviously has not the exact same composition as the manager's property portfolio. The time basis risk is a common issue for standardized derivatives such as futures, but less relevant for OTC contracts where the hedger can specify the maturity himself. Hedging can be seen as an activity that exchanges price risk for basis risk. High basis risk in turn translates into inefficient hedging, which is likely to deter potential hedgers from the market. Hedgers trade off basis risk against the original price risk (see Castelino, 1990).

Consider the following hedge example. A UK company building residential properties faces the risk that the sale price of the properties will fall below the originally expected price due to an unexpected downturn in the market. This risk can be hedged using forward contracts on the Halifax House Price Index. Suppose the company plans to sell a portfolio of houses currently valued at GB £50 million in about one year from now. The company wants to offset any decline in house prices by entering a hedge position; i.e. the company would use a short hedge, such as a one-year short forward position on the Halifax HPI of the corresponding geographic region on a notional amount of GB £50 million. The efficiency of this hedge depends on the correlation between the movement of the house portfolio and the forward contract. If they perfectly correlate and house prices in the region declined over the year by, say, 5%, the company would get GB £2.5 million out of the hedge that offsets the lower-than-expected selling prices. If the company, however, can sell the houses at a total value of only GB £47 million, then it has to bear a loss of GB £0.5 million that the hedge did not compensate for. In this case, correlation was not perfect and cross-hedge basis risk was present.

Unlike a derivative on a stock, a derivative on a property index never perfectly tracks a property portfolio, since the composition of the index and portfolio are not exactly the same. Thus, cross-hedge basis risk is an important issue for property derivatives used as hedging instruments. Regional and sector indices allow a hedge to be refined and hedge efficiency to be improved. A further concern is the likely mismatch between the actual sale dates of the houses and the maturity of the hedge contract. The company does probably not know in advance the precise sale dates for the houses in the portfolio. The time delay inherent in trading physical property can work either in favor or in disfavor of the hedger. However, this time basis risk also reduces the efficiency of the hedge. Hedge efficiency is measured by the amount of total basis risk and of correlation between the portfolio and derivative returns.

As long as the hedge is not perfect, as is typical for property portfolios, a careful assessment of risks must be done to reduce total risk effectively. This is only the case as long as basis risk is smaller for the hedged portfolio than price risk when leaving it unhedged.

In existing derivatives markets, there often seems to be a relation between trading volume and hedge efficiency, since better efficiency attracts more hedgers. However, hedge efficiency is not a strict requirement for the development of a derivatives market. Corkish, Holland and Vila (1997) do not find a significant relation between hedging efficiency and trading volume. Short-term speculative interests can be sufficient to reach a volume that implies success of the market. For long-term contracts, however, hedge efficiency is of great importance, since hedging needs in the property market are also typically long term.

15.3.1 Measuring hedge efficiency

A hedger derives utility from property derivatives if he or she can reduce total risk, i.e. the volatility of the combination of the existing portfolio plus the derivative used for the hedge. The total risk of this combination must be compared to the one of alternative hedging techniques and of the portfolio in isolation. As long as the derivative does not track the portfolio perfectly, there is basis risk. In general, the longer the time to maturity, the bigger is the basis risk. Basis risk can be measured by the variance of the basis

$$\sigma^2 = \mathbb{E}[(\text{Basis} - \overline{\text{Basis}})^2] \tag{15.1}$$

The larger the basis risk, the lower is the hedge efficiency and the less attractive is the use of a property derivative to hedge a real estate portfolio. With regard to cross-hedge basis risk, the correlation $\rho_{V,D}$ between the portfolio V and the derivative D is crucial for an efficient hedge. The total risk is given by

$$\sigma_{\text{total}}^2 = n^2 \sigma_V^2 + x^2 \sigma_D^2 - 2nx \sigma_V \sigma_D \rho_{V,D} \tag{15.2}$$

where σ^2 is variance, n is the net asset value of the portfolio and x is the notional amount of the derivatives that are used to hedge the portfolio. The goal is to minimize σ_{total}^2, or equivalently the volatility of the total position σ_{total}. The minimized total volatility depends on the correlation coefficient as follows:

$$\sigma_{\text{total}} = \sigma_V \sqrt{1 - \rho_{V,D}^2} \tag{15.3}$$

A manager who cross-hedges a portfolio is confronted with a similar issue as a bank that performs a surrogate hedge in an incomplete market (see Chapter 12). If the correlation coefficient is one, the total risk can be reduced to zero. The higher the coefficient, the higher is the utility derived from the derivative by a hedger. A correlation coefficient of 0.85 reduces total risk by about 61 %.

15.3.2   Definition of the hedging index

The definition of the underlying index that is used for the hedge involves several conflicts. Derivatives on a very focused and specialized index, e.g. on an index for shopping malls in a single town, would address the specific hedging needs of a few market participants almost perfectly. A family comprised of regional and sectoral highly focused indices will result in high hedge efficiency to specific property portfolios. On the other hand, the individual markets for the contracts for all these very specialized indices would hardly reach sufficient liquidity since there will probably be very few trades per instrument. Standardization is needed to pool liquidity; i.e. there is a trade-off between index specialization and liquidity. Low liquidity would also result in higher spreads (the market maker wants to be compensated for the assumed liquidity risk), making hedging more costly.

While very specialized indices are desired for hedging purposes, broadly diversified indices are desired for investment. Aggregation of specialized indices to broader indices, e.g. through the use of clusters, is a possible way to pool liquidity.

Moreover, there is an additional problem with regard to regional and sectoral focus. For an index to be representative, there must be a large enough sample of transactions or appraisals. Clearly, when the focus is too narrow, there will not be enough observations to construct a representative, reasonable index.

The question of the appropriateness of an index-hedge for a single house is addressed further in Chapter 19, in the context of home equity insurance.

16
Management of Real Estate Portfolios

Keep alpha, swap beta.

Derivatives are fast becoming a set of investment tools for portfolio managers of more and more asset classes. They are especially useful for real estate portfolio managers, since real estate risk and return is very difficult to transfer or manage flexibly due to the illiquidity that is inherent in property. Whether the goal is to hedge positions, to rebalance existing portfolios or to express a view about one property sector versus another, derivatives allow these strategies to be executed synthetically, without buying or selling physical real estate.

The task of allocating assets of a portfolio optimally to regions and sectors not only depends on their risk and returns but also on their correlations. The lower the correlation, the greater is the diversification benefit. This means that risk can be reduced by adding a new region or sector for any given level of return. Diversification within the asset class of real estate, be it by region or sector, considerably enhances the efficiency of the portfolio. Using derivatives instead of direct investments is beneficial for regions or sector where the portfolio manager has no comparative advantage, i.e. no local or specific know-how.

Further, both strategic and tactical asset allocations can be pursued much easier with property derivatives. So far, portfolio managers could only manage their portfolios on a layer of single objects, but not on an overall portfolio layer. Derivative instruments based on sector and regional indices allow such an approach and thus enable them to hedge portfolios tactically, timely and efficiently. Exposures can be switched or adjusted in a very short time; i.e. portfolio rebalancing is made easy and a manger can trade views on the relative performance of sectors by using property derivatives. Also, property derivatives enable a manager to move quickly towards an optimal portfolio composition.

So far, property management and investment has largely remained a local business and is not as integrated as, for example, equity markets with their global blue chip companies. Demand and prices for properties in two distinct cities, countries or continents do typically not correlate significantly. In contrast, traditional markets such as equities and interest rates mainly move together across borders. In other words, cross-border investing brings a much greater diversification benefit for property portfolios than for equity portfolios. Unfortunately, only a few countries offer real estate investment vehicles that are suitable for foreign investors. Transparency about properties and their transactions terms is also not appealing in many countries (in part due to a lack of data), and regulations often restrict cross-border investments. Even large institutional investors exhibit a significant home bias within the asset class of real estate.

International diversification creates especially large benefits in the asset class of real estate. However, publicly traded real estate assets often tend to correlate with local equity markets. NAV and direct investment returns, on the other hand, show much lower correlation and seem to be mostly independent of other asset classes. Property derivatives, the underlying indices of which track direct investments, make these benefits better available. By entering a derivative contract on an international index, the manager gets pure market returns. Where he or she does not have the expertise of the property market, a property derivative may be the ideal instrument to enter the market.

16.1   TACTICAL ASSET ALLOCATION

In contrast to strategic asset allocation, which is generally targeted for the long term, tactical asset allocation refers to the implementation of shorter-term market views. Tactical asset allocation refers to active portfolio management that rebalances the portfolio composition in order to take advantage of market pricing anomalies or strong market sectors. Tactical allocation allows portfolio managers to create extra value by taking advantage of certain situations and views on the market. Typically, managers return to the portfolio's original strategic asset mix when desired short-term profits are achieved. For example, a portfolio manager who has a bearish view on one sector and favors another will tactically underweight the former and overweight the latter for a period of time, until his or her view gets neutral again and he or she returns to the original allocation.

To pursue tactical allocation, an equity investor can simply reduce or increase exposure by selling and buying shares on the stock market. For a property portfolio manager, however, tactical allocation is very hard to achieve, since it typically takes a long time to buy and sell property. Moreover, because high transaction costs would occur, the benefits of the tactical allocation with physical properties must be large enough to take that cost hurdle. The time delay and transaction costs of entering into and exiting property may even mean that the opportunity identified may have closed by the time the actual investment is transacted. In circumstances where an investor wants to take immediate advantage of a property strategy, a derivative will improve speed of implementation and reduce costs compared to a physical transaction.

16.1.1   Bridge investments

Property derivatives not only suit as an alternative to traditional investments for a long-term horizon, but also allow the capture of property performance in the short term. Some portfolios are excessively long cash, waiting for the right investment opportunities. This gap between raising and spending capital is typically known as cash drag. Using property derivatives, excess cash can be parked during the acquisition period of physical properties, i.e. in the short term, and still generate property performance.

Derivatives allow a quick and flexible investment of cash positions. A manager of a real estate portfolio is often under pressure to invest new money into property assets in order to capture the corresponding performance of the real estate market. Property derivatives enable managers to get exposure quickly and thus to close the investment gap until a suitable physical property is bought.

Conversely, if the manager wishes to reduce property exposure, derivatives can be used to liquidate exposure quickly until the physical sale of buildings takes place.

16.2   GENERATING ALPHA

Commercial property is one of the largest asset classes in the world but remains inefficient, making it a dream asset class for hedge funds. They look for inefficiencies that can be dealt with in large amount. The entry of hedge funds into the property derivatives market in early 2007 indicates significant appetite and that the new instruments are taken seriously.

Just as market-neutral hedge funds do in the equity market, property derivatives allow for the first time to separate and isolate alpha from property portfolios. A hedge fund that focuses on alpha can try to acquire a portfolio of properties that is expected to generate excess returns. The generic property market risk, or beta, can be taken out by entering a short position in a property derivative. In that way, (market neutral) positive returns can also be realized in a bad market environment. The manager can focus on the excess returns of the selected individual objects against the overall market return. The following example illustrates the mechanism.

Imagine that a portfolio manager sells the IPD total return index in exchange for LIBOR plus a spread. Thereby, the portfolio manager hedges the property portfolio by taking a short position in the market index. He or she thus captures the pure alpha of the portfolio, i.e. the excess return of the portfolio over the index. The portfolio manager is likely to be attracted if the spread over LIBOR that is received is high. Further, he or she keeps the assets and thus avoids having to purchase them back if needed at a later stage. Since no physical transaction takes place when property risk is transferred through a derivative, no stamp duty or capital gain tax incurs.

When a new derivatives market develops, often arbitrage opportunities arise; i.e. an arbitrageur can take advantage of price inconsistencies of an asset that is traded in multiple forms or markets. If the price of a futures contract is too high when compared to a physical investment in the same underlying asset, it would be profitable to short sell the relatively expensive future and invest in the relatively cheap underlying asset at the same time. Price fluctuations, which are caused by the general market, of the two will offset each other and the price inconsistency will disappear over time, resulting in a near risk-free profit. Arbitrageurs will continue to pursue such strategies until all prices are in equilibrium. The illiquidity and heterogeneity of properties make arbitrage hard in the physical real estate market. Market participants that have an information advantage either about the base or derivative instruments might be able to extract profits. In an established and information-efficient market, a large number of arbitrageurs who would extract even the smallest possible risk-less profit make sure that prices of different instruments on the same asset are in fair relation.

Hedge funds started to capitalize on arbitrage opportunities using property derivatives. In May 2007, the property firm Cushman and Wakefied announced that they were appointed by the specialist hedge fund company ORN Capital to raise up to US$ 100 million for a global property derivatives fund. According to ORN Capital, which is majority-owned by Morley Fund Management, the fund aims to achieve superior risk adjusted returns by investing in a portfolio of long and short property derivatives positions. The fund is open-ended, does not invest in physical properties and is meant to be market neutral by identifying relative value opportunities between different property markets, sectors and instruments.

In contrast to speculators and hedgers, arbitrageurs typically do not have a directional view of the market. Whether the overall market goes up or down is irrelevant to them. Only the imbalance of at least two instruments is of interest to them.

Traditional investors also have the opportunity to lock in the generic property gains that they have benefited from over the last few years by taking out a hedge on a commercial property index. An investor will continue to have exposure to the extent that their direct investment will not perform in line with the index. Consequently, the investor will be able to retain the specific upside. However, alpha has a flip-side, namely basis risk, as described in the previous chapter.

16.2.1 Cash-and-carry arbitrage

The activity of arbitrageurs has an effect on the efficiency of a derivatives market. In an efficient market, arbitrageurs make sure that the prices of a derivative and of its underlying instrument are closely linked. At any given point, an arbitrage price band for the derivative is a function of the price of the underlying instrument and the cost and time it takes to trade it. Since not all properties in a property index can be traded in reality, the arbitrage band for a property derivative is considered *soft*; i.e. even if a profit is estimated after taking transaction costs and time into account, the potential arbitrage would still not be absolutely risk-free.

Cash-and-carry arbitrage is a strategy whereby an investor purchases the underlying assets, shorts the derivative and holds both positions until maturity. For a stock, the fair price of a forward contract must be equal to the price of the underlying stock plus the cost-of-carry c minus forgone cash flows (dividends) y at any given point in time. This no-arbitrage relationship is described in Chapter 2. If the relation does not hold, i.e.

$$F \neq e^{c-y(T-t)} S \tag{16.1}$$

then cash-and-carry arbitrage can be achieved. If the forward price F is higher than the fair value, an arbitrageur can sell the forward contract short, buy the stock S and finance the purchase by borrowing. If, on the other hand, F is lower than the fair value, the arbitrageur would enter a long position in the forward contract, sell the stock short and lend the proceeds to earn interest. However, this second case involves the need to sell the underlying asset short. This is rarely possible for the objects contained in a property index; thus it will generally be hard to make arbitrage from an "undervalued" forward contract.

Currently, cash-and-carry arbitrage is difficult to undertake with property derivatives because only the largest property portfolio will be able to replicate the returns of the underlying market. However, the emergence of investable funds, which aim to replicate the returns of the entire commercial property market, such as the FTSEpx fund, potentially provides an opportunity for cash-and-carry arbitrage.

16.2.2   Other arbitrage opportunities

Besides the classical cash-and-carry arbitrage, a market participant can use property derivatives and other traded securities to exploit arbitrage opportunities. A popular example is to trade property derivatives against property stocks.

Further, a so-called *curve trade* allows arbitrageurs to take advantage of potential mispricings by taking a view on a specific future time period. For example, going long a five-year swap and going short a three-year swap results in a two-year exposure in three years time, where the combined price of the two swaps might deviate from a reasonable level for that future period.

Finally, different views for different regions or countries can be used for arbitrage trades. For example, an investor might want to trade the residential market of the US against that of the UK, exploiting any unjustified price difference.

16.3   SECTOR AND COUNTRY SWAPS

Real estate is probably the asset class with the most extreme home bias. For most private and institutional investors, it is hardly reasonable to invest directly in international real estate. It would be risky, time-consuming and complex. Moreover, it would be hard to find enough objects to achieve a reasonable diversification abroad. Specific risk would be likely to dominate the portfolio. Further, administration with regard to renting out, paying taxes, buying and selling and other local know-how would be difficult and the portfolio would probably not be optimized. Thus, international investment takes place mostly in the indirect form, be it in listed or nonlisted companies or funds. Listed vehicles are generally more volatile than direct investments and exhibit a higher correlation to their domestic stock or bond market. On the other hand, they are much more liquid than physical investments. Nonlisted indirect investments often have a more stable price development than listed vehicles and are not substantially driven by equity and bond markets. However, nonlisted vehicles usually have lower liquidity, especially closed-end vehicles such as real estate private equity funds.

The argument of diversification benefits and specific know-how also holds for cross-sector investments. For example, a manager who is specialized in office space and has a portfolio that is unbalanced along the different property sectors could swap some office market returns against retail, residential and industrial market returns. Real estate markets exhibit a low correlation between sectors as well as internationally and thus provide large diversification benefits. Reasons include the differences in business cycles and in real estate investment cycles, as well as the different investor basis in specific countries and sectors.

Concentration on a local and specific property market allows high specialization and, at the same time, flexible application and active management of the different market risk components. Derivatives are efficient instruments to diversify real estate market risk.

16.3.1   Cross-border diversification

Investments in real estate are very different around the globe. Real estate markets are internationally by far less integrated than stock markets. Still, it is only possible to invest effectively in few, mostly developed countries. The main share of international investments goes to about 20 to 30 countries. Reasons include the economic stability of these countries, as well as transparency. Transparency means availability of market data and benchmarks, as well as the regulatory framework for investments, such as property guarantees, and zone and building regulations. According to Jones Lang LaSalle, countries that are transparent with regard to real estate investments only include the Anglo-Saxon area, countries in central and western Europe and a handful of Asian countries.

International diversification reduces the overall portfolio risk and allows tactical betting on specific markets. The benefits from international diversification is well known from other asset classes such as equity, but portfolio improvements are even larger for real estate, since correlations of real estate markets are much lower than those of, for example, stock markets.

Cross-continent diversification is generally even more beneficial than international diversification. Investments in real estate are most promising in emerging countries with a strong demographic pressure and excess growth. However, lacking transparency, taxation, regulation and fraud in some emerging economies inhibit investors from diversifying internationally to the economical optimal allocation. The further growth of indirect investment vehicles and derivatives will help to solve this issue.

International taxation can make investments unattractive and can hold capital outside borders. A large share of profits can be lost in the form of profit taxes, withholding taxes or other fees and taxes. Indirect investment vehicles try to optimize taxation by setting up holding companies in low-tax states. Property derivatives provide a very simple, transparent and effective way of taxation and generally reduce international taxation massively.

Consider a French pension fund with a real estate portfolio that is regionally concentrated. The fund manager actively manages the existing portfolio with a domestic focus, and is almost exclusively invested in French property. However, the company is at least as positive on the UK and the German property market and would like to diversify into that region. The company has neither the local know-how nor the contacts to build exposure in these countries in a timely way. The required infrastructure and know-how cannot be easily established in foreign countries, due to a lack of experience. At the same time it would be beneficial for the pension fund to diversify internationally.

The fund can be diversified out of the French real estate market into, for example, the UK and German market by entering a country swap. The fund manager would synthetically give away part of the French exposure in return for UK and German exposure. He or she would pay the domestic, i.e. French, IPD total return in exchange for receiving a basket of foreign, i.e. UK and German, IPD total return plus or minus a spread. The spread arises since there are differences in interest rates, property transactions costs, taxes and market expectation in the three countries. It can take either sign. In other words, the spread depends on the relative levels of the property spreads in the involved countries (see Chapter 8). By doing this transaction, the fund manager can keep the alpha of its domestic portfolio while diversifying into foreign markets. Physical replication of that strategy would require to sell French property and buy UK and German properties, which would result in high costs, due diligence investigations and lagged implementation time. The manager therefore avoids transaction costs in all foreign countries. Also, unwinding the strategy is much quicker with a derivative than with physical investments.

Table 16.1 displays the correlations of France, Germany and the UK for properties and equities. It can be seen that for properties correlations are low or even negative, resulting in great diversification benefits when investing abroad. Equity markets, in contrast, are highly integrated and correlated.

Figure 16.1 compares the total annual returns over the period from 1998 to 2006. There is obviously a strong case in favor of geographical diversification for commercial real estate investors, so that in addition to providing a hedging solution for property investors in their domestic market, property derivatives represent an efficient way to diversify and gain cross-border exposure.

Table 16.1   Upper table: international correlations, based on IPD indices 1998–2006 for the UK, France and Germany. Lower table: international correlations for stock indices over the same period and countries

	UK	France	Germany
UK	1.00	0.60	−0.85
France		1.00	−0.32
Germany			1.00

	UK	France	Germany
UK	1.00	0.85	0.86
France		1.00	0.97
Germany			1.00

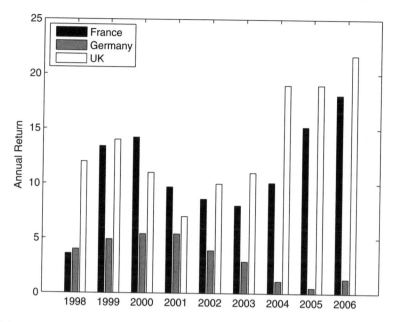

Figure 16.1 Different behavior of returns bring benefits of cross-border diversification. All returns are based on IPD All Property TR measures

16.3.2 Sector diversification

Sector diversification enhances the risk and return profiles further. While office space is very sensitive to economic cycles, residential property and the retail sector, including shopping space, have proved much more resistent to a weak economy in the past. Special sectors such as logistic property can also react very sensitively to the overall economic conditions. There is a need to be aware that regulations and their effects on prices are very different among property sectors and jurisdictions. Especially residential property is heavily regulated in many countries.

In the US, many exchange-traded REITs are specialized and concentrated in a specific sector and can be used by investors according to their allocation desires. There are REITs for office space, shopping centers, residential properties or infrastructure buildings such as hospitals, post offices, hotels and so on. That allows very good sector diversification opportunities along sectors within the US. It would be of great benefit if other countries could develop similar investment opportunities. The emergence of property derivatives can be of great help to develop further sector-differentiated investments.

Derivatives can not only be used for tactical timing but also for tactical sector allocation. A portfolio manager can refine existing direct property exposure by buying or selling derivatives referencing individual property sectors. The manager could swap sector returns against LIBOR to reduce or increase exposure or could swap returns of one sector against the returns of another sector or against the overall property market. The goal of such a transaction is to diversify the portfolio better within the asset class of real estate or to implement a specific market view.

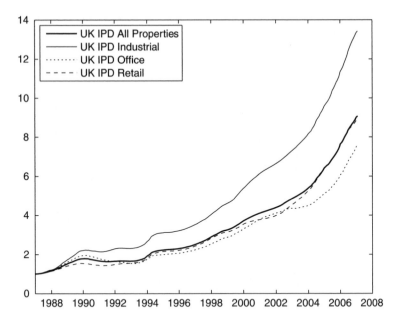

Figure 16.2 Sectors in the UK

Typically, the property market is divided into residential, office, retail and industrial sectors. Figure 16.2 shows the IPD UK sector indices since 1987. It is likely that many investors would prefer even more specific property markets to allow tactical reallocation. If there are sufficient data available, subsector markets can be defined even more closely. In the UK, the IPD Index has a rich data base on commercial properties, but does not track residential real estate. The IPD UK Annual Index is decomposed as listed in Table 16.2.

Table 16.2 Decomposition of the IPD UK Annual Index by the end of 2006

	Number of objects	Capital value	Capital value of total (%)
All retail	4 583	90 543	47.2
Standard retail: South East	1 403	11 140	5.8
Standard retail: rest of UK	1 588	12 930	6.7
Shopping centers	336	32 799	17.1
Retail warehouses	1 256	33 674	17.6
All office	3 461	66 384	34.6
Office: City	442	15 450	8.1
Office: West End and mid town	940	17 372	9.1
Office: rest of South East	1 249	23 400	12.2
Office: rest of UK	830	10 161	5.3
All industrial	3 316	28 318	14.8
Industrial: South East	1 476	15 569	8.1
Industrial: rest of UK	1 840	12 749	6.6
Other commercial	777	6 522	3.4
All property	12 137	191 767	100.0

So far, most sector focused deals have been conducted in the retail sector. Market participants perceive that the retail sector has the most risk attached. Uncertainty about, for example, Marks & Spencer or Tesco in the equity market means uncertainty in the retail property sector. In the UK, there have already been subsector deals on shopping centers (see Chapter 5).

Consider the following example. US-based investors decided to enter into a derivative transaction on 1 January 2000 that would swap office returns for retail returns, based on the NCREIF index series; i.e. the investors would pay the return of the NCREIF Office Index and receive the return of the NCREIF Retail Index. It is assumed that they would also need to pay a spread of 2 %, since the market expects retail space to perform better than offices. The contract terminated on 31 December 2004. Over this particular five-year period retail returns in fact outperformed office returns. The office index increased from 100 to 147.94 whereas the retail index increased from 100 to 189.73. The average annual return (ARR) for each sector was thus as follows:

$$AAR_{Office} = \left(\frac{147.94}{100}\right)^{1/5} - 1 = 8.15\,\%$$

$$AAR_{Retail} = \left(\frac{189.73}{100}\right)^{1/5} - 1 = 13.67\,\%$$

Thus, the investor who swapped office for retail would have earned an average annual return of 13.67 % while paying 8.15 % plus the spread of 2 %. The result is an annual net return of 3.52 %. The investor was not taking the risk of the overall property market but the risk related to the *relative* performance of the retail versus the office sector, betting that retail would outperform office. If the investor had been overexposed to office and underexposed to retail, then he would have achieved a return, by entering the swap, that was closer to the overall property market than without the swap.

17

Corporate Applications

Focus on what you do best.

Why do corporate businesses hold so much property on their balance sheets? The holding and management of properties is not a core business of most corporations. However, because they operate in properties, be it offices, industrial or retail objects, it somehow feels natural to own the place where one works and produces.

Even if the management of a firm's real estate is not conducted by the firm itself but is outsourced, the property risk still remains with the firm. That risk can hit a company hard if real estate prices drop, banks ask for mortgage amortization and the company needs to repay debt. Even worse, if a drop in real estate prices coincides with an economic downturn and a consequent workforce cut, the firm might not need all of its properties and could be stuck with empty buildings. Selling the property at that time will yield low prices and cause high transaction costs (even more so if property is purchased again once an economic upturn kicks in).

This is an unnecessary accumulation of noncore risk and an inefficient allocation of property risk. Rightfully, sale and lease-back transactions became more popular in recent years. The focus on business operations sets free resources and results in a leaner balance sheet, freeing up capital for other investments.

A synthetic alternative to a physical sale and lease-back transaction can be engineered by using property derivatives. Conducting asset and liability management with property derivatives has effects similar to a physical sale. Alongside other forms of finance, a synthetic sale of property is able to raise funds by utilizing existing property assets. Property derivatives are a new tool to manage a corporate balance sheet effectively and to allocate a firm's resources more efficiently.

The Investment Property Forum (IPF) estimates, from Companies House records, that large UK corporations collectively own around GB £160 billion of commercial real estate, with a concentration of 68 retail companies holding GB £38 billion. Some corporations are therefore sitting on a substantial balance sheet exposure to property assets, concentrated in one specific sector. To manage their risks, the corporations could enter a property derivative for a number of reasons:

- As an alternative to a sale and lease-back transaction
- To increase leverage
- To lock in past performance on properties
- To isolate operational returns from exposure to commercial real estate

17.1 SELLING BUILDINGS SYNTHETICALLY

For a company that owns buildings, one possibility to raise cash is via the use of a funded property derivative or a property-linked note. This is potentially cheaper and quicker than other forms of finance, including mortgage finance. Also, issuing a property-linked note reduces the

Table 17.1   Advantages and disadvantages of a synthetic sale over a physical sale

Advantages of a synthetic sale compared to a physical sale
No taxes or fees that arise in a traditional sale
Tax optimization due to income-deductible interest on debt
Maintaining operational control of properties
No property market risk for the term of the deal
Quick and efficient implementation
Potentially positive alpha

Disadvantages of a synthetic sale compared to a physical sale
Liquidity trap if property prices rise sharply
Risk of higher vacancy than the one reflected in the index
Basis risk, i.e. potentially negative alpha

company's property risk, while a mortgage levers it. A property-linked note raises cash on which the issuer does not pay interest, but property performance that is generated by the properties held. Thus, liabilities are aligned with assets. In case property prices drop, debt, i.e. the property-linked note, is reduced accordingly. In case prices rise, debt correspondingly increases, but is offset in the balance sheet since property assets will have risen as well.

Alternatively, a property swap can be entered. Through a swap, the company that holds properties on the balance sheet passes on property performance and receives a fixed or LIBOR-linked interest payment in return. In case the firm has mortgages on its properties, the interest received on the swap can be used to pay the mortgage rates. This might be a more tax-efficient way of property outsourcing than a physical sale, since the interest paid on the mortgages can typically be deducted from taxable income. However, it is important to note that a synthetic sale always leaves the company with basis risk, or alpha. This alpha can be positive or negative. As long as the firm intends to stay in the buildings, alpha is likely to be positive since vacancy risk is not an issue. It can be regarded as the company being the renter. To offset risk in "balance sheet practice," hedge accounting must be applicable.

A synthetic sale of properties has many advantages over a physical sale, with a few disadvantages on the flip side. Table 17.1 list the most important considerations of a synthetic sale.

Using property derivatives in the context of balance sheet management is nothing more than common asset and liability management (ALM). In fact, by issuing a property-linked note, the company manages the liabilities against the assets, i.e. the building owned by the company. If property prices rise sharply, the company needs to make higher debt payment. These payments can result in a liquidity trap, since the capital gain on the buildings is a noncash gain, while the liabilities need to be paid in cash. However, since buildings are more valuable, the company could increase the debt level accordingly, offsetting the shortage of liquidity on the balance sheet. Alternatively, it could simply buy a put option to protect property assets. However, buying a put option is costly and requires a premium payment.

17.1.1   An Illustrative example

The insurance company SafeSide Ltd, based in London, owns office buildings in Paris worth €400 million. The company occupies all of the offices itself. However, the prices of office buildings in Paris have been quite volatile over recent years and are likely to be so in the future. Suppose that five years later, the French economy has fallen into a recession. SafeSide decides to discontinue its operations in France and wants to sell its office buildings in Paris. Prices for offices are sensitive to economic downturns and the company's buildings are now worth only €300 million. By selling them, SafeSide realizes a loss of €100 million caused by the office market in Paris.

SafeSide could have entered a short position in a property swap on an index that tracks Paris offices, e.g. the IPD Paris Offices Capital Growth Index. To offset value fluctuations, a capital growth index is more suitable than a total return index. The insurance company would have received LIBOR-linked or fixed payments, say 2 % annually, and had to pay the capital growth of offices in Paris. If capital growth is negative, SafeSide receives the negative performance on top of the 2 %. The 2 % reflects the market expectation for annual capital growth at the beginning of the swap contract. Over five years, SafeSide would received 10 % (the fixed leg of the swap) plus, in the above scenario, another 25 % due to the negative performace of the office market in Paris. On a notional amount of €400 million, that is €40 million for giving up the expected price appreciation on offices plus €100 million that compensates for the negative actual performance. The company would have been immunized (based on the index) against the adverse price development. However, the idiosyncratic risk, i.e. the basis risk that SafeSide's offices had performed worse than the overall office market in Paris, remained with the company. Figure 17.1 shows the balance sheet of SafeSide at the end of the five-year term, with and without the property swap.

On the other hand, if prices had appreciated by, for example, 25 %, SafeSide had still received the €40 million of the fixed leg of the swap, but had to pay a total of €100 million to the swap counterparty. To raise the necessary cash to pay this amount, the insurance company could increase the mortgage on the buildings, which are now worth €500 million, i.e. €100 million more compared to five years ago.

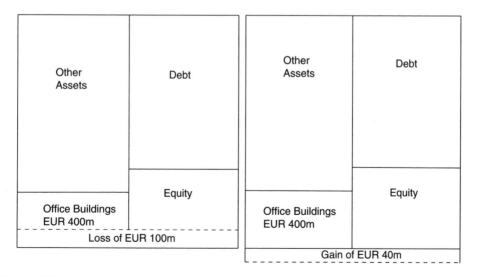

Figure 17.1 By entering a property swap, the balance sheet of SafeSide is stabilized (right graph) compared to the scenario where the company enters no swap (left graph). In fact, the company locks in the expected price growth of 10 %, i.e. €40 million

Conducting asset-liability management by entering a property swap is not a one-sided insurance but an immunization against both a price appreciation and a price decline. The price for the downside protection is to give up some of the upside. Alternatively, keeping the upside while protecting the downside could be implemented by buying a put option on the respective index. That would, however, require the payment of a (potentially costly) premium.

17.2   ACQUISITION FINANCE

By reducing property risk through entering into a swap, a company may find it easier to access acquisition finance from the bank, if the bank has been concerned about the company's exposure to the property sector. Furthermore, the company can take advantage of superior returns offered on a property swap compared to available bank financing terms, as long as the property spread is large enough.

Assume that a company can get a US$ 100 million mortgage financing from a bank at LIBOR plus 1 %. To pay this interest rate, the company could enter a US$ 100 million notional property swap on which it passes on property returns and receives, say, LIBOR plus a property spread of 1.5 %. After paying the mortgage, the company is left with a difference of 0.5 %, i.e. US$ 500 000 per year. Thus, it could achieve a better source of financing than if it simply sold US$ 100 million of its properties. A highly rated company could potentially get even more out of such a swap transaction, since it is likely to have better mortgage terms.

Thus, besides being a tool to manage liabilities against assets, property derivatives have the potential to allow companies cheap funding, as long as they have physical properties and are willing to give up some of the future property returns, whether positive or negative. For many institutions such as insurance companies and banks, which hold large positions in direct property, a property derivative transaction can free up capital to make further investments.

If, on the other hand, the market expectation is bearish on a specific sector, i.e. the property spread is negative, a company that intends to acquire a building is better off by just leasing the building and entering a receiver swap. In early 2007, the property spread for the UK retail sector was significantly negative. In such a situation the company would pay LIBOR *minus* a spread and receive the sector's rental income and capital growth in return. It can use the rental income to pay the lease and accumulate the capital growth performance until the spread turns positive, i.e. when the swap gets more expensive and a physical purchase actually makes sense for the company. By doing this transaction, the company is better off than buying the building from the very beginning and financing it through a mortgage, at a level that would be above LIBOR.

18

Indexed Building Savings

Keep track!

In many countries, tax authorities treat building savings favorably, in order to incentivize homeownership. Spending less on taxes might be a good motivation to start saving for a home, but it does not align the savings plan to the targeted object in any way.

Prospective homeowners typically start to save early to make their dream of then own home come true. Once the decision to buy a home is made, an initial amount is put aside, dedicated to that purpose. Subsequently, periodic savings, e.g. a constant part of the monthly salary, are added to the funds reserved for the home. Depending on the amounts, on the interest rate and on the price of the targeted property, it often takes some years until the purchase can be completed.

However, the prospective buyer is chasing a moving target. House prices may rise and the targeted home could turn out to be more expensive than expected. In this case, the result is a shortfall in cash at the end of the scheduled savings period and the period needs to be prolonged. During that additional savings period, prices can rise even further, causing again a shortfall in cash. Alternatively, a smaller than desired house can be bought, probably not satisfying the buyer entirely. If prices fall, on the other hand, the purchase can be completed earlier than expected, or a bigger house could be afforded.

A solution that addresses house price risk can be provided by using property derivatives. If the savings amount is linked to a local house price index, purchasing power with respect to housing in that region is locked in.

18.1 LINKING THE SAVINGS PLAN TO A HOUSE PRICE INDEX

Consider an example that illustrates the variation of house prices and, as a result, the variation of the savings horizon. The house price data are based on real transactions in East Anglia, measured by the Halifax House Price Index. Prices experienced a similar price development all over the UK.

In early 2000, family Smith has savings of GB £10 000 and decides to buy a home in East Anglia within the next couple of years. The dream home would cost about GB £400 000, anticipating long-term house price inflation of, say, 4 % p.a., in five years time; 80 % of that amount is to be financed by a mortgage. As first-time buyers, the Smiths require GB £80 000 in equity. They can afford to put aside GB £1000 a month. A constant salary and a constant monthly saving amount is assumed. At an interest rate of 5 %, it takes about five years until the targeted GB £80 000 is reached.

However, house prices have more than doubled, i.e. risen by 111 % during the savings period, 89 % more than anticipated by long-term housing inflation. The house now costs GB £690 000. Keeping the mortgage at 80 %, GB £138 000 of home equity is now needed. To save the additional GB £58 000, it takes the Smith family about three and a half additional years of saving. After the additional period, the house can only be afforded if house prices

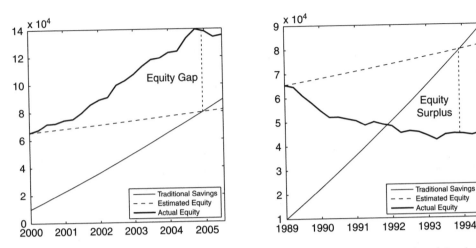

Figure 18.1 From 2000 to 2005, house prices have risen much more than expected, and the dream home cannot be afforded (left graph). A decade earlier, house prices were falling, resulting in an equity surplus in the savings plan (right graph). House price inflation is assumed to be 4 % and the interest rate on the savings account is assumed to be 5 %. An initial equity of GB £10 000 and monthly savings of GB £1000 are assumed

remained stable or weakened. If prices appreciate further during that time, the savings period is again prolonged. Financing the unexpected price increase by a higher loan-to-value (LTV) on the mortgage would further leverage housing risk and strain the budget of the family. Banks do not easily grant high LTVs. Figure 18.1 illustrates the divergence of the savings plan and house prices in East Anglia, as well as the projected house price inflation.

A historical simulation is used to get a likelihood of how often this has happened in the past. In particular, the Halifax House Price Index was used for East Anglia, from 1983 to 2007. The expected saving time is kept, assuming normal house price inflation and interest rates as above, at five years. Approximately 64 % of savers needed to save longer than expected and the ones that started saving after 1995 could not have afforded their dream home until today. Figure 18.2 shows the realized saving time in years along the starting year of saving.

Suppose that the Smith family participated in an index-linked building savings program, where the savings were tied to the Halifax House Price Index for East Anglia. The same savings scheme is assumed as in the above example, i.e. GB £10 000 initial savings and GB £1000 monthly thereafter over five years. At the given interest rate of 5 %, the savings plan has a future value of about GB £80 000 at the end of the savings period. In addition, the Smiths could enter a five-year forward contract on a notional amount of GB £80 000, valued at zero cost at the start.It is assumed that forward prices are in line with expected housing inflation. If an index link is established on this notional amount, purchasing power with regard to house prices is locked in from the very beginning of the savings period. The index link can be implemented in the form of a scheduled index-linked savings account that replaces the traditional savings account. At a normal rate of 4 % of house price inflation, the amount will still be about GB £80 000 in five years. However, should house prices experience a steeper price increase, the savings account will gain in value accordingly, e.g. to about GB £138 000 as in the above example.

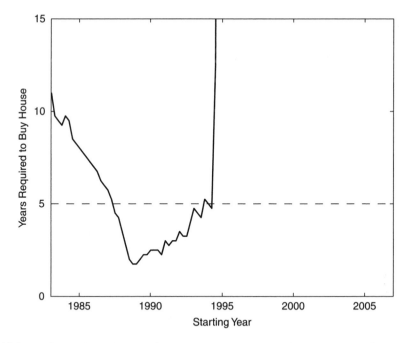

Figure 18.2   It often took much longer than expected: the graph displays the number of years it took to save the required equity along the starting year of saving

If house prices drop, as they did, for example, from 1989 to 1994, the savings plan shrinks accordingly. However, the originally targeted home can still be afforded, since houses are cheaper and less cash is needed to buy the home. Figure 18.3 shows the development of the index-linked savings account, in a scenario of rising or falling house prices. In summary, an index-linked savings account reduces realization risk to purchase a home at a future date

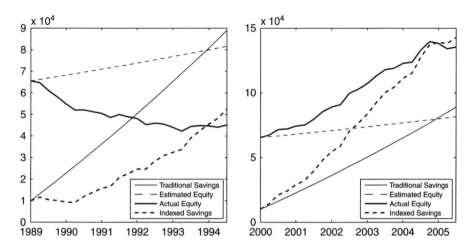

Figure 18.3   Index-linked building savings make sure that the dream home can be bought as scheduled. There is no longer an equity gap or surplus

Table 18.1 Aligning house price development through an indexed savings account: levels at the end of the savings horizon

	Rising prices: 2000 to 2005		Falling prices: 1989 to 1994	
	Traditional account	Index-linked account	Traditional account	Index-linked account
House price development	+111 %	+111 %	−32 %	−32 %
Price of dream home	690 000	690 000	223 000	223 000
Equity needed (20 % of price)	138 000	138 000	44 600	44 600
Account balance	80 000	138 000	80 000	44 600
Surplus (gap) in equity	(58 000)	—	35 400	—

significantly: an appropriate reference index related to house prices defines the account's growth rate. An index-linked account makes the purchase of a targeted home much more calculable and the savings horizon more predictable. Table 18.1 shows the saving account balances for an index-linked and a traditional savings account.

18.2 ENGINEERING A SUITABLE SAVING PLAN

First a typical savings plan is discussed and then the property derivative required to establish a suitable index linkage is added. Generally, a savings plan consists of four variables, of which three can be chosen. The fourth variable is the result of the choices. The variables are:

- Initial saving amount
- Periodic saving amount
- Targeted saving amount
- Time horizon

It is assumed that the periodic saving amount is constant and paid with discipline, i.e. there is no period in which the saving payment is missed. Further, for simplicity reasons, constant interest rates are assumed. In the above example, the initial, the periodic and the targeted saving amounts have been chosen, making the time horizon the residual variable. At an interest rate of 5 %, the time horizon turns out to be approximately five years. In total nominal amounts, the Smith family saves GB £70 000, i.e. GB £10 000 as the initial amount and GB £1000 periodic savings over 60 months. The future value of the savings plan, however, due to interest accumulation, is at GB £80 000, corresponding to the targeted savings amount. Based on that amount, which reflects the expected home equity that is required in five years, the property index link should be established; i.e., a long hedge on a notional value of GB £80 000 is implemented by entering a long forward contract. The forward contract is the financial translation of the purchase of the dream home in five years time.

However, the forward contract will fall in price if house prices weaken, eating up some of the savings. Although houses can also be purchased cheaper in that case, many people do not want to lose any of the saved nominal amounts. To address this desire, the Smith family could alternatively participate in a program where the saved cash amounts are fully capital protected. To finance the protection of the GB £70 000, something else must be given up, e.g. by setting a cap on the upside. In this example, that cap would be at GB £94 000, i.e. the program would track a price appreciation up to 18 % on top of the expected house price inflation (which would result in a final amount of GB £80 000). For the pricing of the capital protection and the cap, the annual volatility is assumed to be at the historic level of 13.3 % with a property forward rate that is in line with housing inflation of 4 %. In return, if house prices drop sharply, the Smith family could afford to buy a bigger home, due to the protection of nominal capital while the house became cheaper. An indexed building savings account could be structured in many more ways and could be tailored to individual clients' needs.

Finally, depending on the contract's reference index, there is little idiosyncratic risk in indexed building savings. Typically, a buyer has a targeted region in mind, where he or she intends to buy a future home. A specific object is only searched when the savings amount is sufficiently large to buy a home in the desired standard. While hedging an individual object with a regional index leaves the homeowner with basis risk, indexed building savings cover the price risk of homes in the targeted region very accurately.

19

Home Equity Insurance

Unload your housing risk.

Once a home is purchased, the sign of the housing risk a household is exposed to turns upside down. Homeowners are typically heavily exposed to house price risk and there are no suitable possibilities to unload it. This leads to suboptimal allocations for most households. Englund *et al.* (2000) show that most Swedish homeowners up to the age of 50 hold a strongly unbalanced portfolio. Flavin and Yamashita (2000) report similar findings for the US where households below 30 years of age invest more than three times their net wealth in owner-occupied housing.

Property derivatives can help to allocate the risk in housing efficiently. However, homeowners' interest in the publicly traded housing futures and options at the Chicago Mercantile Exchange has been limited. Typically, individual homeowner interest gravitates towards longer maturities than the ones offered on a futures exchange. As derivatives markets are notoriously complex and not tailored to the needs of homeowners, large financial institutions or banks are expected to use them to develop home-price insurance programs and offer them to residential buyers alongside traditional property insurance.

Probably the earliest modern project on home equity protection was the home equity insurance program that was launched in 2002 in Syracuse, New York. The project was implemented by joined forces with local and national nonprofit community development organizations, financial institutions and the Yale School of Management. However, the local program remained a pilot project and was not extended to other areas. Only a few homeowners participated in the program.

19.1 INDEX-LINKED MORTGAGES

The academic literature has forcefully attempted to encourage the introduction and the use of property derivatives as a hedge against house price risk (see, for example, Shiller and Weiss, 1999). The economic rationale for these financial instruments is manifest, as many households are heavily invested in housing and standard financial instruments offer a poor hedge. In practice, however, most of the property derivatives available have been targeted to meet the needs of institutional investors, not those of owner-occupiers.

An alternative approach that involves the use of property derivatives is proposed: index-linked mortgages. The payments of these mortgages depend on the corresponding housing market performance. The resulting effect is a stabilization of the homeowner's net wealth and a decrease in the mortgage default risk achieved by immunization effects (see Syz *et al.* (2008) for the full paper on index-linked mortgages).

This new type of mortgage could enable homeowners to reduce housing risk substantially. The basic idea is to link the mortgage to an index of house prices. More precisely, the interest payments and/or the principal are linked to the underlying index movements. If house prices deteriorate, the households have to pay either lower interest on their mortgage or, alternatively, the price decrease is directly subtracted from the mortgage's principal value at its maturity.

In both cases the volatility of a household's home equity is smoothed. Hence, this type of property derivative reduces the homeowner's exposure to house price risk while reducing the credit risk exposure of the mortgage lender through asset-liability immunization. Index-linked mortgages thus provide Pareto improvements by allocating collateral risk more optimally and by reducing the number of defaults and related costs.

The theoretical findings of Iacoviello and Ortalo-Magné (2003) support this approach. The authors investigate the benefits of giving households the possibility to adjust their portfolio holdings through the use of property derivatives. They show that hedging could greatly improve welfare, especially in the case of poorer homeowners who face the highest net wealth volatility and shortfall risk. According to Englund *et al.* (2002) renters would equally benefit from gaining access to housing index investments.

Case *et al.* (1993) advanced the introduction of futures contracts tied to regional house price indices in the US. However, in practice it is difficult for poorer households to enter into short positions of such contracts. Poorer households typically face the highest leverage; i.e. their investment portfolio is significantly out of balance. With index-linked mortgages, households need not enter into short positions since the mortgage is directly linked to a property derivative on a regional house price index.

Most homeowners bear a very high amount of property risk. This may be due to a lack of perception, as owner-occupied housing is often regarded as a consumption asset only and is therefore excluded from the financial portfolio context. However, even risk-savvy home-owners lack the opportunity of financial instruments enabling them to unload housing risk. Furthermore, as mentioned before, poor households would be likely to benefit most from hedging instruments as they have to bear the lumpiest risk in housing. However, it is typically hard for these households to access over-the-counter hedge contracts. It thus appears reason-able to link the hedging instruments to mortgages, such that all homeowners with leveraged housing risk are automatically confronted with the dimension of housing risk and hedging possibilities. Moreover, the expected loss on the mortgage is reduced due to the housing hedge. Hence the client can benefit directly from a reduced credit spread on the package "index-linked mortgage." Recourse mortgages, which are typical in Europe, are exclusively considered here.

19.1.1   Rent or buy?

Today's standard decision when it comes to housing is commonly referred to as "rent or buy." In other words, an individual does either bear a large, lumpy property risk (usually leveraged by mortgage financing) or he or she rents and is thus not exposed to any property risk (the (upward) adjustment of rents is typically heavily regulated and is rarely driven by property performance). Figure 19.1 shows the impact of leverage through a mortgage on home equity.

Considering property risk in a portfolio context, it makes a priori sense for a homeowner to partially unload the property risk, while renters might reasonably take some property risk.

A homeowner's overall financial situation is considered. A typical homeowner finances his or her house partly with a mortgage that comes with fixed nominal and fixed or floating interest payments. In addition, securities such as stocks or bonds may be held in the investment portfolio. Still, the exposure to housing may easily exceed total net wealth, as long as the liability, i.e. the mortgage, is not linked to the price of the property. The result is a poorly diversified overall portfolio of the homeowner. An index-linked mortgage is used to offset housing exposure and therefore significantly contributes to a more efficient portfolio allocation. The following

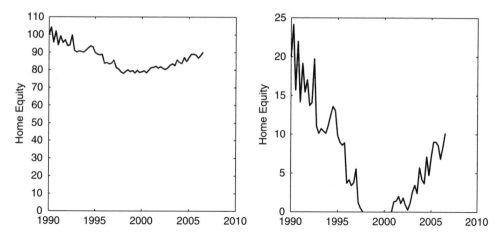

Figure 19.1   Home equity without and with leverage (loan-to-value is 80 %)

example illustrates the risk associated with current property financing that leads to a suboptimal portfolio allocation.

A Swiss-based homeowner buys a house in the Canton of Zurich in 1994, at a price of CHF 500 000. He takes on a five-year mortgage with a notional value of CHF 400 000 (the loan-to-value (LTV) ratio is 80 %) and puts down CHF 100 000 in equity. He or she further possesses a portfolio consisting of various liquid assets amounting to CHF 60 000. Suppose that within five years, house prices in the region decline by 15 %, and so does the value of the house, which is then worth only CHF 425 000. After these five years, the mortgage is due and the house value is reassessed. The bank offers a renewed 80 % mortgage finance, i.e. is willing to provide CHF 340 000. Since the due mortgage amounts to CHF 400 000, the difference of CHF 60 000 needs to be paid out of other funds. Ceteris paribus, the adverse development of house prices leaves the owner with zero liquid assets and home equity of CHF 85 000, i.e. the net wealth has almost halved. A further depreciation of house prices in subsequent years makes the situation worse. Figure 19.2 illustrates what happens to the LTV ratio if house prices move over an eight-year horizon. Starting at an LTV of 80 %, it can rise quickly to 90 % or in some cases even above 100 %.

If the homeowner had financed his or her house with a mortgage linked to the local house price index, e.g. by including a put option on that index, the net wealth would have been stabilized considerably. Instead of losing 15 % on the total house value, he or she would only incur a loss on the equity part of the house plus the cost of the put option of, say, 3.5 % on the mortgage's notional value. The price of the put option is in line with the pricing practice in Switzerland. This would leave a net wealth position of CHF 131 000 instead of CHF 85 000, whereof CHF 46 000 are in liquid assets.

In sum, the owner would have reduced the housing exposure from 312.5 % of net wealth to 62.5 %, which is a much more reasonable level. Still, the share invested in housing might be too high to achieve optimal portfolio allocation. Due to reduced risk, the bank may grant a higher borrowing level, which in turn unloads even more housing risk and makes funds available for investments in other asset classes to optimize the homeowner's overall portfolio further. In this sense, index-linked mortgages greatly improve the risk profile and welfare of many households.

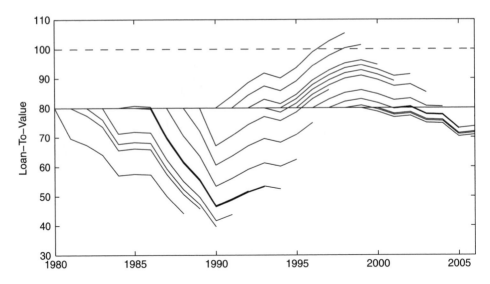

Figure 19.2   The evolution of LTV ratios for Swiss residential properties over eight years

Figure 19.3 shows the impact of a homeowner's portfolio if the housing asset is considered. Due to the low correlation of its returns with those of traditional assets, housing is attractive for diversification. Discussion will focus on the return and standard deviation as well as the correlations of all involved assets, as displayed in Table 19.1. The cash and bond indices are calculated as total returns.

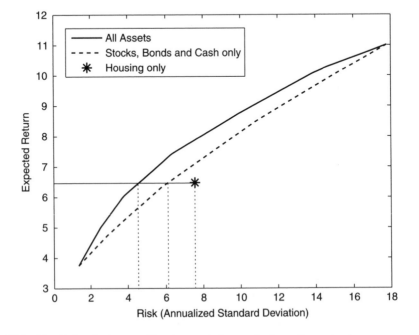

Figure 19.3   Combining the house with other assets is superior to renting or buying

Table 19.1   Returns, standard deviations and correlations of all involved assets. The MSCI Switzerland is used for stock, the 10-year Swiss Government Bond Index for bonds, the J.P. Morgan Switzerland three-month cash index for cash and the index for owner-occupied housing in the Canton of Zurich ZWEX for house prices. All numbers are based on quarterly observations during the period from Q4 1985 to Q4 2005

1985–2005	Return p.a.	Standard Deviation p.a.	Correlation matrix			
			Stock	Bonds	Cash	House prices
Stock	11.01	17.79	1.000			
Bonds	5.41	5.53	0.105	1.000		
Cash	3.75	1.35	−0.075	0.140	1.000	
House prices	6.48	7.56	−0.163	−0.051	0.048	1.000

The figure shows (on an unlevered basis) the risk/return situation of a buyer's portfolio (100 % invested in the house) of a renter's portfolio (100 % invested in an optimized portfolio containing stock, bonds and cash) and of a portfolio with a partial exposure to a property, optimized in context with the other investable assets. Besides the usual caveats of the standard mean-variance portfolio approach, differences in liquidity between housing and other assets are ignored, as well as considerations involved with the fact that housing is held not only as an investment but also for the housing service stream it generates. To make housing returns comparable with pure investment assets, a net rent yield is included that corresponds to the saved rental expense net of maintenance cost.

In this setup, portfolio risk can be reduced considerably using a combined portfolio. In the context of portfolio theory, any risk-averse individual should invest on the efficient frontier to maximize utility. For a given level of return, the buyer (who invested all of the wealth in the house) bears a risk in terms of standard deviations of almost 8 % p.a.. The renter, on the other hand, invests in an efficient portfolio consisting of tradable assets. This leaves him or her with standard deviations of 6 %. However, he or she has zero percent invested in housing. With a partial investment in both housing and the liquid asset portfolio, risk is only around 4.5 %.

19.1.2   Designed to avoid liquidity constraints

Homeowners' characteristics are typically very heterogeneous. Their mortgage financing decisions as well as their risk affinity depend upon their net wealth as well as on their income streams and borrowing constraints (Campbell, 2006). Therefore the design of the mortgage is crucial when it comes to liquidity constraints and solvency risk of individual homeowners.

Assume the principal of the mortgage is linked to the house price index, protecting homeowners against declines in house prices over the life of the mortgage. In order to avoid a liquidity constraint in the case of strongly increasing prices (unrealized gains on housing), an asymmetric payoff profile is proposed by incorporating a put option in the mortgage, such that the principal is directly reduced by a potential negative index performance. The put premium is added to the periodic interest instalments. The put premium is estimated to be approximately 0.7 % p.a. over a five-year term, according to market conditions in 2007, where the premium reflects the pricing practice in Switzerland.

Alternatively, if the principal linkage is symmetric, i.e. the principal rises and falls with the index, then the interest to be paid is typically lower than on a fixed principal. This is because the principal is expected to rise on average with house price inflation. In other words, not the notional amount but the LTV of the mortgage is kept constant. Of course, several more structures of index-linked mortgages would be able to address the constraints.

19.1.3   Index linkage improves credit quality

Traditional asset and liability management targets an immunization effect that smoothes the equity position and reduces default risk. The same effect applies to the portfolio of homeowners and to home equity. Combining mortgages with property derivatives effectively reduces the collateral's volatility with respect to the mortgage liability. This portfolio optimization reduces credit risk and thus has a direct impact on the price of index-linked mortgages.

Finance theory commonly splits debt instruments into a risk-free part and a put option on the collateral. This option is often referred to as credit put, and its premium is charged as a credit spread on top of the risk free rate. In the case of mortgages, the bank sells an *implicit* out-of-the money put option on the financed house, with a strike price equal to the mortgage's nominal amount. An index-linked mortgage, which includes an *explicit* (at-the-money) put option that serves as additional collateral, considerably reduces the probability that the borrower's implicit credit put ends in-the-money. The effectiveness of this credit risk reduction depends on the correlation between the individual house price that underlies the implicit credit put option and the house price index that underlies the explicit index put option. Given that this correlation is significantly positive, the bank's credit risk is considerably reduced. The result is a lower credit spread charged to homeowners or, alternatively, a higher LTV ratio can be granted.

19.2   COLLATERAL THINKING

Consider an index-linked mortgage with an embedded put option such that the principal is directly reduced by a potential negative index performance. A comparison of credit risk of the index-linked mortgage to their traditional counterparts is of interest.

A mortgage can be decomposed into the following securities: an unsecured loan, a credit derivative and, for the index-linked mortgage, a put option. This decomposition follows the logic that an index-linked mortgage equals an unsecured loan plus a credit enhancement through a collateral, i.e. a credit derivative, plus an index put option. This credit derivative, i.e. the mortgage-implicit credit put option, should not be confused with the explicit put option in the index-linked mortgage. From a risk perspective, the risk factor in the unsecured loan is given by the default risk of the borrower. The risk factors of the credit derivative and of the put option are a combination of default risk and house price, i.e. collateral risk (see Akgün and Vanini (2006) for loan pricing).

For the index put option, it is important to note that this option is not valued in its entirety per se, but of interest is the effect of this option on the mortgage conditions; i.e. if the borrower buys such an option, it would amount to an effective increase in the collateral if the bank is contractually able to make use of the option payoff in the case of default. Therefore the amelioration in the mortgage conditions that is brought about by this put option is calculated. For this, it is assumed that both the effective collateral and the index follow correlated processes, which are then simulated to determine the expected additional payoff from the put option.

Table 19.2   Pricing of traditional mortgages. The final price consists of the unsecured loan and the collateral enhancement for the bank as a protection buyer (all amounts are in Tsd. CHF)

Rating	Loan principal	Estimated value of property	Unsecured loan (%)	Collateral enhancement (%)	Terms of mortgage (%)
7	500	625	14.21	8.54	5.67
6	500	625	8.20	3.68	4.52
5	500	625	5.55	1.43	4.12
4	500	625	4.43	0.47	3.96
3	500	625	4.25	0.32	3.94
2	500	625	4.04	0.13	3.91
1	500	625	3.95	0.05	3.90

The prices of traditional mortgage contracts for eight different rating classes, with class eight the defaulted class, are summarized in Table 19.2 (see Syz *et al.* (2008) for details on the pricing of index-linked mortgages). There are two main conclusions from the table. First, the lower the creditworthiness of a borrower, the more expensive are the terms for the unsecured loan. Second, the lower the creditworthiness of the borrower, the more is the bank (as protection buyer) willing to pay for collateral.

If index-linked mortgages are considered, the standard case described above is modified as follows. First, the automatic amortization of the principal if the put ends in the money, i.e. if the property index declined over the mortgage's life, is equivalent to additional collateral. Second, the client pays a put premium. For the best two rating categories one and two, the put premium is approximately 0.7 % p.a. for a five-year term. For borrowers with lower creditworthiness, i.e. a higher risk that they will fail to pay the put premium periodically for the full contract period, the put premium is higher. The variation of the premium is shown in Table 19.3.

Table 19.3 compares the index-linked mortgage with the traditional one. The parameters are the same as for Table 19.2 with the following additional data for the put: correlation between the index and the collateral is estimated at 75 % and the strike of the index put is set equal to the initial value of the index, i.e. at 100 %.

Table 19.3   Pricing of traditional mortgages and index-linked mortgages. Index-linked mortgages are always more expensive than traditional mortgages. However, the lower a homeowner's creditworthiness, the less are the relative additional costs for the index-linked mortgage compared to the traditional one

Rating	Standard mortgage			Index-linked mortgage		
	Unsecured loan (%)	Collateral enhancement (%)	Terms of mortgage (%)	Index put (%)	Credit enhancement (%)	Index-linked mortgage (%)
7	14.21	3.53	10.68	1.09	0.99	10.78
6	8.20	1.52	6.68	0.95	0.67	6.96
5	5.55	0.59	4.96	0.88	0.26	5.58
4	4.43	0.19	4.24	0.81	0.09	4.96
3	4.25	0.13	4.12	0.72	0.06	4.78
2	4.04	0.06	3.99	0.71	0.03	4.67
1	3.95	0.02	3.93	0.71	0.01	4.63

Table 19.3 shows that uniform in borrower creditworthiness the terms of the index-linked mortgage are more expensive than for the classical one. However, it can be seen that the bank is willing to pay slightly more for the credit enhancement to lower rated borrowers than to borrowers with a high creditworthiness: the difference in the final terms between the two mortgages for the rating class seven is 0.10 % whereas the put premium is 1.09 %. It follows that the lower the creditworthiness of the borrower, the more valuable the index put option is as additional collateral.

Today, individual homeowners are often largely overexposed to the asset class of real estate. An index-linked mortgage provides the possibility to improve the balance of individual portfolios and reduce the systematic risk of real estate in these portfolios. Banks will have to offer a menu of options to cater for the individual needs of property owners and investors. Reasonable structures of index-linked mortgages include the linkage of the principal while keeping interest payments fixed or fixing the principal while linking interest payments. Financial engineering will allow the creation of any combination of these structures.

However, it is unclear whether the number of house price observations will be big enough to create the demanded regional focus of indexes, addressing idiosyncratic aspects appropriately. There follows a discussion of whether an index-hedge is appropriate to hedge a single object.

19.3   IS AN INDEX-HEDGE APPROPRIATE?

The price of housing is subject to considerable fluctuations over time, which in turn lead to significant fluctuations in wealth. As pointed out by Sinai and Souleles (2003), the effects of house price risk on consumers' choices are ambiguous. For a household with utility defined over housing consumption, homeownership acts as a hedge against changes in the cost of consumption, i.e. against rent risk. Housing market risk may thus increase homeownership rates. The extent to which hedging considerations affect tenure choice is mitigated by the existence of frictions on the real estate and on the mortgage market. Transaction costs coupled with borrowing constraints restrict the number of house trades and investors' ability to implement first-best strategies significantly (see Cocco, 2000). In this context, the existence of home equity insurance is of great interest to investors. However, the extent to which an investor may take advantage of the property derivatives market is limited by its effectiveness for hedging purposes, i.e. by the amount of the idiosyncratic risk of individual properties compared to the risk of the respective index.

Results from previous research indicate substantial variability in returns to particular properties relative to the market. For the Swedish market, Englund et al. (2002) report a standard deviation in the returns of individual properties of 11.3 %, compared with 7.6 % for the market as a whole. Goetzmann (1993) also documents a substantially higher variation for individual properties, with standard deviations 1.5 to 3 times higher than the respective four US metropolitan area indices. For New Zealand, Bourassa et al. (2005) find standard deviations 1.4 to 2 times higher than those of the general market. They relate the degree of variation in price changes among houses within a market to their characteristics and to the prevailing conditions of the housing market at the time of the sale. Atypical houses and houses with characteristics in limited supply, e.g. waterfront houses, are generally more risky.

Iacoviello and Ortalo-Magné (2003) found a weakly positive correlation of 0.13 between the London housing returns and simulated individual returns at a short horizon (one quarter) but a very strong correlation (0.87) at a 10-year horizon. The capital returns to a single housing unit, r_t^h, are defined as

$$r_t^h = (p_t^I + v_t) - (p_{t-1}^I + v_{t-1}) \qquad (19.1)$$

where p_t^I is the log of the house price index and v is the idiosyncratic noise term with $E(v_t) = 0$ and $E(v_t^2) = \sigma_v^2$. Syz *et al.* (2008) perform an analysis on idiosyncratic house price risk in the greater Zurich area. The availability of geographically disaggregated indices allows the returns on individual properties to be approximated. They assume that the idiosyncratic variation of individual housing returns is captured by the variation of the local index returns around the returns of the market index. Note that this method is likely to underestimate true idiosyncratic risk, as the regional segmentation only represents one source of idiosyncratic risk. The estimated idiosyncratic volatility of the returns σ_v is equal to 0.082 while the volatility of the yearly index returns σ_I is 0.054. The correlations are indeed very high, ranging from 0.77 for 4-year, to 0.89 for 8-year and 0.96 for 12-year periods. These results confirm the importance of designing hedging instruments with maturities of at least five years, as correlations are higher at longer horizons.

Appendix

A.1 HEDGING WITH CORRELATED ASSETS

At time $t = 0$, the trader's portfolio contains n derivatives based on the property index $\tilde{S}$. The portfolio includes linear claims such as swaps as well as nonlinear claims such as options. Each derivative has a value $H_{i,t}$ at time t. The value of the portfolio at $t = 0$ is

$$V_0 = \sum_{i=1}^{n} \psi_{i,0} H_{i,0} \tag{A.1}$$

where ψ_i is the dollar weight of each derivative. The trader can engage in a hedging position W by trading $k - 1$ hedging assets S_j that are correlated with $\tilde{S}$. In addition, there is a risk-free asset S_1 which can be used to lend or borrow. The hedging strategy is assumed to be self-financing; i.e. it neither receives nor pays out anything during its life. The hedging position in each asset S_j is denoted ϕ_j. The hedge portfolio at time 0 reads

$$W_0 = \sum_{j=1}^{k} \phi_{j,0} S_{j,0} \tag{A.2}$$

Using a self-financing strategy, the value of the two portfolios at the hedge horizon T are

$$V_T = V_0 + \sum_{t=0}^{T-1} \sum_{i=1}^{n} \psi_{i,t} \delta H_{i,t} \tag{A.3}$$

and

$$W_T = W_0 + \sum_{t=0}^{T-1} \sum_{j=1}^{k} \phi_{j,t} \delta S_{j,t} \tag{A.4}$$

where $\delta H_{i,t} = H_{i,t+1} - H_{i,t}$ and $\delta S_{j,t} = S_{i,t+1} - S_{i,t}$. The hedged portfolio is thus

$$V_T - W_T = V_0 - W_0 + \sum_{t=0}^{T-1} \left(\sum_{i=1}^{n} \psi_{i,t} \delta H_{i,t} - \sum_{j=1}^{k} \phi_{j,t} \delta S_{j,t} \right) \tag{A.5}$$

A vector of weights ϕ is chosen for the hedging assets such that the portfolio variance is minimized

$$\text{var}(V_T - W_T) \rightarrow \min \tag{A.6}$$

subject to the constraint

$$E[V_T - W_T] = r \tag{A.7}$$

The scalar products are defined as

$$\langle \psi, \delta H \rangle_{0 \to T}^n \equiv (\psi_{1,1}, \ldots, \psi_{n,1}, \psi_{1,2}, \ldots, \psi_{n,2}, \ldots, \psi_{n,T-1}) \begin{pmatrix} \delta H_{1,1} \\ \ldots \\ \delta H_{n,1} \\ \delta H_{1,2} \\ \ldots \\ \delta H_{n,2} \\ \ldots \\ \delta H_{n,T-1} \end{pmatrix} \tag{A.8}$$

and

$$\langle \phi, \delta S \rangle_{0 \to T}^k \equiv (\phi_{1,1}, \ldots, \phi_{k,1}, \phi_{1,2}, \ldots, \phi_{k,2}, \ldots, \phi_{k,T-1}) \begin{pmatrix} \delta S_{1,1} \\ \ldots \\ \delta S_{k,1} \\ \delta S_{1,2} \\ \ldots \\ \delta S_{k,2} \\ \ldots \\ \delta S_{k,T-1} \end{pmatrix} \tag{A.9}$$

Using this notation,

$$V_T - W_T = V_0 - W_0 + \langle \psi, \delta H \rangle_{0 \to T}^n - \langle \phi \delta S \rangle_{0 \to T}^k \tag{A.10}$$

The expected value of the hedged portfolio is

$$\begin{aligned} E[V_T - W_T] &= V_0 - W_0 + E[\langle \psi, \delta H \rangle_{0 \to T}^n] - E[\langle \phi \delta S \rangle_{0 \to T}^k] \\ &=: V_0 - W_0 + \langle \psi, \mu \rangle - \langle \phi, \nu \rangle \\ &= r \end{aligned} \tag{A.11}$$

where $\mu = E[\delta H]$ and $\nu = E[\delta S]$. Next the exposures of the derivatives H_i with underlying $\tilde{S}$ are linearized and aggregated as

$$\begin{aligned} \sum_i^n \delta H_{i,t} \psi_{i,t} &= \sum_i^n H_{i,t}(\tilde{S}_{t+1}) \psi_{i,t} - \sum_i^n H_{i,t}(\tilde{S}_t) \psi_{i,t} \\ &\approx \sum_i^n H_{i,t}(\tilde{S}_t) \psi_{i,t} + \delta \tilde{S}_t \sum_i^n \frac{\partial H_{i,t}}{\partial \tilde{S}_t}(\tilde{S}_t) \psi_{i,t} - \sum_i^n H_{i,t}(\tilde{S}_t) \psi_{i,t} \\ &= \delta \tilde{S}_t \sum_i^n \frac{\partial H_{i,t}}{\partial \tilde{S}_t}(\tilde{S}_t) \psi_{i,t} \\ &=: \delta \tilde{S}_t \Delta_t \end{aligned} \tag{A.12}$$

Then

$$z = \begin{pmatrix} \Delta \\ \phi \end{pmatrix} \tag{A.13}$$

$$q = \begin{pmatrix} \delta \tilde{S} \\ \delta S \end{pmatrix} \tag{A.14}$$

and

$$X_{k,l} = \mathrm{cov}(q_k, q_l) \tag{A.15}$$

where the variance–covariance block matrix reads

$$X_{k,l} = \left(\begin{array}{c|c} X_{\tilde{S},\tilde{S}} & X_{\tilde{S},S} \\ \hline X_{S,\tilde{S}} & X_{S,S} \end{array} \right) \tag{A.16}$$

where $X_{\tilde{S},\tilde{S}}$ is the variance of the underlying index, $X_{\tilde{S},S}$ is a $1 \times n$ vector, $X_{S,\tilde{S}}$ is an $n \times 1$ vector and $X_{S,S}$ is an $n \times n$-matrix.

The variance of the hedged portfolio can be written as

$$\mathrm{var}(V_T - W_T) = \langle z, Xz \rangle \tag{A.17}$$

Using this notation, the Lagrange function can now be applied

$$L = \langle z, Xz \rangle + 2\lambda (V_0 - W_0 + \langle \psi, \mu \rangle - \langle \phi, \nu \rangle - r) \tag{A.18}$$

where 2λ is the Lagrange multiplier to solve the optimization problem. The first partial derivative of the Lagrange function with respect to the hedge ratios ϕ reads

$$\frac{\partial L}{\partial \phi} = 2X_{SS}\phi + 2X_{S\tilde{S}}\Delta - 2\lambda\nu \tag{A.19}$$

Setting Equation (A.19) equal to zero and solving for ϕ leads to the optimal hedge ratios

$$\phi^* = -X_{SS}^{-1}X_{S\tilde{S}}\Delta + \lambda X_{SS}^{-1}\nu \tag{A.20}$$

Then

$$\beta = X_{SS}^{-1}X_{S\tilde{S}} \tag{A.21}$$

where β is the partial regression coefficient of a multiple OLS linear regression. The vector of weights that minimizes the variance of the hedged portfolio can now be written as

$$\phi^* = -\beta\Delta + \lambda X_{SS}^{-1}E[\delta S] \tag{A.22}$$

Inserting Equation (A.20) into (A.11) and solving for λ results in

$$\lambda = \frac{V_0 - W_0 - r + \Delta\langle \beta, \nu \rangle + \langle \psi, \mu \rangle}{\langle \nu, X_{SS}^{-1}\nu \rangle} \tag{A.23}$$

A.2   ADJUSTING FOR CONVEXITY

If the portfolio consists mainly of linear derivatives such as forwards, futures and swaps, the linearization in Equation (A.12) provides a good approximation. If the portfolio is highly nonlinear however, there is a need to adjust for convexity. Thus Equation (A.12) is expanded to its second order:

$$\sum_i^n \delta H_{i,t}(\tilde{S}_t)\psi_{i,t} \approx \delta\tilde{S}_t \sum_i^n \frac{\partial H_{i,t}}{\partial \tilde{S}_t}(\tilde{S}_t)\psi_{i,t} + \delta\tilde{S}_t^2 \frac{X_{\tilde{S}\tilde{S}}}{2} \sum_i^n \frac{\partial^2 H_{i,t}}{\partial \tilde{S}_t^2}(\tilde{S}_t)\psi_{i,t}^2$$

$$=: \delta\tilde{S}_t \Delta_t + \delta\tilde{S}_t^2 \frac{X_{\tilde{S}\tilde{S}}}{2}\Gamma_t \tag{A.24}$$

Consequently,

$$z = \begin{pmatrix} \Delta \\ X_{\tilde{S}\tilde{S}}/2\Gamma \\ \phi \end{pmatrix} \tag{A.25}$$

and

$$q = \begin{pmatrix} \delta\tilde{S} \\ \delta\tilde{S}^2 \\ \delta S \end{pmatrix} \tag{A.26}$$

and the variance–covariance block matrix extends to

$$X_{k,l} = \begin{pmatrix} X_{\tilde{S},\tilde{S}} & X_{\tilde{S},\tilde{S}^2} & X_{\tilde{S},S} \\ X_{\tilde{S}^2,\tilde{S}} & X_{\tilde{S}^2,\tilde{S}^2} & X_{\tilde{S}^2,S} \\ X_{S,\tilde{S}} & X_{S,\tilde{S}^2} & X_{S,S} \end{pmatrix} \tag{A.27}$$

The first partial derivative of the Lagrange function with respect to the hedge ratios ϕ is now

$$\frac{\partial L}{\partial \phi} = 2X_{SS}\phi + 2X_{S\tilde{S}}\Delta + 2\frac{X_{\tilde{S}\tilde{S}}}{2}\Gamma X_{\tilde{S}^2 S} - 2\lambda v \tag{A.28}$$

and setting Equation (A.28) equal to zero, the vector of optimal hedge ratios is

$$\phi^* = -X_{SS}^{-1}X_{S\tilde{S}}\Delta - \frac{X_{\tilde{S}\tilde{S}}}{2}\Gamma X_{SS}^{-1}X_{\tilde{S}^2 S} + \lambda X_{SS}^{-1}v \tag{A.29}$$

Finally, λ reads

$$\lambda = \frac{V_0 - W_0 - r + \Delta\langle \beta, v \rangle + (X_{\tilde{S}\tilde{S}}/2)\Gamma\langle X_{SS}^{-1}X_{\tilde{S}^2 S}, v \rangle + \langle \psi, \mu \rangle}{\langle v, X_{SS}^{-1}v \rangle} \tag{A.30}$$

A.3   HEDGING WITH OPTIONS

Finally, if hedging assets and options on the hedging assets can be used, delta and gamma can be treated separately. Two independent Lagrange problems are solved, one for the delta hedge and one for the gamma hedge. Since gamma addresses the curvature in the derivatives portfolio, the convexity adjustment delta hedge is not applied. The delta position is thus hedged according to Equation (A.22). The second term of the Taylor expansion remains, i.e.

$$\sum_i^n \delta H_{i,t}(\tilde{S}_t)\psi_{i,t} - \delta\tilde{S}_t \sum_i^n \frac{\partial H_{i,t}}{\partial \tilde{S}_t}(\tilde{S}_t)\psi_{i,t} \approx \delta\tilde{S}_t^2 \frac{X_{\tilde{S}\tilde{S}}}{2}\sum_i^n \frac{\partial^2 H_{i,t}}{\partial \tilde{S}_t^2}(\tilde{S}_t)\psi_{i,t}^2$$

$$=: \delta\tilde{S}_t^2 \frac{X_{\tilde{S}\tilde{S}}}{2}\Gamma_t \tag{A.31}$$

The hedged portfolio with the weights ϕ^* according to Equation (A.22) is defined as

$$Y_t^* = V_t - W_t(\phi_t^*) \tag{A.32}$$

and a new hedge account U that addresses gamma risk is introduced. The hedging position for the gamma in each asset S_j is denoted $(X_{SS}/2)\gamma_j = \xi_j$. Hence,

$$U_0 = \sum_{j=1}^k \xi_{j,0} S_0^2 \tag{A.33}$$

Following the same reasoning as above and with

$$r = \begin{pmatrix} (X_{\tilde{S}\tilde{S}}/2)\Gamma \\ \xi \end{pmatrix} \tag{A.34}$$

$$s = \begin{pmatrix} \delta\tilde{S}^2 \\ \delta S^2 \end{pmatrix} \tag{A.35}$$

and

$$Q_{k,l} = \text{cov}(s_k, s_l) \tag{A.36}$$

gives a second Lagrange function that reads

$$L = \langle r, Qr \rangle + 2\lambda_\Gamma(Y_0 - U_0 + \langle \omega, \iota \rangle - \langle \xi, \kappa \rangle - r_\Gamma) \tag{A.37}$$

where ω is the portfolio exposure in $\tilde{S}^2$, $\iota = E[\delta\tilde{S}^2]$, $\kappa = E[\delta S^2]$, $r_\Gamma = E[Y_T - U_T]$ and λ_Γ is the Lagrange multiplier. The first partial derivative of the Lagrange function with respect to ξ is

$$\frac{\partial L}{\partial \xi} = 2Q_{S^2 S^2}\xi + 2Q_{S^2\tilde{S}^2}\frac{X_{\tilde{S}\tilde{S}}}{2}\Gamma - 2\lambda_\Gamma\kappa \tag{A.38}$$

This gives the optimal weights

$$\xi^* = -Q_{S^2 S^2}^{-1} Q_{S^2\tilde{S}^2}\frac{X_{\tilde{S}\tilde{S}}}{2}\Gamma + \lambda_\Gamma Q_{S^2 S^2}^{-1}\kappa \tag{A.39}$$

and λ_Γ as

$$\lambda_\Gamma = \frac{Y_0 - U_0 - r_\Gamma + (X_{\tilde{S}\tilde{S}}/2)\Gamma \langle Q_{S^2\tilde{S}^2} Q_{S^2 S^2}^{-1}, \kappa \rangle + \langle \omega, \iota \rangle}{\langle \kappa, Q_{S^2 S^2}^{-1}\kappa \rangle} \tag{A.40}$$

Bibliography

Ahn, C. (1992) Option pricing when jump risk is systematic, *Mathematical Finance*, **2**, 299–308.

Akgün, A. and Vanini, P. (2006) The pricing of index-linked mortgages: technical documentation, Working Paper, Cantonal Bank of Zurich.

Amin, K. (1993). Jump diffusion option valuation in discrete time, *The Journal of Finance*, **48**(5), 1833–1863, December.

Armonat, S. and Pfnür, A. (2001) Ergebnisbericht zur empirischen untersuchung immobilienkapitalanlage institutioneller investoren – risikomanagement und portfolioplanung, *Arbeitsbereich Öffentliche Wirtschaft am Fachbereich Wirtschaftswissenschaften der Universität Hamburg*, 26 January 2001.

Artzner, P., Delbaen, F., Eber, J.-M. and Heath, D. (1999) Coherent measures of risk, *Mathematical Finance*, **9**(3), 203–228.

Ball, C. and Torous, W. On jumps in common stock prices and their impact on call option pricing, *The Journal of Finance*, **40**(1), 155–173.

Banks move in on property derivatives (2007). *The Financial Times*, 5 March 2007.

Barkham, R. and Geltner, D. (1994) Unsmoothing British valuation-based returns without assuming an efficient market, *Journal of Property Research*, **11**(2), 81–95.

Barkham, R. and Geltner, D. (1995) Price discovery and efficiency in American and British property markets, *Real Estate Economics*, **23**, 21–44.

Basel Commitee on Banking Supervision (1996) *amendment to the Capital accord to Incorporate Market Risks*.

Baum, A. (1991) Property futures, *Journal of Property Valuation and Investment*, **9**(3), 235–245.

Baum, A., Beardsley, C. and Ward, C. (1999) Using rental swaps and sales to manage portfolio risk and to fund property development, Working Paper.

Bellamy, N. and Jeanblanc, M. (2000) Incompleteness of markets driven by a mixed diffusion, *Finance and Stochastics*, **4**, 201–222.

Benartzi, S. and Thaler, R. (1995) Myopic loss aversion and the equity premium puzzle, *The Quarterly Journal of Economics*, **110**(1), 73–92, February.

Bjork, T. and Clapham, E. (2002) On the pricing of real estate index linked swaps, *Journal of Housing Economics*, **11**(4), 418–432, December.

Black, F. (1976) The pricing of commodity contracts, *Journal of Financial Economics*, **3**, 167–179.

Black, F. and Scholes, M. (1973) The pricing of options and corporate liabilities, *The Journal of Political Economy*, **81** (3), 637–654.

Blundell, G. and Ward, C. (1987) Property portfolio allocation: a multi-factor model, *Journal of Property Research*, **4**(2), 145–156, May.

Bollen, N. (1998) A note on the impact of options on stock return volatility, *Journal of Banking and Finance*, **22**, 1181–1191.

Bond, S. and Hwang, S. (2003) A measure of fundamental volatility in the commercial property market, *Real Estate Economics*, **31**(4), 577–600.

Borio, C. (1995) The structure of credit to the non-government sector and the transmission mechanism of monetary policy: a cross-country comparison, in *Financial Structure and the Monetary Policy Transmission Mechanism*, Bank for International Settlements, pp. 59–105.

Borio, C. and McGuire, P. (2004) Twin peaks in equity and housing prices?, *BIS Quarterly Review*, 79–93, March.

Borio, C., Furfine, C. and Lowe, P. (2001) Procyclicality of the financial system and financial stability: issues and policy options. *BIS Papers*, **1**.

Borsani, C. (2002) Stabilität hedonischer immobilienpreisindizes – eine empirische untersuchung anhand des zkb-immobilienpreisindex, Master's Thesis, Universitäre Hochschule St Gallen –HSG.

Bourassa, S., Haurin, D., Haurin, J., Hoesli, M. and Sun, J. (2005) House price changes and idiosyncratic risk: the impact of property characteristics, Working Paper, University of Geneva.

Box, G. and Cox, D. (1964) An analysis of transformations, *Journal of the Royal Statistical Society*, **26**(2), 211–252.

Brown, G. and Matysiak, G. (1995) Using commercial property indices for measuring portfolio performance, *Journal of Property Finance*, **6**(3), 27–38.

Buraschi, A., Porchia, P. and Trojani, F. (2006) Correlation hedging, Working Paper, Imperial College London and University of St Gallen.

Buttimer, R., Kau, J. and Slawson, V. (1997) A model for pricing securities dependent upon a real estate index, *Journal of Housing Economics*, **6**(1), 16–30.

Campbell, J. (2006) Household Finance, *The Journal of Finance*, **61**(4), 1553–1604.

Case, B. and Quigley, J. (1991) The dynamics of real estate prices, *The Review of Economics and Statistics*, **73**(1), 50–58, February.

Case, K. and Quigley, J. (2007) How housing booms unwind: income effects, wealth effects, and sticky prices, Paper prepared for a joint session of the American Economic Association and the American Real Estate and Urban Economics Association, Chicago, 5 January, 2007.

Case, K. and Shiller, R. (1987) Prices of single-family homes since 1970: new indices for four cities, *New England Economic Review*, 45–56.

Case, K., Shiller, R. and Weiss, A. (1993) Index-based futures and options markets in real estate, *Journal of Portfolio Management*, **19**(2), 83–92.

Castelino, M. (1990) Minimum variance hedging with futures revisited, *Journal of Portfolio Management*, **16**(3), 74–80.

Catte, P., Girouard, N., Price, R. and André, C. (2004) Housing markets, wealth and the business cycle, *OECD Economics Department Working Papers*, (394).

Cho, H., Kawaguchi, Y., and Shilling, J, (2003) Unsmoothing commercial property returns: a revision to Fisher–Geltner–Webb's unsmoothing methodology, *Journal of Real Estate Finance and Economics*, **27**(3), 393–405, November.

Clapp, J. and Giaccotto, C. (1992) Estimating price indices for residential property: a comparison of repeat sales and assessed value methods, *Journal of the American Statistical Association*, **87**(418), 300–306, June.

Cocco, J. (2000) Hedging housing price risk with incomplete markets, Working Paper, London Business School.

Commercial Real Estate: The Role of Global Listed Real Estate Equities in a strategic asset allocation, (2006) Ibbotson associates, 2 November 2006.

Conrad, J. (1989) The price effect of option introduction, *Journal of Finance*, **44**, 487–498.

Corkish, J., Holland, A. and Vila, A. (1997) The determinants of successful financial innovation: an empirical analysis of futures innovation on LIFFE, Bank of England Working Paper, 70, October.

Cox, J. and Ross, S. (1976) The valuation of options for alternative stochastic processes, *Journal of Financial Economics*, **3**, 145–166.

Deep, A. and Domanski, D. (2002) Immobilienmarkt und Wirtschaftswachstum: Lehren aus dem Refinanzierungsboom in den USA, *BIS Quarterly Report*, 42–51, September.

Diewert, W. (2004) Consumer Price Index Manual: Theory and Practice, Quality change and hedonics, Chapter 21 in International Labour Office, Geneva. ILO/IMF/OECD/UNECE/Eurostat/The World Bank.

Dombrow, J., Knight, J. and Sirmans, C. (1995) A varying parameters approach to constructing house price indexes, *Real Estate Economics*, **23**.

Dresig, T. (2000) *Handelbarkeit von Risiken – Erfolgsfaktoren von Verbriefungen und derivativen Finanzinstrumenten*, Deutscher Universitäts-Verlag, Wiesbaden.

Ederington, L. (1979) The hedging performance of the new futures market, *Journal of Finance*, **34**, 157–170.

Englund, P., Hwang, M. and Quigley, J. (2002) Hedging housing risk, *The Journal of Real Estate Finance and Economics*, **24**(1–2), 167–200.

Ferri, M. (1977) An application of hedonic indexing methods to monthly changes in housing prices: 1965–1975, *Real Estate Economics*, **5**(4), 455–462, December.

Fisher, J., Gatzlaff, D., Geltner, D. and Haurin, D. (2003) Controlling for the impact of variable liquidity in commercial real estate price indices, *Real Estate Economics*, **31**(2), 269–303.

Fisher, J., Geltner, D. and Webb, R. (1994) Value indices of commercial real estate: a comparison of index construction methods, *The Journal of Real Estate Finance and Economics*, **9**(2), 137–164, September.

Fitzgerald, D. (1993) *Financial Futures*, 2nd edition Euromoney Institutional Investor.

Flavin, M. and Yamashita, T. (2002) Owner-occupied housing and the composition of the household portfolio, *American Economic Review*, **92**(1), 345–362.

Föllmer, H. and Schweizer, M. (1991) Hedging of contingent claims under incomplete information, Discussion Paper Series B 166, University of Bonn, Germany.

Four more banks to trade US property swaps (2007) *Reuters*, 14 February 2007.

Gatzlaff, D. and Geltner, D. (1998) A transaction-based index of commercial property and its comparison to the NCREIF index, *Real Estate Economics*, **15**(1), 17–22.

Gau, G. and Wang, K. (1990) A further examination of appraisal data and the potential bias in real estate return indexes, *Real Estate Economics*, **18**(1), 40–48.

Geltner, D. (1989) Bias in appraisal-based returns, *Journal of the American Real Estate and Urban Economics Association*, **17**, 338–352.

Geltner, D. and Fisher, J. (2007) Pricing and index considerations in commercial real estate derivatives, *Journal of Portfolio Management – Special Issue Real Estate*, **34**, 99–118.

Geltner, D. and Miller, N. (2001) *Commercial Real Estate Analysis and Investments*, Reiter's Books.

Geltner, D., MacGregor, B. and Schwann, G. (2003) Appraisal smoothing and price discovery in real estate markets, *Urban Studies*, **40**(5–6), 1047–1064, May.

Geltner, D., Miller, N. and Snavely, J. (1995) We need a fourth asset class: HEITS, *Real Estate Finance*, **12**, 71–81.

Gibson, R. and Schwartz, E. (1990) Stochastic convenience yield and the pricing of oil contingent claims, *Journal of Finance*, **45**(3), 959–976.

Goetzmann, W. (1993) The single family home in the investment portfolio, *Journal of Real Estate Finance and Economics*, **6**(3), 201–222,

Gordon, J., Canter, T. and Webb, J. (1998) The effect of international real estate securities on portfolio diversification, *Journal of Real Estate Portfolio Management*, 83–91.

Guttery, R. and Sirmans, C. (1998) Aggregation bias in price indices for multi-family rental properties, *Journal of Real Estate Research*, **15**(3).

Harris, L. (1989) S&P 500 cash stock price volatility, *Journal of Finance*, **44**, 1155–1176.

Heravi, S. and Silver, M. (2004) Hedonic price indexes and the matched models approach, *The Manchester School*, **72**(1), 24–49.

Hinkelmann, C. and Swidler, S. (2006) Trading house price risk with existing futures contracts, Working Paper, Auburn University.

Hull, J. (2000) *Options, Futures and Other Derivatives*, Prentice-Hall. Englewood chilp, New Jersey.

Hwang, S. and Satchell, S. (2000) Market risk and the concept of fundamental volatility: measuring volatility across asset and derivative markets and testing for the impact of derivatives markets on financial markets, *Journal of Banking and Finance*, **24**(5), 759–785.

Iacoviello, M. and Ortalo-Magné, F. (2003) Hedging housing risk in London, *The Journal of Real Estate Finance and Economics*, **27**(2), 191–209.

Janssen, C., Söderberg, B. and Zhou, J. (2001) Robust estimation of hedonic models of price and income for investment property, *Journal of Property Investment and Finance*, **19**(4), 342–360.

Jarrow, R. and Rosenfeld, E. (1984) Jump risks and the intertemporal capital asset pricing model, *The Journal of Business*, **57**(3), 337–351.

Johnson, L. (1960) The theory of hedging and speculation in commodity futures, *The Review of Economic Studies*, **27**(3), 139–151.

Kaplanski, G. and Kroll, Y. (2002) VAR risk measures versus traditional risk measures: an analysis and survey, *Journal of Risk*, **4**(3), 1–20.

Kumar, R., Sarin, A. and Shastri, K. (1998) The impact of options trading on the market quality of the underlying security: an empirical analysis, *Journal of Finance*, **53**(2), 717–732.

Leishman, C. and Watkins, C. (2002) Estimating local repeat sales house price indices for British cities, *Journal of Property Investment and Finance*, **20**(1), 36–58.

Liang, Y., Seiler, M. and Chatrath, A. (1998) Are REIT returns hedgeable? *Journal of Real Estate Research*, **16**(1), 87–98.

McKenzie, M., Brailsford, T. and Faff, R. (2001) New insights into the impact of the introduction of futures trading on stock price volatility, *Journal of Futures Markets*, **21**(3), 237–255.

Mahal, G. (2001) Pricing weather derivatives, Chapter 4 in *Weather Derivatives – An Introduction*, ICFAI University Press.

Markowitz, H. (1952) Portfolio selection, *The Journal of Finance*, **7**(1), 77–91, March.

Mercurio, F. and Runggaldier, W. (1993) Option pricing for jump-diffusions: approximations and their interpretation, *Mathematical Finance*, **3**, 191–200.

Merton, R. (1976) Option pricing when the underlying stock returns are discontinuous, *Journal of Financial Economics*, **5**, 125–144.

Moss, S. and Schneider, H. (1996) Do EREIT returns measure real estate returns? *Journal of Property Finance*, **7**(2), 58–74.

Myer, N., Chaudhry, M. and Webb, J. (1997) Stationarity and co-integration in systems with three national real estate indices, *Journal of Real Estate Research*, **13**(3), 369–381.

OECD Economic Outlook (2005) Chapter III, Recent house price developments: the role of fundamentals, pp. 193–234, No. 78, December, Issue 2, Organization for Economic Cooperation and Development.

Pagliari, J., Lieblich, F., Schaner, M. and Webb, J. (2001) Twenty years of the NCREIF property index, *Real Estate Economics*, **29**(1), 1–27.

Patel, K. and Pereira, R. (2006) Pricing property index linked swaps with counterparty default risk. Working Paper, University of Cambridge.

Platen, E. and Schweizer, M. (1998) On feedback effects from hedging derivatives, *Mathematical Finance*, **8**(1), 67–84.

Plewka, T. and Pfnür, A. (2006) *Immobilien Manager*, 7–8:16.

Property derivatives, homes with hedges (2006) *The Economist*, 20 April.

Property derivatives: US (2007) *Risk Magazine*, **20**(9), September 2007.

Pyhrr, S., Roulac, S. and Born, W. (1999) Real estate cycles and their strategic implications for investors and portfolio managers in the global economy, *Journal of Real Estate Research*, **18**(1), 7–68.

Quan, D. and Quigley, J. (1991) Price formation and the appraisal function in real estate markets, *The Journal of Real Estate Finance and Economics*, **4**(2), 127–146, June.

Roche, J. (1995) *Property Futures and Securitisation – The Way Ahead*, Cambridge University Press.

Roehner B. (2000) Real estate price peaks – a comparative overview, *Evolutionary and Institutional Economics Review*, **2**(2), 167–182.

Ross, S. (1976) Options and efficiency, *Quarterly Journal of Economics*, **90**, 75–89.

Sharpe, W. (1964) Capital asset prices: A theory of market equilibrium under conditions of risk, *The Journal of Finance*, **19**(3), 425–442.

Shiller, R. (1993) Measuring asset values for cash settlement in derivative markets: hedonic repeated measures indices and perpetual futures, *Journal of Finance*, **48**(3), 911–931.

Shiller, R. (1998) Macro Markets: Creating Institutions for Managing Society's Largest Economic Risks, Oxford University Press.

Shiller, R. and Weiss, A. (1999) Home equity insurance, *The Journal of Real Estate Finance and Economics*, **19**(1), 21–47.

Sinai, T. and Souleles, N. (2003) Owner-occupied housing as a hedge against rent risk, NBER Working Paper 9462, January.

Stein, J. (1961) The simultaneous determination of spot and futures prices. *The American Economic Review*, **51**(5), 1012–1025.

Stoken, D. (1993) *The Great Cycle: Predicting and Profiting from Crowd Behavior, the Kondratieff Wave and Long-Term Cycles*, Probus Publishing Company.

Syz, J., Salvi, M. and Vanini, P. (2008) Property derivatives and index-linked mortgages, *Journal of Real Estate Finance and Economics*, **36**(1), 25–35.

The Surgery of Independent Forecasts: UK Property Investment (2004) Investment Property Forum (IPF), May 2004

Thomas, R. (1996) Indemnities for long-term price risk in the uk housing market, *Journal of Property Finance*, **7**(3), 38–52.

Tsetsekos, G. and Varangis, P. (2000) Lessons in structuring derivatives exchanges. *The World Bank Research Observer*, **15**(1), 85–98.

Turbulence in asset markets: the role of micro policies (2002). *G10 Contact Group on Asset Prices.*

Use of property derivatives recommended by the PDIG (2005). *The Financial Times, 29 August 2005.*

Wofford, L. (1978) A simulation approach to the appraisal of income producing real estate, *Real Estate Economics*, **6**(4), 370–394, December.

Zhu, H. (2003) The importance of property markets for monetary policy and financial stability, *BIS Papers*, (21), 9–29.

Index

Abbey National 39
Aberdeen Property Investors 37
ABN Amro 38–42, 47, 48
ABS HPI *see* Australian Bureau of Statistics
    House Price Index
accounting practices 24–5, 29, 30, 32–3, 62, 184
acquisition finance 186
adverse selection 165
agricultural sector, historical derivatives 7, 106
AI *see* Appraisal Institute
ALM *see* asset-liability management
alpha
    concepts 24–5, 162–4, 174–81, 184
    hedge funds 174–5
    portfolios 174–81
alternative asset classes, concepts 3–4
AME Capital 156–7
American Stock Exchange (Amex) 50
American-style options
    see also options
    concepts 14, 17–18
anticipatory hedging, concepts 169–70
appendices 203–7
applications
    corporate applications 25, 27, 146–7, 167–8,
        183–6
    property derivatives 26–7, 106–8, 145–7,
        162–4, 165–72, 183–6
Appraisal Institute (AI) 58–9
appraisal-based indices 5, 11, 30, 31, 35, 36–43,
    47–9, 51, 55–68, 73, 83, 93–108, 110–11,
    149–64, 170–1, 175, 179–80, 186
    see also commercial real estate
    autocorrelation 93–6, 97–9
    concepts 55–68, 73, 83, 93–100, 102, 152,
        160–1
    critique 58–9, 68, 93–100, 152
    dynamics 93–6
    FTSE UK Commercial Property Index 36,
        42–3, 63–4, 94, 158–61

internal/external appraisals 58–9
IPD 11, 30, 31, 36–43, 47–9, 51, 57–63, 93–6,
    97–100, 101–8, 110–11, 149–64, 170–1,
    175, 179–80, 186
NCREIF 36, 43–4, 57, 64–7, 85, 94, 98, 150
non-synchronous appraisals 94
practices 51, 58–9
problems 58–9, 93–100
smoothing factors 93–9, 152–6
sticky prices 94, 108
unsmoothing factors 95–9, 152–6
volatility 93–100, 102, 152, 160–1
appropriateness issues, indexes 172
arbitrage
    autocorrelation 93
    cash-and-carry arbitrage 104–5, 175–6
    concepts 7, 8–9, 14–21, 30, 93, 101–7, 109–10,
        175–6
    curve trades 176
    market frictions 105–6, 112–13
    price bands 106–7, 176
    soft arbitrage price bands 176
    speculator/hedge-fund contrasts 175
arms-length sales, repeat sales indices 71–2
arrangements, swaps 10–11, 26–7, 35–6, 147,
    162–4, 176–81, 184–6
asking prices, concepts 72–3
asset allocations
    see also strategic . . . ; tactical . . .
    concepts 150–1, 174–81
asset classes, concepts 3–6, 53–4, 149–64
asset-backed securities 3, 129–30, 156–61, 168
asset-liability management (ALM) 145–7, 184–6
at-the-money options, concepts 15–16, 20, 119,
    198
auctions 47, 118–21
Australia 35, 47, 60, 84, 90, 127, 159
Australian Bureau of Statistics House Price Index
    (ABS HPI) 84
Austria 60, 63

autocorrelation 58, 71, 92–9, 112–14, 130,
    137–9
    see also volatility
    appraisal-based indices 93–6, 97–9
    arbitrage 93
    concepts 92–9, 112–14, 130, 137–9
    empirical index analysis 97–9
    transaction-based indices 96, 97–9, 137–9
autoregressive fractionally integrated moving
    average (ARFIMA) 94, 153
AXA Real Estate Investment Managers 47–8

back-to-back matching, risk management
    strategies 118–21
balance sheets, corporates 183–6
Bank of America 39, 44
Bank of International Settlement (BIS) 7
banks
    see also mortgage . . .
    derivatives 7, 118–25, 145–7
    market development 118–25
Barclays Capital 36, 37, 39
barrier options 50
barriers to entry 146
base aggregate approaches 79
Basel Committee on Banking Supervision 122
Basel II 122–4
basis risk
    concepts 170–2, 175, 184, 191
    types 170, 171
    variance 172
bear markets 91–4, 167, 174, 186
Bear Stearns 46
Belgium 60, 63, 159
benchmarks
    see also indexes
    concepts 30–1, 45, 53–85, 122–3, 146–7, 150
    property development hurdles 30–1, 45, 146–7,
        150, 155–6, 172
    requirements 53–4
beta
    see also indexes
    concepts 162–4, 165
biases, indexes 72, 77, 94–8, 130, 176–7
bibliography 209–13
bid–offer spreads 24–5, 106, 117, 120, 145
BIS *see* Bank of International Settlement
Black–Scholes option pricing formula
    concepts 7, 14–18, 21, 99, 106, 109, 112–15,
        131
    constant parameters 114, 131
    critique 99, 109, 114–15, 131
    definition 14–15
    jumps in the diffusion process 115
    Merton's extension 115
    property derivatives 21, 109, 112–15

Bloomberg 104
BNP Paribas 48
bonds 5, 10, 16, 37–8, 101–2, 129–30, 149–64,
    196–7
    see also Property Index Certificates
boring perceptions, real estate market 5, 155–6
Box/Cox transformation 70
bricks and mortar
    see also real estate market
    financial risks 3–6, 30, 31
bridge investments 174
British Land 37
Brownian motion, concepts 14, 113, 114–15
bubbles, real estate market 90–2, 187–91,
    193–201
builders 25, 145, 165–6, 167–8
building savings 25, 146, 187–91
bull markets 157
buyers
    property derivatives 25, 35–9, 92–3, 145–7,
        162–4
    rent or buy decisions 194–7

call options
    see also options
    concepts 12–21, 113–15, 119, 133–4, 138–41
    definition 12
    payoffs 13–21
    pricing 14–21, 113–15
call warrants 42, 169
Canada 60, 90, 128, 159
capital adequacy requirements 122, 138, 140–1,
    168
capital asset pricing model (CAPM) 99
capital gains tax 32–3
    see also taxes
capital growth (CG) performance
    empirical index analysis 97–9
    IPD 61–3, 97, 150–2
    NCREIF 66–7
capital guarantees 24–5
capital protection 163, 190–1
capital value
    appraisals 58–9, 64–7
    empirical index analysis 97–9
    growth forecasts 33–4, 51
    IPD 61–3
    NCREIF 66–7
capital-at-risk (CaR) 122–5
capital-only contracts 6–7
capital-protected products 163, 190–1
capitalization weighted indexes 57
CaR *see* capital-at-risk
Case, Karl 3
Case–Shiller *see* S&P/Case–Shiller Index
cash drag 174

cash-and-carry arbitrage, concepts 104–5, 175–6
CB Richard Ellis (CBRE) 38–9, 44
CBOE *see* Chicago Board Options Exchange
CBRE *see* CB Richard Ellis
central limit theorem 97
CFDs *see* contracts-for-difference
CFE *see* Chicago Board Options Exchange
CG *see* capital growth . . .
CGBI *see* Citigroup Bond Index
characteristics
    real estate market 4–5, 109–15, 117
    underlying assets 54–7, 109–15, 117
Charles Schwab Investment Management 78–9
chartered surveyors 51, 57–8
Chau, Professor K.W. 84
cherry picking 25
Chicago Board Options Exchange (CBOE) 7,
    45–7, 50
Chicago Mercantile Exchange (CME) 33, 43–7,
    78–9, 119, 193
Citigroup Bond Index (CGBI) 129–30, 151–5
City Index Financial Markets 42, 119
clearing houses, futures 10
CMBS 47
CME *see* Chicago Mercantile Exchange
CMHPI *see* Conventional Mortgage Home Price
    Indices
CMOs *see* collateralized mortgage obligations
coefficient of determination 135–6
collateral risk, concepts 198–201
collateralized mortgage obligations (CMOs) 168
collective investment funds 5, 29, 46–7, 48–9, 61,
    63–4, 65, 129–30
    see also Real Estate Investment Trusts
Colliers International 48–9
commercial real estate 35–7, 38–41, 44–5, 50–1,
    55–67, 73, 93–100, 128, 145–7, 149–64,
    170–1, 175, 179–80, 183–6
    see also appraisal-based indices
    CME expansion 46
    economic dependencies/cycles 128, 130, 183,
        185
    IPD 11, 30, 31, 36–43, 47–9, 51, 57–63, 93–6,
        97–100, 101–8, 110–11, 149–64, 170–1,
        175, 179–80, 186
    statistics 38–41, 50–1, 97–108, 146, 149–64,
        183
commodities markets 3, 10, 106
compensation payments, forwards 10
constant parameters, Black–Scholes option
    pricing formula 114, 131
constant-quality indices *see* Hedonic models
contingent claims
    see also options
    concepts 16–21, 112–15
contracts-for-difference (CFDs) 36, 42–3

contrarians 33
convenience yields
    see also commodities . . .
    definition 10, 18
Conventional Mortgage Home Price Indices
    (CMHPI), concepts 82
convexity 206
coordination and limitation strategies, market
    development 120–1
corporate applications 25, 27, 146–7, 167–8,
    183–6
corporate bonds
    see also bonds
    statistics 149–52
corporates
    acquisition finance 186
    ALM 184–6
    balance sheets 183–6
    property derivatives 25, 27, 146–7, 167–8,
        183–6
    property-linked notes 183–6
    synthetic corporate building sales 183–6
corporation tax 32–3
    see also taxes
correlated assets 131–2, 137–41, 153–5, 159–61,
    172, 173, 178–9, 196–7, 201, 203–5
cost-of-carry arbitrage 9–10, 18
costs, transaction costs 5, 21, 23–4, 26–7, 90–4,
    104–6, 128, 131, 145–7, 163
cotton, historical derivatives 7
counterparties
    property development hurdles 30, 31–2, 33–4,
        149–50
    swaps 11–12, 35, 37–8, 147, 162–4, 176–81,
        184–6
counterparty risk
    see also default risks
    concepts 11–12, 101, 118–19, 147
country swaps, concepts 176–81
covered forwards, concepts 9–10
Cox and Ross model 115
crashes, property market crash (1990–1992) 101
credit derivatives 198–201
credit ratings 124–5, 198–201
credit risk 122, 198–201
Credit Suisse First Boston (CSFB) 39, 43–4
creditworthiness 198–201
CREX *see* S&P/GRA Commercial Real Estate
    Indices
cross-border investments
    hurdles 177–8
    portfolios 173–4, 176–81
    taxes 177–8
    transparency concerns 177–8
cross-hedge basis risk 170–2
CSFB *see* Credit Suisse First Boston

currency swaps 11
see also swaps
curve trades, arbitrage opportunities 176
Cushman and Wakefield BGC (CW BGC) 39
CW BGC *see* Cushman and Wakefield BGC
cycles, real estate market 89–97, 127–30

DCF *see* discounted cash flows
default risks 10, 11–12, 101, 118–19
see also counterparty risk
delivery quantities, forwards concepts 8–10
delivery times, forwards concepts 8–10
delta
see also gamma
concepts 19–20, 132, 138–9, 206–7
definition 19
delta hedging
concepts 19, 132–4, 139–41, 206–7
definition 19
demand/supply factors, real estate market 89–90
Denmark 60, 90, 128
Department for Communities and Local
Government (DCLG) 85
derivatives 3–6, 7–21, 23–38, 49–51, 106–7,
109–15, 131–2, 145–7, 153, 156–64,
165–72, 173–4, 183–4, 186, 193–201
see also forwards; futures; options . . . ;
property . . . ; swaps
banks 7, 118–25, 145–7
basics 7–21
benefits 5–6, 7–8, 12–13, 19, 21, 23–7, 29–30,
49–51, 106, 145–7, 153, 156–64, 173–4,
183–4, 186, 193–201
categories 7–8
concepts 3–6, 7–21, 165–72
credit derivatives 198–201
definition 7
historical background 7, 29, 31, 32, 33–4,
35–51
leverage benefits 12, 21, 24–5, 108, 156–64,
183–4, 194–6
linear/nonlinear categories of derivatives 7–8
statistics 7, 40–7
types 7–21, 35–8, 106–7, 109–10, 117, 131–2,
198–201
uses 5–6, 7–8, 25, 35–9, 145–7, 165–70, 183–6
volatility effects 49–51
Deutsche Bank 37, 40, 44, 46, 48, 118–19
diffusion processes, jumps 114–15
direct investments 5, 29–30
disaggregation 38
discounted cash flows (DCF) 14, 51, 55–6, 58–9
discounts, indirect investments 5, 26, 157
discrete time settings, hedging 132–41
distribution of returns 14–15, 97, 99–100, 107–8,
112–13, 123–4

diversification benefits
cross-border investments 173–4, 176–81
real estate market 5–6, 24–7, 29, 33, 54, 145–7,
149–56, 162–4, 173–81
sector swaps 38–42, 54, 171, 179–81
dividends
see also yields
concepts 9–10, 18, 26
forward prices 9–10
DIX 63
documentation, property derivatives 36, 162–3
downturns, real estate market 90–4, 128, 183,
185, 189–91, 193–201
Drivas Jonas 59
DTH *see* dummy time Hedonic method
DTZ 39
due diligence 5
dummy time Hedonic method (DTH) 70–1, 80–1
Durbin–Watson statistic 97–8, 130
Dutch auctions 47, 118–19
dynamics
appraisal-based indices 93–6
indexes 89–100, 127–30
transaction-based indices 96–7

early-stage market development 117–21
economic dependencies/cycles 89–97, 127–30,
183, 185, 187–91, 193–201
economic significance, property derivatives 3–4
education and acceptance, property development
hurdles 30, 31, 45
efficient frontiers 153–6
efficient markets 21, 26, 99, 153–6, 174–6
emerging economies 177–8
emotional aspects, real estate market 23, 33, 89
empirical index analysis 97–100
EPRA *see* European Public Real Estate
Association
equities
real estate market 3–4, 5, 27, 127, 128–30,
149–64, 173, 177, 178–9, 196–7
returns 127, 128–30, 151–64, 196–7
statistics 149–50, 151–64
ETFs *see* Exchange Traded Funds
EuroHypo 37–8
European INREV indices 84–5
European Public Real Estate Association Index
(EPRA) 129–30, 137, 139, 149, 158–61
European Union
see also individual countries
IPD 59–62
property derivatives 6, 23, 31, 36, 47–9, 57
real estate statistics 3, 149–50, 157–61
European-style options
see also options
concepts 14–21, 112

excess returns 101–8, 139–40
  see also returns
Exchange Traded Funds (ETFs) 162
exchange-traded contracts
  futures trading 8, 10
  options trading 12
  property derivatives 35, 36–43, 47, 118–21
  statistics 7, 40–1
exercising the option, concepts 14, 17–18
exotic derivatives 23, 50
explanatory factors, prices 127–30
external appraisals, concepts 58–9

Fannie Mae (FNMA) 45–6, 82
FASB see Financial Accounting Standards Board
'fat tail' returns 97, 99–100
  see also kurtosis
Federal Reserve 147
feedback effects, property derivatives 49–51
Fenlon, Andrew 42
final transaction prices
  see also transaction prices
  concepts 73
finance view, real estate market 3–6
Financial Accounting Standards Board (FASB) 32
financial engineering, index-linked mortgages 200
financial risks
  see also risks
  bricks and mortar 3–6, 30, 31
Financial Services Authority (FSA) 29, 32
The Financial Times 44, 85
Finland 60, 90, 127
fixed payments, swaps 10–12, 35, 147, 162–4,
  176–81, 184–6
floating payments, swaps 10–12, 35, 147, 162–4,
  176–81, 184–6
forecasts
  downturns 91–2
  property spreads 107–8, 136–41
  returns 33–4, 51, 107–8, 136–41
forward price curves 51, 91–2, 109–11, 163–4
forward prices
  see also strike prices
  calculation 8–9, 105–6, 109–11
  concepts 8–10, 51, 105–6, 109–11, 136–41,
    163–4, 176
  dividends 9–10
  HPI 110–11, 137–9
  IPD 110–11
  property spreads 105–6, 109–15, 136–41
forwards
  compensation payments 10
  concepts 7, 8–10, 36, 37–8, 47, 91–2, 105–6,
    131, 136–41, 156, 176
  contract terms 8
  curve trades 176

definition 8
hedging 112–15
payoffs 8–9, 16, 109–11
trading 8
FOX see London Futures and Options Exchange
FOX Mortgage Interest Rate Index (MIR)
  36–7
France 35, 47–8, 59, 60, 84, 90, 128, 149–50,
  159, 178–80, 184–5
Frank Russell Company 65
fraud dangers, indexes 53–4
Freddie Mac (FHLMC) 46, 82
Frischer–Kranz delta rent model 83
FSA see Financial Services Authority
FTSE property indices 36, 42–3, 57, 63–4, 94,
  158–61
FTSE UK Commercial Property Index (FTSEpx)
  36, 42–3, 63–4, 94, 158–61, 176
  see also appraisal-based indices
  cash-and-carry arbitrage 176
  concepts 63–4, 176
FTSE100 index 50, 129–30, 149–62
fund managers 36, 173–81
  see also management issues
funded investments, concepts 36
fungibility issues 4, 8, 155–6
future prospects, property derivatives 47–51
futures
  clearing houses 10
  concepts 7, 8, 10, 33, 45–6, 112–15, 129–30,
    131, 145–6, 156, 175
  contract terms 8
  definition 8, 10
  hedging 112–15, 129–30
  margin settlement 10
  marked-to-market processes 10
  options 12, 112–15
  payoffs 10, 16, 112–15
  perpetual futures 10
  trading 8, 10

gamma
  see also delta
  concepts 19–20, 117, 133–4, 139–41, 206–7
  definition 19, 133
Geltner and Miller unsmoothing techniques 95
General Electric 12–13
geographical factors 38–42, 54
geometrical Brownian motion, concepts 14,
  114–15
Germany 35, 48, 59, 60, 63, 90, 127, 149–50,
  159, 178–80
GFI 38–9, 48, 49, 104
Global Investment Performance Standards (GIPS)
  63
Global Real Analytics (GRA) 43, 46–7, 78–9

Goldman Sachs 38–42, 44, 46, 48, 82, 118–19,
  129, 169
government bonds 16, 101–2, 129–30, 149–64,
  196–7
  see also bonds
  statistics 149–64
GRA *see* Global Real Analytics
gross domestic product (GDP) 127
Grosvenor 48–9

Halifax House Price Index (HPI) 36, 40–3, 73–5,
  98, 99, 110–11, 129–30, 137–9, 169, 171,
  187–8
  see also residential housing; transaction-based
    indices
  concepts 40–3, 73–5, 98, 99, 110–11, 129–30,
    137–9, 187–8
  construction processes 73–4
  correlated tradable assets 129–30
  distribution of returns 99
  'fat tail' returns 99
  forward prices 110–11, 137–9
  indexed building savings 187–8
  NAHP comparison 75
hedge funds 3, 5, 7–8, 25, 27, 39, 47, 49–50, 129,
  145–7, 174–5
  alpha 174–5
  costs 129
  critique 129
  property derivatives 25, 27, 145–7, 174–5
hedging
  accounting practices 24–5, 29, 30, 32–3, 184
  anticipatory hedging 169–70
  concepts 8, 14, 19, 24–5, 29, 31–2, 33–4, 37,
    49–50, 104–5, 112–15, 117, 121–5, 127–30,
    131–41, 165–72, 174–6, 200–1, 203–7
  correlated assets 131–2, 137–41, 153–5, 172,
    173, 178–9, 196–7, 201, 203–5
  definition 8, 131–2, 165
  discrete time settings 132–41
  efficiency issues 170–2
  forwards 112–15
  futures 112–15, 129–30
  home equity insurance 169, 193–201
  incomplete markets 121, 125, 131–41,
    172
  long hedges 165–6, 169–70
  optimal hedge ratios 133–41, 203–7
  property portfolio managers 167
  remaining risks 134–6
  replicability factors 30, 31–2, 105–6, 117,
    120–1, 127, 131–41
  risk transfers 140–1, 165, 193–201
  short hedges 165–9
  strategies 31–2, 104–5, 112–15, 131–41,
    165–72, 175–6

trading portfolio example 138–41
  types 165–70
  VaR 124–5, 138–41
  volume links 171
hedging assets
  concepts 132–41
  definition 132
hedging errors 31–2, 33–4, 134–6, 138–41
Hedonic models
  see also transaction-based indices
  concepts 4–5, 68–71, 73, 75, 80–1, 96–7,
    129–30
  construction processes 69–71, 73, 96–7,
    129–30
  repeat sales indices 72
heterogeneity factors
  property development hurdles 30, 31–2, 155–6,
    172
  real estate market 4, 27, 30, 31–2, 155–6,
    172
heteroskedasticity 77–8, 96
high-frequency preferences, indexes 53–4
historical background, derivatives 7, 29, 31, 32,
    33–4, 35–51
HKU-REIS *see* Hong Kong Real Estate Index
  Series
home equity insurance, concepts 169, 193–201
home suppliers, property derivatives 25, 145–7
Hong Kong 35, 48, 60, 83–4, 159
Hong Kong Real Estate Index Series
  (HKU-REIS) 83–4
hotel and convention indices categories 55–6
HPI *see* Halifax House Price Index
HSBC 39
hurdles
  cross-border investments 177–8
  property derivatives 29–34, 37, 105–6, 117,
    146–7, 149–50, 155–6, 172, 177–8

IAZI 80
ICAP 46
idiosyncratic risk 24, 54–5, 146, 162, 176–7, 191,
    200–1
IG Index 42, 119
IMMEX Index 84–5
implied volatility
  see also volatility
  concepts 17, 24–5, 113–15
in-the-money options, concepts 15–16, 18,
    198
income return (IR) performance
  IPD 61–3, 97, 150–2
  NCREIF 66–7
income tax 32–3
  see also taxes
income-only contracts 6–7

incomplete markets
    hedging 121, 125, 131–41, 172
    options pricing 112, 131–41
    trading portfolio hedging example 138–41
incremental risk, concepts 137–41
index options, concepts 14
index-linked mortgages
    collateral issues 198–201
    concepts 169, 193–201
    credit quality improvements 198
    financial engineering 200
    liquidity issues 197–8
    pricing 198–201
indexed building savings
    concepts 170, 187–91
    plan variables 190–1
indexes 4–5, 10, 11, 14–15, 23–7, 30–1, 35–51,
        53–85, 89–108, 109–15, 127–30, 149–64,
        170–1, 172, 175, 179–80, 186
    see also benchmarks; individual indexes;
        price . . .
    appraisal-based indices 5, 11, 30, 31, 35,
        36–43, 47–9, 51, 55–68, 73, 83, 93–108,
        110–11, 149–64, 170–1, 175, 179–80, 186
    appropriateness issues 172
    autocorrelation 93–6, 97–9, 112–14, 130,
        137–9
    beta 162–4, 165
    biases 72, 77, 94–8, 130, 176–7
    building savings 170, 187–91
    categories 55–6
    characteristics of underlying indices 54–7,
        109–15, 117
    concepts 4–5, 23–7, 30–1, 35–6, 42–7, 53–85,
        89–100, 109–15, 127–30, 149–64, 172
    cycles 89–97, 127–30
    decomposition 127–30
    definition 172
    distribution of returns 14–15, 97, 99–100,
        107–8, 112–13
    drivers 89–97, 127–30
    dynamics 89–100, 127–30
    economic dependencies/cycles 89–97, 127–30,
        185, 187–91, 193–201
    empirical analysis 97–100
    explanatory factors 127–30
    fraud dangers 53–4
    high-frequency preferences 53–4
    HPI 36, 40–3, 73–5, 98, 99, 110–11, 129–30,
        137–9, 169, 187–8
    idiosyncratic risk 24, 54–5, 146, 162, 176–7,
        191, 200–1
    incomplete markets 121, 125, 131–41, 172
    IPD 11, 30, 31, 36–43, 47–9, 51, 57–63, 93–6,
        101–8, 110–11, 149–64, 170–1, 175,
        179–80, 186

    options pricing 112–15
    perpetual futures 10
    publication dates 110, 115, 117, 132, 152–3
    randomness considerations 92–3
    requirements 53–4
    sample sizes 54–5, 71, 96–7, 99
    total returns 57, 61–7, 97–100, 101–8, 110–11,
        150–2, 162–4
    track records 53–4
    transaction-based indices 35, 37, 40–3, 55–6,
        68–85, 96–100, 129–30, 180–1, 187–91
    types 5, 35–6, 55–6, 150, 180–1
    variances 54–5
    volatility 93–100, 102, 152, 160–1, 201
    weightings 57
indirect investments
    concepts 5, 26, 29, 156–64, 177
    critique 156–61, 177
    discounts 5, 26, 157
    interest rates 29, 161
    NAV 5, 26, 63–4, 108, 136–7, 157, 161, 173
    premiums 5, 26, 157
    statistics 156–61
    types 156–61
inefficient markets 21, 26, 99, 153–6, 174–6
inflation
    derivatives 117, 131–2
    house prices 188–9
initial amount, indexed building savings 190–1
INREEX see International Real Estate Exchange
INSEE Index 84
institutional investors 5, 25–6, 36–43, 44–5, 53–4,
        62, 145–7, 150–1, 162
    see also insurance companies; pension funds
    property derivatives 25–6, 36–43, 44–5, 145–7,
        162
insurance
    home equity insurance 169, 193–201
    risk transfers 140–1, 165–6, 193–201
insurance companies 32, 38, 145–9, 185–6
interest rate swaps 11, 34
    see also swaps
    historical background 34
interest rates 11, 14, 16, 19, 29, 35–6, 37, 43–4,
        49, 59, 81, 101–5, 127–30, 137, 147, 161,
        167, 175, 179, 184–6, 187–91
    see also mortgage . . . ; rho
    indirect investments 29, 161
    LIBOR 11, 35, 37, 43–4, 49, 81, 101–5, 147,
        167, 175, 179, 184–6
    property derivatives 19, 35–6
    property prices 127–30
    risk-free interest rates 14, 16, 101–2, 109–10,
        138–9
intermediaries, market development 118–25
internal appraisals, concepts 58–9

internal rates of return 67
international investments *see* cross-border
    investments
International Real Estate Exchange (INREEX)
    45–6
International Securities Exchange (ISE) 47,
    118–19
International Swaps and Derivatives Association
    (ISDA) 36
International Valuation Standards Committee
    (IVSC) 58
intrinsic risk
    concepts 136–41
    definition 136
    prices 137–8
intrinsic value, options pricing 17–18
investable real estate, definition 149
investment banks 29–30, 38–43
investment committees 29–30
Investment Property Databank (IPD)
    see also appraisal-based indices; commercial
        real estate
    CG performance 61–3, 150–2
    concepts 11, 30, 31, 36–43, 47–9, 51,
        57–63, 93–6, 97–100, 101–8,
        110–11, 149–64, 170–1, 175, 179–80,
        186
    construction processes 62–3, 93–6
    countries benchmarked 59–63
    distribution of returns 100
    forward prices 110–11
    historical background 30–1, 36–43, 59–60
    index types 59–63
    investment banks 38–43
    IR performance 61–3, 97, 150–2
    Pan-European index 63
    performance measures 61–3, 150–2
    quality issues 59–60
    reporting requirements 40
    sector diversification 180
    TR performance 61–3, 97–100, 101–8, 110–11,
        150–2, 179–80
    unsmoothing methods 95–6
Investment Property Forum (IPF) 25, 29, 33–4,
    38, 107–8, 183
investor types 39–40, 145–7, 149–64
IPD *see* Investment Property Databank
IPF *see* Investment Property Forum
IR *see* income return ...
Ireland 60, 90, 127
ISDA *see* International Swaps and Derivatives
    Association
ISE *see* International Securities Exchange
Italy 35, 48, 60, 90, 159
IVSC *see* International Valuation Standards
    Committee

J-REITS 48, 61, 108, 159
Japan 7, 30, 35, 48–9, 60–2, 90–1, 108, 159
    historical derivatives 7, 30
    J-REITS 48, 61, 108, 159
    real estate bubbles 90–1
Jones Lang LaSalle 177
JP Morgan 39, 197
jumps, diffusion processes 114–15

kurtosis
    see also 'fat tail' returns
    concepts 99–100

Lagrange multiplier 205–7
Land Registry 73, 84–5
Laspeyres Index family 70
Lehman Brothers 44, 46
leverage issues 12, 21, 24–5, 108, 156–64, 183–4,
    194–6
LIBOR *see* London Interbank Offered Rate
limited access to investments, real estate market
    5–6
linear claims category of derivatives
    see also forwards; futures; swaps
    concepts 7–8
liquidity 3, 10, 23–5, 27, 29, 30–1, 33–4, 47,
        50–1, 93, 105–6, 117–21, 129, 146, 149–50,
        156–64, 172, 177
    determinants 23, 30–1, 33–4, 50, 93, 105–6,
        155–6, 172, 177
    index-linked mortgages 197–8
    market development 117–25, 149–50,
        156
    market frictions 105–6, 112–13
listed real estate vehicles 146, 159–61, 177
    see also real estate ...
loan-to-value ratios (LTV) 128, 188, 194–8
log-linear models 70–1
London Futures and Options Exchange (FOX) 34,
        36–7, 45, 75
London Interbank Offered Rate (LIBOR) 11, 35,
        37, 43–4, 49, 81, 101–5, 147, 167, 175, 179,
        184–6
long hedges
    see also hedging
    concepts 165–6, 169–70
long positions
    concepts 8, 13–14, 37, 104–5, 109–11, 145–7,
        163–4, 175–6
    definition 8
LTV *see* loan-to-value ratios

management issues
    ALM 145–7, 184–6
    arbitrage 7, 8–9, 14–21, 30, 93, 101–7, 109–10,
        175–6

country swaps 176–81
mismanagement risks 5
portfolios 27, 167, 173–81
sector swaps 38–42, 54, 171, 179–81
margin settlement, futures 10
marked-to-market processes, futures 10
market clearing prices 119
market development 117–25, 149–64
  liquidity 117–25, 149–50, 156
  stages 118–20
  subsidies 120–1
market expectations, role 106–7,
  110–15
market frictions, arbitrage 105–6,
  112–13
market information 21, 24–5
market making strategies 119–20
market risk 23, 117–25, 177
  see also risks
Markowitz-efficient allocation 26, 99,
  153–6
Marks & Spencer 181
martingales 132
mature-stage market development 117–21
maturity dates
  Black–Scholes option pricing formula 14–18,
    112–15
  options 12–21
maximum likelihood methods 80
mean reversion 110
mean-variance 95, 99–100, 197–8
Merrill Lynch 38–42, 44, 46–8, 50, 104, 107–8,
  129
Merton's extension, Black–Scholes option pricing
  formula 115
metropolitan statistical areas (MSAs) 76–80,
  82
minimal martingale measure 132
mismanagement risks 5
MIT Center for Real Estate 85
mix-adjusted method, transaction-based indices
  68–9, 75, 84–5
modified Dietz formula 67
Monte Carlo simulations 109
Moody's/REAL Commercial Property Price
  indices 85
moral hazard 165
Morgan Stanley 39, 43, 44, 46
mortgage agreed prices
  see also transaction prices
  concepts 73
mortgage completion prices
  see also transaction prices
  concepts 73
mortgage-backed securities (MBSs) 129–30,
  156–61, 168

mortgages
  index-linked mortgages 169, 193–201
  property derivatives 25, 145–7, 165, 168, 169,
    193–201
  property prices 127–9
  rates 3, 127–8
  repayment penalties 128
  US subprime mortgage crisis 38, 43, 168
moving averages 58, 94
MSAs see metropolitan statistical areas
MSCI 197
MSS Capital 42, 63

NAHP see Nationwide Anglia House
  Price Index
NAR see National Association of Realtors
National Association of Realtors (NAR) 45, 82
  concepts 82
National Council of Real Estate Investment
  Fiduciaries Index (NCREIF) 36, 43–4, 57,
    64–7, 85, 94, 98, 150, 181
  see also appraisal-based indices
  breakdown 65–6
  concepts 64–7, 85, 94, 98, 150, 181
  construction processes 66–7
  historical background 65, 150
  requirements 66
Nationwide Anglia House Price Index (NAHP)
  concepts 36–7, 74–5
  HPI comparison 75
NAV see net asset values
NCREIF see National Council of Real Estate
  Investment Fiduciaries Index
net asset values (NAVs) 5, 26, 63–4, 108, 136–7,
  157, 161, 173
net operating income (NOI) 66–7
net yields 18
  see also yield
Netherlands 59, 60, 90, 128, 159
New York Cotton Exchange 7
New York Real Estate Securities Exchange
  (NYRESE) 43
New York Stock Exchange (NYSE) 50
New Zealand 60, 90
NOI see net operating income
non-synchronous appraisals, appraisal-based
  indices 94
noninvestable real estate, definition 149
nonlinear claims category of derivatives
  see also options
  concepts 7–8
normal probability distributions 14–15, 97,
  99–100, 112–13
Norway 60, 90
NPI see National Council of Real Estate
  Investment Fiduciaries Index

NYRESE *see* New York Real Estate Securities
Exchange
NYSE *see* New York Stock Exchange

OECD *see* Organization for Economic
Cooperation and Development
Office of Federal Housing Enterprise Oversight
Index (OFHEO) 36, 45–6, 82
concepts 82
office sector 55–6, 180–1, 184–6
OFHEO *see* Office of Federal Housing Enterprise
Oversight Index
oil derivatives 40, 106, 110
OLS *see* ordinary least squares
open market value (OVM) 58–9
optimal hedge ratios, concepts 133–41, 203–7
optimal portfolio allocation 26, 153–6, 195–6
options
    see also American . . . ; call . . . ; European . . . ;
      put . . .
    barrier options 50
    benefits 12–13, 21, 156–64, 193–201
    buyers/sellers 12–13
    concepts 7, 8, 12–21, 37–8, 46–7, 96, 112–15,
      156, 206–7
    contract elements 12
    critique 21
    definition 12
    exercising the option 14, 17–18
    futures 12, 112–15
    leverage benefits 12, 21, 24–5, 108, 156–64,
      183
    maturity dates 12–21
    payoffs 13–14, 16–21, 198–9
    premiums 7, 12–21, 195–201
    risks 12, 21
    strategies 12–14
    strike prices 12, 14–21, 138–9
    trading 12
    types 12–14, 37–8, 50
    underlying assets 12, 14–21, 23, 37–8, 46–7
options pricing 7, 14–21, 37–8, 99, 106–8, 109,
    112–15, 131–41, 195–201
    see also Black–Scholes option pricing formula
    call options 14–21, 113–15, 133–4
    concepts 7, 14–21, 37–8, 99, 106–8, 112–15,
      131–41
    delta 19–20, 138–9, 206–7
    gamma 19–20, 133–4, 139–41, 206–7
    incomplete markets 112, 131–41
    intrinsic value 17–18
    property indices 112–15
    put options 15–21, 133–4, 138–41, 195–201
    rho 19
    sensitivities 19–20
    vega 19

ordinary least squares (OLS) 81, 129–30
Organization for Economic Cooperation and
Development (OECD) 90, 128
OTC *see* over-the-counter contracts
out-of-the-money options, concepts 15–17, 198
over-the-counter contracts (OTC)
    concepts 7–8, 11, 26–7, 35–6, 40, 46–7, 107,
      119, 171
    forwards trading 8
    property derivatives 35–6, 40, 46–7, 107, 119,
      171
    statistics 7
    swaps trading 11, 35–6
overseas demand, UK 39
OVM *see* open market value
owner-occupiers, short hedges 169

Paasche Index family 70
Pacific Stock Exchange (PSE) 50
Pakistan 159
Pan-European index, IPD 63
Pareto improvements 194
partnerships 156
passive property exposure, concepts 162–3
past-time weighting *see* Laspeyres Index family
payoffs
    forwards 8–9, 16, 109–11
    futures 10, 16, 112–15
    options 13–14, 16–21, 198–9
    swaps 11–12
PDIG *see* Property Derivatives Interest Group
peaks, real estate market 90–2, 128–9, 187–91,
    193–201
pension funds 5, 36–7, 38, 47, 145–7, 149–50,
    157–8, 178
perceptions, real estate market 3, 5–6, 89–90,
    155–6
performance measures
    comparisons 149–64, 173, 177, 178–80, 196–7
    IPD 61–3, 150–2
periodic saving amount, indexed building savings
    190–1
permanent disadvantages, property derivatives 25
perpetual bonds 10
perpetual futures
    see also futures
    concepts 10
Philadelphia Stock Exchange (PHLX) 50, 158
PHLX *see* Philadelphia Stock Exchange
physical underlying assets, concepts 9–10, 51, 93,
    105–6, 117
PICs *see* Property Index Certificates
PIFs *see* Property Index Forwards
plain vanilla options
    see also options
    concepts 14

population effects, property prices 127
portfolios 5–6, 7–8, 14–21, 24–7, 29, 30–4, 54,
    94, 95–6, 121–5, 137–41, 145–7, 149–64,
    173–81, 195–6
  alpha 174–81
  cash-and-carry arbitrage 104–5, 175–6
  country swaps 176–81
  cross-border investments 173–4, 176–81
  diversification benefits 5–6, 24–7, 29, 33, 54,
    145–7, 149–56, 162–4, 173–81
  management issues 27, 167, 173–81
  Markowitz-efficient allocation 26, 99, 153–6
  optimal portfolio allocation 26, 153–6,
    195–6
  property derivatives 25, 30–4, 137–41, 146–7,
    167, 173–81
  real estate assets 149–64, 173–81
  rent or buy decisions 194–7
  sector swaps 38–42, 54, 171, 179–81
  strategic asset allocations 174
  tactical asset allocations 174–81
  trading portfolio hedging example 138–41
  unsmoothing factors 95–6, 152–6
  VaR 123–4, 138–41
Portugal 60
power laws 80
premiums 5, 7, 12–21, 26, 50, 106–8, 137–8, 157,
    195–201
  see also options pricing
  indirect investments 5, 26, 157
  intrinsic risk 137–8
  options 7, 12–21, 195–201
present-time weighting see Paasche Index family
price bands, arbitrage 106–7, 176
price return swaps 44–7
price-to-income ratios, real estate market 89
price-to-rent ratios 90
prices 71–3, 89–100, 106–8, 114–15, 127–30,
    187–91, 193–201
  see also indexes
  Brownian motion 14, 113, 114–15
  bubbles 90–2, 187–91, 193–201
  downturns 90–4, 128, 183, 185, 189–91,
    193–201
  drivers 89–97, 127–30
  economic dependencies/cycles 89–97, 127–30,
    183, 185, 187–91, 193–201
  elasticities of demand 89
  explanatory factors 127–30
  index-linked mortgages 169, 193–201
  interest rates 127–30
  jumps in the diffusion process 114–15
  peaks 90–2, 128–9, 187–91, 193–201
  sticky prices 94, 108
  transaction prices 71–3
prices of options see options pricing; premiums

pricing
  see also options . . .
  incomplete markets 131–2, 136–41
  index-linked mortgages 198–201
  property derivatives 21, 106–7, 109–15, 127,
    131–2, 136–41
private equity 3, 39, 53–4, 156–61, 177
private housing market 145, 146–7
professional investors 5, 25–6, 36–43, 44–5,
    53–4, 62, 145–7
profitability
  see also returns
  property derivatives 121
property derivatives
  see also derivatives; real estate market
  acquisition finance benefits 186
  additional pricing variables 106–7
  ALM 184–6
  alpha 24–5, 162–4, 174–81, 184
  applications 26–7, 106–8, 145–7, 162–4,
    165–72, 183–6
  appraisal practices impacts 51
  benefits 5–6, 19, 23–7, 49–51, 106, 145–7, 153,
    156–64, 173–4, 183–4, 186, 193–201
  Black–Scholes option pricing formula 21, 109,
    112–15
  building savings 170, 187–91
  buyers/sellers 25, 35–9, 92–3, 145–7, 162–4
  cash-and-carry arbitrage 104–5, 175–6
  challenges 29–34
  concepts 3–6, 10, 19, 21, 23–7, 29–34, 35–51,
    92–3, 101–8, 112–15, 117–25, 145–7, 153,
    156, 162–4, 173–81
  corporates 25, 27, 146–7, 167–8, 183–6
  critique 3–6, 10, 19, 21, 23–7, 29–34, 106–8,
    145–7, 156, 162–4
  cross-border investments 173–4, 176–81
  definition 5
  disadvantages 23–5, 29–34, 156, 184
  documentation 36, 162–3
  economic significance 3–4
  European Union 6, 23, 31, 36, 47–9, 57
  exchange-traded contracts 35, 36–43, 47,
    118–21
  experiences 7, 29, 31, 32, 33–4, 35–51
  feedback effects 49–51
  FOX debut 34, 36–7, 45, 75
  future prospects 47–51
  home equity insurance 169, 193–201
  hurdles 29–34, 37, 45, 105–6, 117, 146–7,
    149–50, 155–6, 172, 177–8
  incomplete markets 121, 125, 131–41, 172
  index-linked mortgages 169, 193–201
  indexed building savings 170, 187–91
  institutional investors 25–6, 36–43, 44–5,
    145–7, 162

property derivatives (*Continued*)
  interest rates 19, 35–6
  market development 117–25, 162–4
  market expectations 106–7, 110–15
  mortgage lenders 25, 145–7, 165, 168
  mortgages 25, 145–7, 165, 168, 169, 193–201
  needs 5–6, 92–3, 117, 165
  OTC 35–6, 40, 46–7, 107, 119, 171
  permanent disadvantages 25
  portfolios 25, 30–4, 137–41, 146–7, 167,
    173–81
  pricing 21, 106–7, 109–15, 127, 131–2, 136–41
  profitability 121
  property developers 25, 145, 165–6, 167–8
  property spreads 106–8, 109–15, 136–41,
    162–4, 178–81, 186
  rationales 23–7, 145–7
  risk premium impacts 50
  sensitivities 19
  settlement 10
  standardization issues 4–5, 8, 30, 31–2,
    36, 172
  statistics 40–7, 101–8, 163–4
  structures 35–6, 43
  synthetic corporate building sales 183–6
  tactical asset allocations 174–81
  temporary disadvantages 25
  types 25–6, 35–47, 147, 156, 162–4
  UK 23, 25, 29, 31, 32, 33–4, 35, 36–43, 50–1,
    91–2, 163–4
  US 32, 35, 36, 43–7
  uses 25, 26–7, 35–9, 106–8, 145–7, 162–4,
    165–70, 183–6
  VaR 124–5, 138–41
  volatility 19, 24–6, 49–51, 113–15
  volumes and activity 40, 51, 166, 171–2
Property Derivatives Interest Group (PDIG) 25,
  37–8
property developers 25, 145, 165–6, 167–8
Property Index Certificates (PICs) 33, 37
  see also bonds
Property Index Derivatives Definitions 36
Property Index Forwards (PIFs) 37
property indices 4–5, 23–7, 30–1, 35–6, 42–7,
  112–15, 172
  see also indexes
property notes 163
property portfolio managers, hedging 167
property securitization *see* securitization
property spreads
  concepts 101–8, 109–15, 136–41, 162–4,
    178–81, 186
  definition 101
  estimates 107–8, 136–41
  forward prices 105–6, 109–15, 136–41
  market expectations 106–7, 110–15

market frictions and arbitrage 105–6, 112–13
  term structure 103–5, 110–11
property total return swaps (PTRS) 35, 43–7,
  101–8, 110–11, 147, 162–4
property type swaps 44–7
property value-at-risk (PVaR), concepts 122–5
property-linked notes 183–6
Prudential 37
PSE *see* Pacific Stock Exchange
psychological factors, housing cycles 89–90, 94
PTRS *see* property total return swaps
public exchanges, risk management strategies
  118–21
publication dates, indexes 110, 115, 117, 132,
  152–3
purchasing power, real estate market 150–1
put options
  see also options
  concepts 12–21, 133–4, 138–41, 195–201
  definition 13
  home equity insurance 195–201
  payoff types 13–14, 198–9
  pricing 15–21, 138–41, 195–201
put warrants 42, 169
PVaR *see* property value-at-risk

Radar Logic's Residential Property Index (RPX)
  36, 46, 79–80, 85
random walks 112
randomness considerations, indexes 92–3
Real Capital Analytics (RCA) 85
real estate certificates 156–61
real estate companies 5, 156–61
real estate funds 156–61
real estate index futures 3–4
Real Estate Investment Trusts (REITs) 5, 29,
  46–7, 48–9, 61, 63–4, 65, 94, 108, 129–30,
  136, 149–50, 156–61, 179
  booming demand 156–7, 158–9
  concepts 156–9, 179
  countries 159, 179
  definition 156
  historical background 158–9
  sector diversification 179
real estate market
  see also indexes; property derivatives
  benefits 5–6, 19, 23–7, 49–51, 106, 145–7,
    149–64
  boring perceptions 5, 155–6
  bubbles 90–2, 187–91, 193–201
  characteristics 4–5, 109–15, 117
  concepts 3–6, 23–7, 29–34, 89–100, 127–30,
    149–64
  corporates 25, 27, 146–7, 167–8, 183–6
  cycles 89–97, 127–30
  demand/supply factors 89–90

diversification benefits 5–6, 24–7, 29, 33, 54,
    145–7, 149–56, 162–4, 173–81
downturns 90–4, 128, 183, 185, 189–91,
    193–201
economic dependencies/cycles 89–97, 127–30,
    183, 185, 187–91, 193–201
emotional aspects 23, 33, 89
equities 3–4, 5, 27, 127, 128–30, 149–64, 173,
    177, 178–9, 196–7
explanatory factors 127–30
finance view 3–6
forecasts 33–4, 51
heterogeneity factors 4, 27, 30, 31–2, 155–6,
    172
indirect investments 5, 26, 29, 156–64, 177
investable/noninvestable contrasts 149
investment universe overview 156
limited access to investments 5–6
liquidity issues 3, 23–5, 27, 29, 30–1, 33–4, 47,
    50–1, 93, 105–6, 117–21, 129, 146, 149–50,
    172, 177
market development 117–25, 149–64
peaks 90–2, 128–9, 187–91, 193–201
perceptions 3, 5–6, 89–90, 155–6
price-to-income ratios 89
property spreads 101–8, 109–11, 136–41,
    162–4, 178–81, 186
purchasing power 150–1
rent or buy decisions 194–7
round-trip costs 23–4, 105–6
short positions 5, 37, 104–5, 109–11, 145–7,
    163–4, 175–6
standardization needs 4–5, 30, 31–2, 36, 66,
    69–70, 155–6, 172
statistics 3–4, 33–4, 38–9, 42–3, 97–108,
    149–64, 183, 200–1
suitable investments 25–6
tactical asset allocations 174–81
turnover statistics 3–4
valuations 4–5, 51, 55–6, 58–9, 66, 93–6,
    128–9, 152
real estate private equity 3, 39, 53–4, 156–61, 177
recourse mortgages 194–201
'Red Book' 57
regression analysis 4–5, 81, 129–30, 136–7
regulations 26, 30, 32–3, 37, 73, 122, 138
    see also taxes
    background 30, 32–3, 37, 73
    capital adequacy requirements 122, 138,
        140–1, 168
    hurdles 30, 32–3, 37, 177–8
    rents 73
Reid, Ian 37
REITs see Real Estate Investment Trusts
rent or buy decisions 194–7
rent guarantee contracts 167

rental swaps 27
rental value growth forecasts 33–4, 51
rents 10, 27, 33–4, 51, 55–6, 58–9, 61–3, 73, 83,
    90, 128, 150–2, 167, 185, 194–7
    categories, residential apartment renters 55–6
    DCF 58–9
    economic dependencies/cycles 128, 185
    empirical index analysis 97–9
    IPD performance 61–3, 150–2
    perpetual futures 10
    price-to-rent ratios 90
    regulations 73
    transaction-based indices 73, 83
repeat sales indices
    see also transaction-based indices
    concepts 68, 71–2, 76–8, 82, 85, 97
    construction processes 71–2, 97
    Hedonic models 72
    S&P/Case–Shiller Index 36, 45–6, 76–80, 97
replacement costs 58
replicability factors
    see also hedging
    definition 131–2
    property development hurdles 30, 31–2, 105–6,
        117, 120–1, 127, 131–41
residential apartment renters, indices categories
    55–6
residential housing 25, 33–4, 37, 40–3, 44–9,
    53–4, 55–6, 68–85, 97–100, 128, 145–7,
    149–64, 169, 170, 179–81, 187–91
    see also transaction-based indices
    building savings 25, 146, 170, 187–91
    economic dependencies/cycles 128, 187–91,
        193–201
    emotional aspects 23, 33, 89
    home equity insurance 169, 193–201
    property derivatives 25, 33–4, 37, 40–3, 44–9,
        53–4, 145–7, 179–81, 187–91
    statistics 44–7, 54, 147, 149, 200–1
    US 44–7, 54, 147, 149, 179
retail investors, property derivatives 25, 145–7
retail sector
    concepts 55–6, 180–1, 183
    sector diversification 180–1
returns
    autocorrelation 58, 71, 92–3, 112–14, 130,
        137–9
    comparisons 149–64, 173, 177, 178–80, 196–7
    distributions 14–15, 97, 99–100, 107–8,
        112–13, 123–4
    excess returns 101–8, 139–40
    'fat tail' returns 97, 99–100
    forecasts 33–4, 51, 107–8, 136–41
    FTSE100 index 50, 129–30, 149–62
    FTSEpx 36, 42–3, 63–4, 94, 158–61, 176
    IPD 61–3, 97–100, 101–8, 110–11, 150–2

returns (*Continued*)
  kurtosis 99–100
  NCREIF 64–7, 98, 181
  property spreads 101–8, 109–11, 136–41,
    162–4, 178–81, 186
  risk-free returns 101–2, 109–10
  risks 3, 5–6, 7, 101–2, 109–10, 121, 146–7,
    150–64, 197–8
  total rate of return swaps 44–7, 147, 162–4
Rexx Index LLC 47, 83, 118
rho, definition 19
RICS *see* Royal Institution of Chartered
    Surveyors
Rightmove 85
risk aversion 15, 89–90
risk management 3–4, 7–8, 43–4, 50, 115,
    117–25, 145–7, 149–64, 193–201
  CaR 122–5
  concepts 3–4, 7–8, 43–4, 50, 115, 117–25,
    145–7, 149–64, 193–201
  market development 117–25
  PVaR 122–5
  strategies 118–25, 145–7, 149–64, 183–6,
    193–201
  VaR 121–5, 138–41
risk premiums, property derivatives
    impacts 50
risk transfers, methods 140, 165, 193–201
risk-free arbitrage 9
risk-free interest rates 14, 16, 101–2, 109–10,
    138–9
risk-free returns 101–2, 109–10
risks
  see also hedging
  attitudes 15, 89–90
  basis risk 170–2, 175, 184, 191
  bricks and mortar 3–6, 30, 31
  CaR 122–5
  concepts 3–4, 5–6, 7–8, 43–4, 50, 115, 117–25,
    145–7, 149–64, 193–201
  counterparty risk 11–12, 101, 118–19, 147
  credit risk 122, 198–201
  idiosyncratic risk 24, 54–5, 146, 162, 176–7,
    191, 200–1
  incremental risk 137–41
  intrinsic risk 136–41
  market risk 23, 117–25, 177
  measurement 115, 117–25
  options 12, 21
  PVaR 122–5
  reduction methods 125, 154–6
  returns 3, 5–6, 7, 101–2, 109–10, 121, 146–7,
    150–64, 197–8
  systematic risk 50, 165, 167
  tail risk 125, 141
  transfer methods 140, 165, 193–201

  VaR 121–5, 138–41
  volatility 121–2
round-trip costs 23–4, 105–6
Royal Bank of Scotland (RBS) 38–42, 48–9
Royal Institution of Chartered Surveyors (RICS)
    51, 57, 59
RP Data–Rismark Index, concepts 84
RPX *see* Radar Logic's Residential Property
    Index

S&P/Case–Shiller Index, concepts 36, 45–6,
    76–80, 97–8, 168
S&P/GRA Commercial Real Estate Indices
    (CREX)
  concepts 46–7, 78–9, 85, 97
  construction processes 79
  underlying assets 97
SafeSide Ltd example 184–6
sale and lease-back transactions 183
sales pairs, repeat sales indices 71–2, 76–8,
    82, 97
sample sizes, indexes 54–5, 71, 96–7, 99
Santander Global Banking & Markets 42–3
savings, building savings 25, 146, 170, 187–91
SEC 43
secondary markets 24–5, 117
sector swaps 38–42, 54, 171, 179–81
  see also swaps
Securities and Exchange Commission (SEC)
    122
securitization 3, 129
  see also mortgage-backed securities
sellers/buyers, property derivatives 25, 35–9,
    92–3, 145–7, 162–4
sensitivities, options prices 19–20
shape-fitting method, transaction-based indices
    68–9, 80
short hedges
  see also hedging
  concepts 165–9
short positions
  concepts 8, 13–14, 37, 104–5, 109–11, 145–7,
    163–4, 165–9, 175–6
  definition 8
  real estate market 5, 37, 104–5, 109–11, 145–7,
    163–4, 175–6
signal-to-noise ratios 95
Singapore 49, 60, 85, 159
smoothing problems, appraisal-based indices
    93–9, 152–6
soft arbitrage price bands 176
'Sourcebook COLL' collective investment
    scheme 33
South Africa 60, 159
South Korea 60, 62, 159
Spain 60, 90, 127, 159

speculation 8, 33, 46–7, 49–50, 90, 145–7, 165–7, 175
  concepts 8, 49–50, 90, 165–7, 175
  definition 8
spreads *see* property spreads
stamp duties 32, 158
standardization issues
  concepts 4–5, 8, 30, 31–2, 36, 66, 69–70, 155–6, 172
  real estate market 4–5, 30, 31–2, 36, 66, 69–70, 155–6, 172
sticky prices 94, 108
stochastic behaviour, volatility 50
stock 3–4, 5, 27, 127, 128–30, 149–64, 173, 177, 178–9, 196–7
  see also equities
strategic asset allocations, concepts 174
strategies
  auctions 118–21
  back-to-back matching 118–21
  hedging 31–2, 104–5, 112–15, 131–41, 165–72, 175–6
  incomplete markets 131–41
  options 12–14
  public exchanges 118–21
  risk management 118–25, 145–7, 149–64, 183–6, 193–201
  warehousing 119–20, 138
strike prices
  see also forward prices
  Black–Scholes option pricing formula 14–16, 112–15
  forwards concepts 8–10
  options 12, 14–21, 138–9
strips 40
structured products 156, 163
structures, property derivatives 35–6, 43
Student's *t*-distribution 100
submarkets 53–4
subsidies, market development 120–1
Sun Hung Kai Financial 48
supply factors, real estate market 89–90
Survey of Independent Forecasts 33–4
swaps 7, 8, 10–12, 26–7, 34, 35–6, 37–47, 91–2, 112, 147, 156, 162–4, 166–7, 176–81, 184–6
  arrangements 10–11, 26–7, 35–6, 147
  concepts 7, 8, 10–12, 26–7, 34, 35–8, 147
  corporate applications 184–6
  counterparties 11–12, 35, 37–8, 147
  country swaps 176–81
  curve trades 176
  definition 8, 10–11
  fixed/floating payments 10–11, 35, 147
  historical background 34
  payoffs 11–12
  PTRS 35–6, 43–7, 101–8, 110–11, 147

sector swaps 38–9, 54, 171, 179–81
statistics 40–1, 91–2, 101–8
total returns 26–7, 91–2, 101–2, 147, 162–4
trading 11, 26, 35–6, 40–1
types 11, 35–6, 37, 38, 43–7, 147
Sweden 60, 90, 128, 200–1
Switzerland 35, 49, 60, 80–1, 90, 195–201
synthetic corporate building sales, concepts 183–6
systematic risk 50, 165, 167
  see also risks

tactical asset allocations, concepts 174–81
tail risk 125, 141
Taiwan 159
targeted saving amount, indexed building savings 190–1
taxes 5, 24–5, 29, 30, 32–3, 37, 105, 131, 156–8, 163, 177–8, 184
  see also regulations
  background 32–3, 37, 131
  building savings 187
  cross-border investments 177–8
  hurdles 30, 32–3, 37, 105, 163, 177–8
  types 32–3
  UK 32–3, 37
Taylor expansion 207
templates 36
temporary disadvantages, property derivatives 25
term structure of property spreads 103–5, 110–11
Tesco 181
TFS *see* Traditional Financial Services
Thailand 159
time basis risk 170
time horizons, indexed building savings 190–1
time to maturity
  Black–Scholes option pricing formula 14–18, 112–15
  concepts 17–18
Toernqvist Index method 71
total rate of return swaps 44–7, 147, 162–4
total returns
  indexes 57, 61–7, 97–100, 101–8, 110–11, 150–2
  swaps 26–7, 91–2, 101–2, 147, 162–4
total returns (TR) index
  IPD 61–3, 97–100, 101–8, 110–11, 150–2, 179–80
  NCREIF 66–7, 98, 181
track records, indexes 53–4
trading portfolio hedging example, incomplete markets 138–41
Traditional Financial Services (TFS) 39, 40, 85, 104
transaction costs 5, 21, 23–4, 26–7, 90–4, 104–6, 128, 131, 145–7, 163

transaction prices
  concepts 71–85
  definition 72–3
transaction values 4–5
transaction-based indices 35, 37, 40–3, 55–6,
    68–85, 96–100, 129–30, 180–1, 187–91
  see also residential housing
ABS HPI 84
autocorrelation 96, 97–9, 137–9
base aggregate approaches 79
building savings 170, 187–91
challenges 68–9
CMHPI 82
concepts 55–6, 68–85, 96–100, 102, 129–30,
    160–1, 180–1, 187–91
critique 68–9, 96–100
dynamics 96–7
Hedonic indices 4–5, 68–71, 73, 75, 80–1,
    96–7, 129–30
HKU-REIS 83–4
HPI 36, 40–3, 73–5, 98, 99, 110–11, 129–30,
    137–9, 169, 187–8
mix-adjusted method 68–9, 75, 84–5
NAHP 36–7, 74–5
NAR 82
OFHEO 82
rental indices 73, 83
repeat sales indices 68, 71–2, 76–8, 82, 85, 97
Rexx Index LLC 47, 83, 118
RP Data–Rismark Index 84
RPX 36, 46, 79–80
S&P/Case–Shiller Index 36, 45–6, 76–80,
    97–8, 168
S&P/GRA Commercial Real Estate Indices
    46–7, 78–9, 85, 97
shape-fitting method 68–9, 80
volatility 96–9, 102, 160–1
ZWEX 49, 80–1, 96–9, 197
transparency issues
  concepts 24–5, 27, 30–1, 49, 53–4, 146, 150,
    155–6, 173, 177–8
  cross-border investments 177–8
Treasury Bills 16, 101–2, 129–30, 153
trustees 29–30
tulips, historical derivatives 7
turnover statistics 3–4

UBS 149–50
UK 7, 23–5, 29, 31, 32, 33–4, 35, 36–43, 50–1,
    54, 58–64, 66, 84–5, 90–2, 107–8, 127–8,
    149–52, 157–61, 163–4, 178, 180, 187–91
  see also FTSE . . .
  commercial property statistics 38–9, 50–1,
    97–108, 149–52
  cross-border investments 178–80
  downturn predictions 91–2

EPRA 129–30, 137, 139, 149, 158–61
  experiences 34, 36–43, 45
  FOX 34, 36–7, 45, 75
  historical derivatives 7, 29, 31, 32, 33–4, 35,
    36–43
  HPI 36, 40–3, 73–5, 98, 110–11, 129–30,
    137–9, 169, 187–8
  IPD 11, 30, 31, 36–43, 51, 57–63, 97–100,
    101–8, 175, 179–80, 186
  IPF 25, 29, 33–4, 38, 107–8, 183
  mortgage rates 127–8
  overseas demand 39
  property derivatives 23, 25, 29, 31, 32, 33–4,
    35, 36–43, 50–1, 91–2, 163–4
  property market crash (1990-1992) 101
  sector diversification 180
  statistics 38–43, 50, 97–108, 149–52, 157–61,
    163–4
  taxes 32–3, 37
  valuation practices 66
  volumes and activity 40
underlying assets
  see also delta; indexes; volatility
  Black–Scholes option pricing formula 14–18,
    112–15
  Brownian motion 14, 113, 114–15
  characteristics of indices 54–7, 109–15, 117
  concepts 7–10, 12–21, 23, 35, 36–51, 53–85,
    101–8, 109–15
  correlated assets 131–2, 137–41, 153–5,
    159–61, 172, 173, 178–9, 196–7, 201, 203–5
  cross-border investments 173–4, 176–81
  exercising the option 14, 17–18
  incomplete markets 121, 125, 131–41, 172
  market risk 23, 117–25, 177
  options 12, 14–21, 23, 37–8, 46–7, 206–7
  property derivatives feedback effects 49–51
  requirements 23
  S&P/GRA Commercial Real Estate Indices 97
  sample sizes 54–5
  types 7–8, 9–10, 12, 21, 23, 35, 36–51, 109–15
unit trusts 31
unsecured loans 198–201
unsmoothing factors, portfolios 95–9, 152–6
US 3, 32, 35, 36, 38, 43–7, 54, 58–9, 66, 76–8,
    81–5, 90, 128, 149, 157–61, 181
  experiences 43–7
  NCREIF 36, 43–4, 57, 64–7, 85, 94, 98, 150,
    181
  property derivatives 32, 35, 36, 43–7
  real estate statistics 3, 43–7, 97–100, 149,
    157–61
  residential housing 44–7, 54, 147, 149, 179
  S&P/Case–Shiller Index 36, 45–6, 76–80,
    97–8, 168
  sector diversification 181

statistics 3, 43–7, 97–100, 149, 157–61
subprime mortgage crisis 38, 43, 168
valuation practices 66
uses, property derivatives 25, 26–7, 35–9, 106–8,
    145–7, 162–4, 165–70, 183–6

valuations
    problems 58–9, 93–6, 152
    real estate market 4–5, 51, 55–6, 58–9, 66,
        93–6, 128–9, 152
value-at-risk (VaR)
    concepts 121–5, 138–41
    critique 122
    definition 122, 123–5
    formula 123–4
    hedge horizons 124–5, 138–41
    historical background 122
    merits 122–3
    portfolios 123–4, 138–41
    property derivatives 124–5
    reduction methods 125
variance 54–5, 132, 172, 206
variance–covariance block matrix 206
variance-optimal martingale measure 132
vega, definition 19
volatility
    see also implied . . . ; underlying assets
    appraisal-based indices 93–100, 102, 152,
        160–1
    autocorrelation 58, 71, 92–9, 112–14, 130,
        137–9
    Black–Scholes option pricing formula 14–18,
        112–15
    comparability considerations 93–9, 152–6

concepts 16–17, 24–6, 49–51, 94–100, 102–8,
    112–15, 152–6, 201
derivatives effects 49–51
empirical index analysis 97–9
indexes 93–100, 102, 152, 160–1, 201
property derivatives 19, 24–6, 49–50,
    113–15
risk measures 121–2
smile concepts 114
smoothing problems 93–9, 152–6
stochastic behaviour 50
transaction-based indices 96–9, 102, 160–1
types 17
vega 19
volumes
    downturns 94
    hedging efficiency 171
    property derivatives 40, 51, 166, 171–2

warehousing strategies 119–20, 138
warrants 42, 169
weather derivatives 109, 131–2
weightings, indexes 57

Yale School of Management 193
yields
    see also dividends; returns
    Black–Scholes option pricing formula 14–18,
        112–15
    concepts 18

ZKB 49, 80–1
Zurich Housing Index (ZWEX), concepts 49,
    80–1, 96–9, 197

Index compiled by Terry Halliday